SAVING AFRICAN NATURE

An Ecological Mission and the Violence of History

Guillaume Blanc

Translated by Helen Morrison

polity

Originally published in French as *La nature des hommes. Une mission écologique pour "sauver" l'Afrique*
© Éditions La Découverte, Paris, 2024
This English translation © Polity Press, 2026

This book is supported by the Institut français (Royaume-Uni) as part of the Burgess programme.

Polity Press
65 Bridge Street
Cambridge CB2 1UR, UK

Polity Press
111 River Street
Hoboken, NJ 07030, USA

ISBN-13: 978-1-5095-6868-0 – hardback
ISBN-13: 978-1-5095-6869-7 – paperback

A catalogue record for this book is available from the British Library.

Library of Congress Control Number: 2025948470

Typeset in 11.5 on 14 Adobe Garamond
by Fakenham Prepress Solutions, Fakenham, Norfolk NR21 8NL
Printed and bound in Great Britain by Ashford Colour Press

The publisher has used its best endeavours to ensure that the URLs for external websites referred to in this book are correct and active at the time of going to press. However, the publisher has no responsibility for the websites and can make no guarantee that a site will remain live or that the content is or will remain appropriate.

Every effort has been made to trace all copyright holders, but if any have been overlooked the publisher will be pleased to include any necessary credits in any subsequent reprint or edition.

For further information on Polity, visit our website:
politybooks.com

Contents

North Tanganyika, 5 September 1961. A sea of cloud drifts around the summit of Mount Meru. The rising sun suffuses the slopes with a soft red glow and, 3,000 metres below, the group of people gazing at the former volcano are already basking in the warmth of its rays. More than a hundred visitors have gathered in the small town of Arusha, all with the shared goal of discussing the future of wildlife and natural resources in the African countries as, one after the other, they gain independence. This is the focus of the major international conference they will all be attending later this same morning.

Gathering on the terraces of the town's handful of hotels, some are getting to know each other over a black tea or a *café-cerise*, the two local specialities cultivated on the plateau surrounding Mount Kilimanjaro. Others are savouring the pleasure of renewing old acquaintances. Some are dressed in suits and ties and carry small leather briefcases. These are the senior officials and heads of the African states. They have come from Dahomey, from the Congo or from Burundi to act as spokespersons for their new nations which gained their independence just a few months ago or are on the point of doing so. Others are dressed in the uniform of the modern traveller – a hint of stubble, jeans, back-pack, linen shirt half-unbuttoned. Many have come from the USA and some from Canada. They are ecologists or agronomists.

And then there are the Europeans. These represent the majority amongst this cosmopolitan crowd. Some have come from 'the Old Continent' of Europe and others from neighbouring colonies: Uganda, Rwanda, Northern and Southern Rhodesia. The layer of dust visible on their safari jackets suggests that some of them have travelled by car from Nairobi, the capital of neighbouring Kenya. Here too, as all over the continent, decolonization is in the process of making them redundant. But most of them have already found new jobs and are now working for the international institutions responsible for organizing the conference.

The idea behind this event was first proposed a year earlier by the International Union for the Conservation of Nature (IUCN). The undisputed leader of non-governmental organizations for the protection of the environment ever since its creation in 1948, the IUCN had unveiled its 'African Special Project' on the occasion of its 7th General Assembly, which had taken place in Warsaw, Poland, in June 1960. The organization was therefore the mastermind behind this ambitious ecological mission, but it had the support of some solid allies in the form of the Fauna Preservation Society (FPS), the United Nations Educational, Scientific and Cultural Organization (UNESCO) and the Food and Agriculture Organization of the United Nations (FAO). It also had the backing of the Commission for Technical Cooperation in Africa South of the Sahara (CCTA), a sort of inter-imperial agency created six years previously by Great Britain, France, Belgium and Portugal.[1]

From inside Europe, these institutions had therefore launched their African Special Project, which was planned over three separate stages: stage 1, meetings 'to discuss the principles and practices of nature conservation with leaders of African opinion'; stage 2, organizing 'a conference on the conservation of nature and natural resources' in Africa; stage 3, sending staff into the field in order 'to help Governments to help themselves'.[2]

Gerald Watterson, originally from Great Britain, was in charge of the first stage. Forestry Officer for Africa for the FAO, he had recently become secretary-general of the IUCN. It was in this capacity that he flew to Ghana in November 1960 for a tour of the continent which took him from the Ivory Coast to Ethiopia, via Cameroon, Nigeria, Uganda, Kenya and Somalia. During the course of his trip, this conservation traveller met the leaders of sixteen African states. 'Although several of these countries have not very much left in the way of large, conspicuous wild life areas … each of them still contains extensive tracts of undeveloped land where the wild flora and fauna is dominant to the tame', he observed, on completion of his trip.[3] Clearly, the myth of an African Eden persisted, the very same myth that had been shaped by nineteenth-century European scientists: travelling naturalists who dreamed up the idea of Africa as a doomed paradise, a virgin land still untouched – a true Eden, to be saved from the people who threatened to destroy it. As the colonial period drew to an end, the myth lingered on in the minds of western nature professionals.

While Watterson was criss-crossing Africa, Julian Huxley, former director-general of UNESCO, was sounding the alarm in Europe. 'Does the wildlife of the continent now face extinction … ?', he demanded, in an article published in 1960.[4] In the hope of saving this threatened wildlife, Huxley brought together scientists, business men and former game hunters from Europe and the United States. In April 1961, fifteen of these lent their signatures to the Morges Manifesto, named after the Swiss town which was home to the headquarters of the IUCN. The European colonial order was not yet over, yet these men were already holding the Africans to blame for the devastation of African nature. 'Vast numbers of fine and harmless wild creatures are losing their lives, or their homes, in an orgy of thoughtless and needless destruction', they proclaimed in their Manifesto. From their perspective 'the eleventh hour has struck'. Hope nevertheless remained, since 'skilful and devoted men and admirable organisations are struggling to save the world's wild life'. It remained simply to find 'the support and resources' in order to 'send out experts ... and to train more local wardens and helpers in Africa and elsewhere ... before it is too late'.[5]

All of which explains why these delegates have gathered in Arusha in September 1961. The town has become the stage on which the second act of the Special Project is being played out – this is the first international conference on 'the conservation of Nature and Natural Resources in modern African states'. On the morning of 5 September, once breakfast is over, 130 men gather at the foot of the steps of the largest concrete building in Arusha – a conference centre built ten years previously. The atmosphere is relaxed, even friendly. The delegates then disappear inside the building and silence descends. Along the walls of the long corridor leading to the main lecture hall are framed photographs of lions, elephants, zebras and savanna landscapes. The men take up their seats in the centre of the room on wooden folding chairs meticulously polished for the occasion, and a small number of women gather to the right of the central podium, ready to assume their secretarial duties. A solemn atmosphere descends on all those assembled.

The conference is chaired by Julius Nyerere, the prime minister of Tanganyika. He speaks in the name of his country, due to obtain national sovereignty in three months' time, but he also assumes the role of spokesperson for all the representatives of independent Africa. In shirt-sleeves, his voice shrill and penetrating, Nyerere reiterates in their name his 'earnest desire ... to continue and actively expand the efforts already made in the field of wildlife management'. It is a highly strategic manoeuvre. In order to govern their countries, the leaders of the new African states are in need of recognition and financial aid from the international institutions. They are understandably keen to provide reassurance to their European and American emissaries. And they are successful in doing so. As Julian Huxley puts it, Nyerere's declaration marks 'a landmark for Africa'.

This is something of an understatement. On 11 September 1961, the day before the end of the conference, the news is on everyone's lips: a worldwide fund for nature is in the process of being created in Morges, Switzerland.[6] Thanks to subsidies from this World Wildlife Fund (WWF), a bank set up to finance the work of the IUCN, the third stage of the Special Project can now begin. The era of the colonial nature professionals has come to an end and that of the international conservation experts is just beginning. These men had feared they would be forced to leave the national parks they had watched over for more than twenty years but now they are reassured. Until the end of the 1970s they will remain in Africa 'to help Governments to help themselves'.

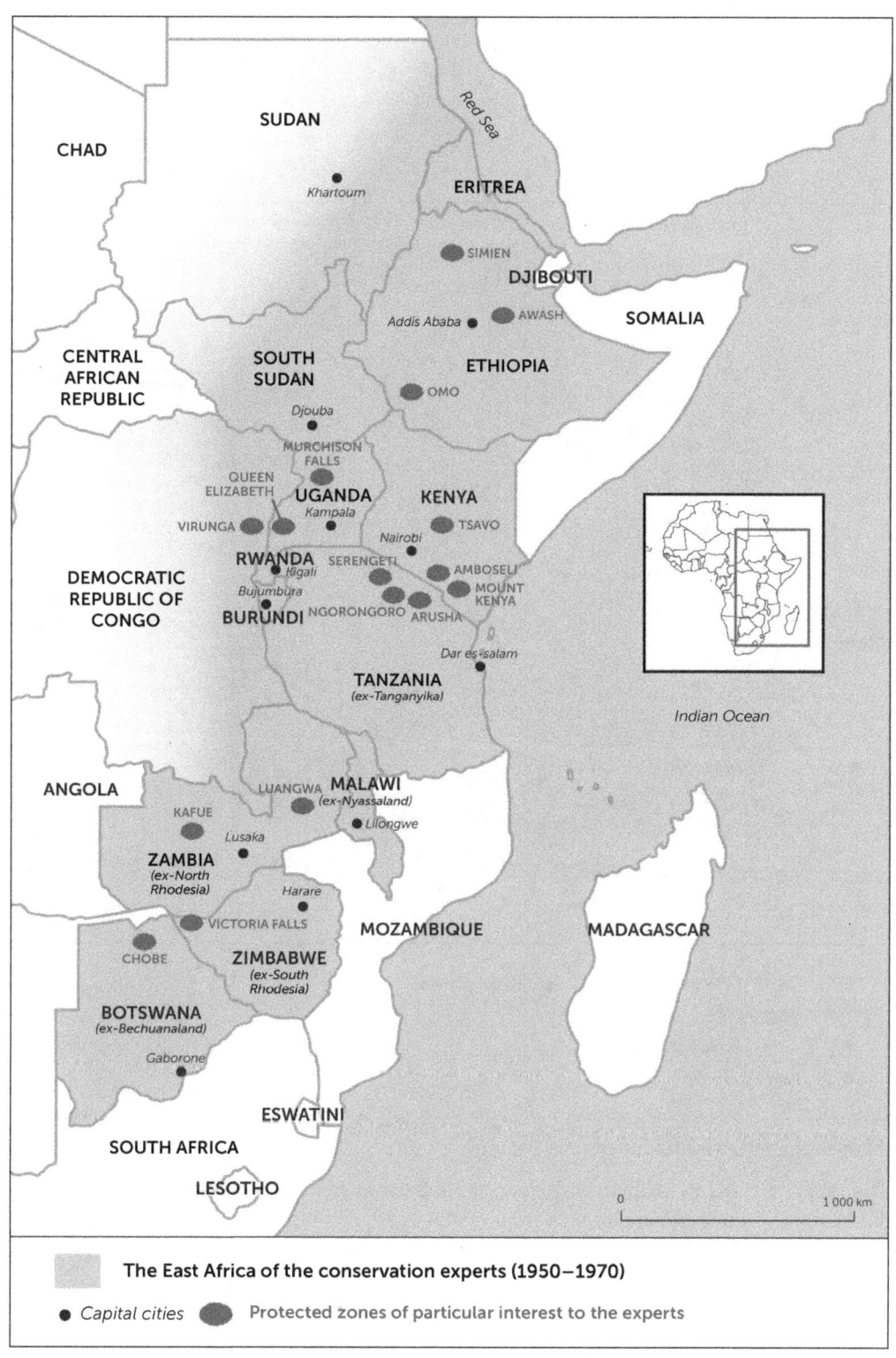

Map 1: Eastern Africa and world nature

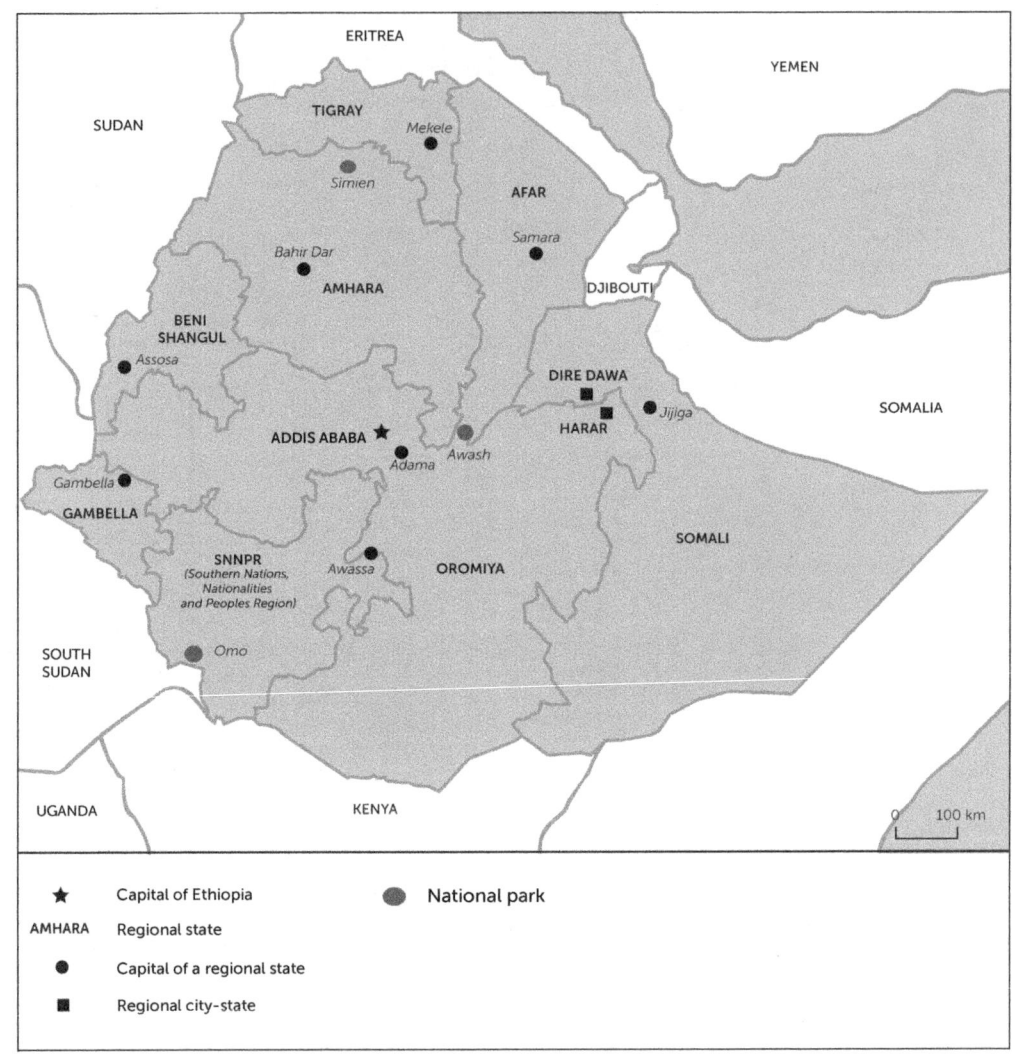

Map 2: Ethiopia and its (inter)national parks

Both maps created by Guillaume Blanc, Marie Bridonneau and Clara Delboé (drawing on CSA, 2007, *Atlas of Ethiopia*).

Introduction

Violence in a natural environment: From why to how

Each book owes a debt to the books which came before it. This one owes much to Karl Jacoby's powerful study *Shadows at Dawn: An Apache Massacre and the Violence of History*. In his book, the American historian describes the Camp Grant massacre in Arizona, when at dawn on 30 April 1871, a group of Americans, Mexicans and Tohono O'odham Indians slaughtered more than 140 Apaches. The attack lasted little more than an hour, but Jacoby uses it to weave a historic tapestry of American violence. He does so by rejecting the sense of duty historians generally feel under an obligation to honour. Instead of creating a 'single, authoritative narrative of the past', he offers four separate accounts, each of which focuses on the experience of the four different communities involved in the Camp Grant massacre. Jacoby insists that by choosing this method he is not seeking to evade the issues inherent in historical interpretation. On the contrary, his aim is to accept the complexity of the past in order to show it in a clearer light.[1]

In the following pages I have adopted a similar approach. The argument which lies at the core of this book is that, by singling out a relatively banal subject – the Arusha conference in 1961 – it is possible to portray the distinctive nature of the different worlds which were brought together on that occasion and, in so doing, gain a clearer understanding of the postcolonial moment and of the individuals who were part of it.

The event itself is both anecdotal and paradigmatic. Anecdotal, because this conference was attended by only a hundred or so people who would spend a week discussing nature reserves. Paradigmatic, because it provided an opportunity to witness colonial administrators in the process of reconverting themselves into international experts and extending their field of activity throughout Africa, working under the supervision of European based institutions, in close interaction with

African elites and in a more distant but very real sense with the villagers accused of destroying nature. My aim here is to study such 'contact situations' over the course of a story intended to be told 'in equal parts', in the manner proposed by the historian Romain Bertrand. Giving each actor in the global encounter their own space means refusing 'to arbitrarily construct a common world', choosing instead to 'give a voice to each of the groups present'.[2]

This point of view forces us to accept an undeniable fact: the actors involved in the conservation of African nature each belong to a specific context – in other words they do not *inhabit* the same places and, even more importantly, they do not *talk about* the same places.

First of all, came the great conservation experts, recognized all over the world and nicknamed by the historian Raf de Bont as the 'expert gentlemen'.[3] These were men like Julian Huxley, the elegant Englishman, always dressed in an impeccable white suit whether in the UNESCO offices or in the Tanzanian wildlife parks. Trained as a biologist and very much in demand by all the international agencies specializing in 'development', Huxley thought very much in terms of 'Africa' as a whole. Throughout the 1950s, 1960s and 1970s, preoccupied by the issue of overpopulation, which he believed posed a severe threat to the future of the continent, he travelled from one major city to another. In New York, London or Rome, he attended numerous international conferences, many of which he had helped to organize.

Then there were the field experts, whose day-to-day existence was played out in Eastern Africa. This group included, amongst others, John Blower, formerly a warden in the Tanganyika nature reserve during the colonial period and now an international expert. Bald-headed and with an imperious gaze and aggressive manner, Blower was convinced that action on a regional scale was imperative. With this in mind, from the 1950s to the 1970s, he divided his time between Kampala (Uganda), Dar es Salaam (Tanzania), Nairobi (Kenya) and Addis Ababa (Ethiopia), using these places as a base from which to embark on expeditions to observe nature, and then urging his managers to instigate the measures needed to save it.

For these managers, day-to-day life was organized on a national scale. These were men like Major Gizaw Gedlegiorgis. A proud representative of Ethiopia, an empire which had, since the end of the nineteenth century, jealously guarded its independence, he had fought against the Italians during the Second World War and his uniform was adorned with an impressive array of medals. Made into a senior official after the war, since 1965 Gizaw[4] had been director of the agency responsible for the country's national parks in Addis Ababa. In that capacity the major travelled frequently to Gondar, Mui or Metehara, keeping in close contact with his employees, the park guards who were responsible for preserving the jewels of nature so prized by the western world.

And, finally, there were the 'Africans' – constantly referred to but never by name. These were agro-pastoralists, who generally lived self-sufficiently from agriculture and pastoral farming. They were called Dehaw, Mengest or Tekelakay and they lived in the nature reserves now placed under supervision, for example in the Ethiopian parks of the Awash, the Omo or the Simien. Between the 1950s and the 1970s, each of these parks was home to several thousand farmers and shepherds. For the expert gentlemen, the field experts and those responsible for managing nature, these agro-pastoralists were very often the 'third state': the *tertium quid*[5] of those who get left behind and who can be sacrificed if the cause is a just one. But for these people, whose role in society is played out on the level of the village, 'nature' is not a cause but rather a constraint to which they must constantly adapt.

These four worlds are of course connected to each other. But each of them also exists independently of the others, each has its own history. This is why, by examining the 1950s, 1960s and 1970s, this book will successively shine a spotlight on each of these geographies of the postcolonial moment. First of all, it will focus on the Africa of the 'expert gentlemen', originating from Europe and North America. The next chapter will look at East Africa with its field experts, all former colonialists and subsequently transformed into international experts. The third and fourth chapters will respectively examine the world-nation of the Ethiopian leaders, that is to say a nation which uses the outside world in order to more effectively impose itself on an internal level; and finally, the global village of the inhabitants of Ethiopia's first national parks – the Awash, the Omo and the Simien – each of them isolated territories yet nevertheless firmly bound, in spite of themselves, to the globalized world of 'African nature'.

In the light of the present

This book tells the story of a period of transition – the passage of time between the colonial era and the postcolonial era. But it is important to state from the outset that by telling the story of 'the Arusha years' the first aim of this book is to throw light on the present – a present marked by the violence which still today continues to affect those living in the protected areas of Africa. In Zimbabwe, in Rwanda, in Uganda, in Tanzania, in Kenya, in Ethiopia and in many other African countries, in the heart of the national parks and in the adjoining areas, hundreds of thousands of farmers and shepherds are being punished with fines and prison sentences for cultivating the land, grazing their animals and hunting small game. Tens of thousands of men and women are also being expelled from their land, forced to abandon their homes, their fields and the familiar places of their everyday lives. Worse still, in the most atrocious cases, African eco-guards, trained and funded by western organizations, assault and sometimes kill residents accused of poaching.[6] Why?

In a book published in 2020, I attempted to give a response to this 'why' by unravelling the origins and the ongoing consequences of a form of green colonialism.[7] This way of ruling both nature and individuals first emerged at the end of the nineteenth century when Europeans in quest of new opportunities in the colonies were turning their backs on landscapes which had been radically transformed by urbanization and industrialization. Convinced that they would find in Africa a nature which no longer existed in Europe, they set about creating game reserves which, from the 1930s onwards, were then transformed into national parks. And in all these natural sanctuaries, from the Belgian Congo to South Africa, they invented the myth of the good and bad hunter. The former is a white man who confines himself to trophy hunting, armed simply with a gun and his own courage. The latter, a black man, hunts for food, using a bow, a spear, snares and, above all, cruelty – a string of preconceptions which served to justify the expropriation of African people and later the imposition of criminal penalties on them. And when they were not being expelled from the park areas, their use of the land was restricted and sanctioned.

In Africa, nature therefore became synonymous with violence. But, for the rest of the world, this violence was concealed behind images of a Garden of Eden. This confused version of reality begins with the travel accounts published in the newly expanding national newspapers, accounts like those written in the 1880s by Henry Morton Stanley and David Livingstone, and later by Winston Churchill and Theodore Roosevelt in the 1910s, all of which depicted a vast African garden, still preserving its natural state in spite of its destructive inhabitants. Then, in the mid-1930s, it was the turn of literature, with Ernest Hemingway's *The Snows of Kilimanjaro* and Karen Blixen's *Out of Africa*. Thanks to books like these, western readers discovered a fairy-tale Africa, a continent where large wild animals reigned supreme, where lions, buffalo, elephants, giraffes and rhinoceros roamed free. In the period following African independence such accounts proliferated. There were more novels, for example, *The Roots of Heaven* by Romain Gary, magazines such as *National Geographic*, guidebooks like those published by *Lonely Planet*, manga adapted for the cinema, such as *The Lion King*. All described an identical Africa – green, unspoilt, teaming with animal life and wild – the ecological sanctuary of the entire world. Yet this version of a nature more universal than African does not exist. Africa is inhabited and farmed, just like Europe. If today the majority of African parks are empty, it is purely because they have been emptied of their inhabitants.

This dehumanization of nature is intrinsically linked to the accepted wisdom disseminated by colonial scientists, and which still persists even today. Like that associated with 'primary' forests, for example. In reality, such forests scarcely existed in Africa. Here, as in Europe, most existing forests are human-made. But when colonization first began in Africa, European foresters and botanists convinced themselves that the African continent had previously been home to an original forest once dense and extensive but recently deforested as a result of the excessive population of local peasants. The figures appeared to support their claim. In the 1890s, almost 65,000 elephants were slaughtered each year for their highly prized ivory. From 1850 to 1920, more than 90 million hectares of forest were cleared within European empires, in other words, four times more than in the preceding century. This, according to European scientists keen to protect the environment, explained why it was important to create hunting reserves and subsequently national parks. But their argument failed to take into account a fundamental fact – if these forests were indeed cleared on a large scale, it was first of all to free land for cultivation in order to serve the European economy. And if elephants were killed, it was because ivory was particularly sought after on the world market. Unable to accept that imperial capitalism was responsible for the ongoing destruction, scientists transferred responsibility to the Africans themselves and persuaded the colonial administrators to forbid them access to the protected zones which had ostensibly been set aside in order to redress the catastrophe. The administrators lost no time in doing just that. Thanks to science, they could legitimately expropriate the agro-pastoralists and assume the right to exploit the lands in a 'rational' manner.

The process continued, and even intensified, following independence. Copper, gold, cobalt, oil, cocoa, peanuts, coffee, cotton – throughout Africa, the exploitation of raw materials destined to supply the world market continued to ravage the entire continent, and at the same time the introduction of protected zones continued to be seen as the best way of combatting the ongoing destruction. Since the 1960s, hand in glove with the multinational companies and the international organizations for the protection of nature, the majority of the governments of African states have continued to support both overexploitation and overprotection. In these countries, as in other parts of the world, in certain areas nature has indeed been totally destroyed; but within Africa, in certain areas nature had also been enclosed within national parks where it was more rigorously protected than anywhere else in the world. In this way, Africa is still today a favoured setting for this strange pairing of predation–protection, a direct inheritance from the colonial period.

Even today, most of the conservation experts involved in this overprotection of African nature are still westerners. Because they were unable to save nature in their own countries or chose not to do so, they continue to focus their attention on an Africa they want to remain untouched and wild. The majority of tourists who visit the African national parks also come from industrialized western countries. Their longing for nature involves a heavy toll in terms of pollution – a return plane trip, a tent with aluminium poles, a fleece jacket produced from petroleum residues, a Gore-Tex jacket manufactured using bauxite, etc. But, as in the case of the experts, for tourists too, African nature belongs more to the realm of dreams than to that of reason. By definition, 'nature' is born on the very day it begins to disappear. For example, in France, for anyone living in a city and travelling only within their own country, it was only in the 1960s, with the urbanization of rural areas within the 'Hexagon', that 'nature' started to be used in reference to isolated hamlets and mountain pastures where eagles and chamois could still be sighted. And then, for those Europeans and North Americans who could travel far from their own homes, there was also another version of 'nature', all the more natural since it had long since disappeared from their own countries. This was nature as encountered in Africa, where, since time immemorial, animals and the savannah grasslands seemed to take precedence over a time of human activities, of agriculture and of the city.

Such are the western legacies of green colonialism. But there is also another indisputable fact which must not be forgotten, notably that colonialism could not have taken root without the participation, as much imposed as chosen, of certain African elites. And, following independence, the same applies to the power associated with the protection of nature. Marking out boundaries (in the form of protected areas), providing spaces for the public and for tourists (like national parks), defining how resources should be exploited (in order to have better control over them) or imposing state authority on those inhabitants who live far from the centre of power (by transforming their mountains into parks) – all of these sovereign prerogatives which originated from green colonialism are familiar to African leaders who use western norms on a daily basis to suit their own purposes; even if it means perpetuating the colonial idea that many international experts still have of Africa.

This narrative of nature and power has been at the heart of my research for a number of years but I am by no means the first to have followed this path. Indeed, I might not even have developed any interest in it at all had certain heritage specialists not already pointed to the existence, in the twentieth century, of a single management model for tropical nature which was founded on the belief that, in the countries of the southern hemisphere, protecting the environment meant protecting it from its inhabitants. This model, researchers tell us, was established in the colonial period and then reproduced by the international organizations created after the Second World War – UNESCO, the IUCN and the WWF. And seventy years later, it remains the dominant model amongst conservation professionals. Regarded as innovative in the 2000s, this approach rapidly became groundbreaking and remains as powerful today as it was in the past.[8] But it has failed to provide an answer to the question: why and how did colonial policies on nature continue to be universally applied even after independence?

I think I have answered the 'why' part of the question by demonstrating the triple ongoing persistence of perceptions, beliefs and practice which continued to depict a lush and verdant Africa, destructive Africans, and a natural world which needs to be emptied of humans in order to be saved. And, in the course of this history of green colonialism, the overprotection of African ecological systems is seen as a counterweight to the overexploitation of natural resources across the entire planet: the more nature is destroyed *here* (especially in the west), the more we can fantasize about its untouched and virgin state *there* (especially in Africa). All of which explains why colonial policies on African nature continued to exist after independence.

The 'how' remains to be investigated. There is a 'before' (the colonial era which began in the 1880s) and an 'after' (the postcolonial era which began in the 1960s and which is still very much in place today). But, between these two, what about the postcolonial moment itself? How, in practical terms, was continuity maintained between the two eras?

Seizing the moment

In the wake of subaltern studies and postcolonial studies, specialists in African studies have defined postcolonialism as both a process and a method. A process because it involves the interweaving of the so-called colonial and post-colonial (with a hyphen) eras. This is the famous before-and-after of the process of independence, a particular moment best considered not in terms of the passage of time, but rather of its accumulation: colonial past + post-colonial present = postcolonial societies (without a hyphen since the past continues to weigh on the present).[9] As well as a process, postcolonialism is also a method which involves the claim that rather than suffering at the hands of the world, African societies were built *with* the world. In Africa, colonization was certainly a time of intense violence, but there was more to it than merely confrontation and domination. There was also interaction, and, in the end, hybridization.[10] The same is true following independence. Africa's relationship with the outside world continued to change according to an unequal balance of power, but, like everywhere else, African societies were as much subjected to the transmission of power as they were participants in it – they were the driving force of their own global history.[11] So much for the process and the method. It is however necessary to see postcolonialism as also being a moment in its own right, one which belongs to a postcolonial Africa with its origins in time as well as in space. My hypothesis is that the postcolonial moment did indeed exist, and that, consequently, its history deserves to be written.

Environmental history is one of the potential entry points for this investigation. Specialists of the colonial period generally conclude their narratives by quickly looking ahead to the postcolonial era. 'Most of the ideas and practices that had long underpinned wildlife protection in the tropics remained intact', writes, for example, the historian Corey Ross towards the end of his book on ecology in the age of empire. Then, on the subject of postcolonial Africa, he refers both to the international experts and to the African heads of state. The former acted as though they were 'the only competent custodians of the land', writes Ross, whilst the latter took advantage of conservation policies 'to bolster their control over remote hinterlands, to profit from the natural resources of their territories, and to demonstrate their credentials as "civilised countries"'.[12] This brief glance ahead to the postcolonial era concludes most environmental histories of the colonies. And, conversely, the specialists of the postcolonial period very often begin their accounts with a rapid reminder of the colonial past. William Adams, for example, begins his famous *Decolonizing Nature* by listing what current conservationism has conserved from its colonial heritage: 'colonial ideas' which separate nature from humans; the 'colonial mind' which provides a bureaucratic and elitist control of social relationships with nature; 'colonial coercion' which seeks to impose discipline on everything, both humans and their environment; then the 'repeated failure of colonial strategies' intended to protect nature on the one hand by imposing a tightly organized structure and on the other by ensuring maximum exploitation of resources.[13]

For both Corey Ross and William Adams, the caesura between colonization and decolonization is therefore far from obvious. Many other writers have also drawn attention to this and some have even made a case for continuity by conducting case studies running from the end of the nineteenth century to the beginning of the twenty-first, and focusing either on a specific environment such as the Sahara,[14] on a state, such as South Africa,[15] or on a nature reserve such as the Serengeti National Park in Tanzania.[16] Each in their own way, such accounts demonstrate that it is impossible to consider the management of African nature through the simplifying prism of a chronological rupture along the lines of colonization–decolonization.

Conversely, when we turn our attention to the process through which continuity operates, no real clarity emerges either. Some historians have focused on the origins of postcolonial conservation but, oddly, have taken at face value the discourse of the institutions responsible for implementing it. According to the narrative presented by the leaders of UNESCO or the IUCN, their history underwent a radical change in the 1950s when they abandoned their mission of 'preservation' which involved protecting nature by radically separating it from humans, and instead adopted the goal of 'conservation', aimed at managing natural environments in a rational manner in order to exploit them in a sustainable way. In keeping with this institutional rationale, some historians claim that UNESCO or the IUCN switched to 'humanistic' conservation in the mid-1950s, in response to new imperatives in terms of world food security.[17] Others go so far as to claim that 'the decolonization process sounds the death knell for an authoritarian colonial preservation process with an emphasis on wildlife sanctuaries', as demonstrated by the Arusha conference during which, in September 1961, the international institutions were responsible for 'the demise of preservation of nature'.[18] Moreover, according to these historians, the movement was already in existence by this date, since in 1956, that is to say, eight years after its official creation, the International Union for the Protection of Nature renamed itself the IUCN, with the P for *Protection* (wrapping nature in cotton wool in order to preserve it from humans) being replaced with the C for *Conservation* (limiting the exploitation of the environment so that humans can use it in a sustainable manner). These historians seem therefore to have confused the discourse of the institutions with the reality of the work they carry out in the field.

Yet anthropologists and sociologists specializing in development have already exposed the contradictions of this international discourse. With reference to the 350 African national parks, Daniel Brockington and James Igoe identified evictions of local people in 30 per cent of national parks in Tanzania and Congo-Kinshasa, in 40 per cent of Rwandan national parks and in 65 per cent of national parks in Gabon.[19] Charles Geisler and Ragendra de Sousa listed between 900,000 and 14.4 million farmers and pastoralists evicted from protected areas within Africa – the chronology extends right through the twentieth century, but the authors emphasize that such displacements became more common after the 1960s.[20] While this removal of people from certain spaces was organized by the national governments of Africa, their officials still worked hand in hand with the experts from international institutions who offered them guidance on their conservation policies.[21] Before independence, most of these experts *decided*; since independence, they *advised*. And this is where the first major change of direction can be identified, a change brought about by the advent of a coproduction of African nature, as witnessed precisely by the Arusha conference in 1961.

The first stage of the African Special Project was launched in June 1960 and took the form of a series of meetings bringing together officials from the IUCN and the leaders of the new African nations. The month of September 1961 saw the second act of the project coming to fruition with a major conference in Arusha on the future of African wildlife. Then, immediately following this event, came the third stage during which experts were sent to Africa.

These included men like John Blower. It was the archives of the Ethiopian Wildlife Conservation Authority (EWCA) that set me on the trail of this man – born in Britain and as passionate about nature as he was proud of his authority as a former colonial administrator. On behalf of the institutions in charge of the Special Project (UNESCO, the IUCN and FAO), a number of conservationists travelled to Ethiopia in 1963. They met with the Ethiopian emperor, Haile Selassie I, and recommended that he employ John Blower. After studying forestry, Blower had learned his trade in British East Africa as a warden in the Tanganyika Park, a ranger in Kenya and then chief game warden of the Ugandan national parks. Immediately following independence, and having attended the Arusha conference, he set himself up as a conservation expert and it was in this capacity that he arrived in Ethiopia in 1965. In his role of 'Adviser to the Imperial Ethiopian Government on Wildlife Conservation', over a period of five years, Blower, along with members of the Ethiopian Wildlife Conservation Organization (EWCO, forerunner of the EWCA), oversaw the creation of the first three national parks in the country, But, in spite of his insistence that farmers and pastoralists should be evicted, progress on the ground was slow. He subsequently requested the Ethiopian authorities at least to impose fines on the men and women who cultivated the land and grazed their livestock in what would eventually be the Awash, Omo and Simien parks.[22]

The archives show that the Ethiopian government complied with these recommendations: an indication of the continuity of patrimonial practices, and also of the continued importance of experts in issues relating to patrimony and heritage. At the time of independence – that is to say shortly before and after the Arusha conference – many Europeans, former colonial scientists, subsequently converted into international experts, and continued to pursue their mission within the continent: a mission which involved enclosing African nature within parks and protecting it from those living there. The postcolonial moment had arrived.

Nevertheless, this Ethiopian episode indicates the ongoing presence of colonial actors while at the same time revealing the capacity for action held by the leading African elites, whether heads of state, senior officials, directors of national institutions or heads of regional government agencies. John Blower and the experts he summoned to Ethiopia certainly wielded a genuine power over both nature and people. But the same was also true of the Ethiopian leaders. In creating these parks, they received enough external funding to enable them to plant the national flag in the territories they struggled to control – in the Awash with its population of Karayu and Afar agro-pastoralists opposed to central power; in the Omo, inhabited by the Surma who refused to recognize either the authority or even the existence of the Ethiopian state; and in the Simien mountains, a region which had become a stronghold for Tigrayan rebels from the north.

It would therefore be oversimplistic to see the continuity between the colonial and postcolonial eras as the sign of a neo-imperialism driven by international experts keen to impose western norms. Of course, many of these experts suffered from '"The empire strikes back" syndrome' and their attitudes were so deeply rooted in the imperial experience that they had difficulty shaking off the sense of authority which legitimized their colonial mission.[23] But these experts were not alone. Local people were under no obligation to obey them and each day they found themselves having to deal with governments who were themselves pursuing their own goals and their own objectives. Whether they were spokespersons for the international institutions, field experts, national managers or peasant farmers, they would still find themselves having to negotiate on the way nature and people should be governed. The historian therefore must undertake to unravel the threads of the relationships linking these different groups during this unique postcolonial moment, a period which was no longer wholly imperial nor yet completely international.

Making choices

A close study of the encounters between an 'International' body made up of heritage experts and the actors of an African nation enables us to think beyond the confines of the colonization–decolonization caesura. The complex social depths of African nature can also be better understood by observing how subalterns reconfigure, on the ground, ideas and norms which have come from outside. These hypotheses seem to me highly pertinent. But they are nevertheless the product of choices made in order to present in an orderly manner – and therefore a comprehensible one – a history of connections which have been thoroughly disconnected – and are therefore incomprehensible.

These choices take place in the archives. The researcher must never draw a distinction between what supports the story he or she would like to tell and what might contradict it. In the interests of honesty, the archives should guide the narrative, not the reverse. And, if sincerity is also regarded as important, we must accept that if we are to engage with the rhetoric of the experts, we will find ourselves constantly confronted with 'the effect of surprise – or perhaps of torpor – induced by the reading of UN texts, or of any other texts couched in "managerial" language'.[24] Gilbert Rist bravely describes the sense of 'torpor' he has himself experienced – an apt word given the often unsettling nature of such archives. In the minutes and proceedings of conferences, international recommendations and development programmes for management, states are rarely named, and individuals even less so. Instead, such documents refer only to the 'less developed countries', to the 'political leaders of the continent' or to the 'local stakeholders'. In reality, these archives are written in a vocabulary which conceals the social dimension of any given situation. Where reports on activities only rarely mention sanctions imposed on farmers or pastoralists, debriefings on specific missions are couched in an even vaguer vocabulary when they touch on the attitude of African heads of state and senior officials towards international norms. In such cases reference might be made to 'measures' designed to 'improve conservation', to the 'reorganization of the protected area' or to 'raising awareness amongst stakeholders' or 'good governance'. In order to dispel the fog created by this administrative rhetoric, we need to read between the lines and, in particular, to seek additional sources, such as, for example, the correspondence between international conservation experts and those responsible for nature on a national level.

My research for this book was no exception. The investigation involved studying materials in eight separate archive collections over a period of two years. In England there were the Foreign Office and Foreign and Commonwealth Office records in the National Archive at Kew, the papers of Peter Scott and of the WWF in the university library in Cambridge and the London archives of the Fauna Preservation Society (FPS) at the Natural History Museum. On the internet were all issues of *Oryx*, the official review of the FPS and its experts. In Paris there were the archives of UNESCO, in Gland, Switzerland, the archives of the IUCN, in Rome, those of the FAO and in Addis Ababa, those of the Ethiopian Wildlife Conservation Authority. Further archives could also have been consulted. The contents of these eight archive collections were however sufficiently wide-ranging to provide an objective search for the traces of the past which were of interest for this research and this sample therefore offers a reassuring scientific guarantee. But when it came to analysing the material, the sheer extent of the task was almost crippling. What, for example, should be done with this file entitled 'Saving African Nature', carefully stored in the left-hand corner of the computer screen and now too daunting to open given that it contains precisely 1,318 digitalized documents – in other words around 130,000 pages of archives? A certain number of choices clearly needed to be made.

The first of these was to accept the confusion which is characteristic of the beginning of the postcolonial era. First there was confusion over the various roles involved. For example, when an archive mentions a 'scientific expert', the phrase generally refers to an influential conservationist, someone who travelled to Africa from time to time, but was based in Europe where he, or she, sat on the management committees of the IUCN, the WWF or UNESCO. On the other hand, where reference is simply made to an 'expert' this often means a conservationist working in the field – he or she may occasionally have travelled to the European headquarters of the IUCN, or of UNESCO, but generally lived and worked locally, and in particular in an African country. The nature professionals knew each other and resembled each other, operating in worlds which overlapped but which were nevertheless very different – like those of the 'chief wardens', of the 'wardens' and of the park 'guards' or 'rangers'. These individuals worked closely together but it is important to differentiate between them. So, for example, in the colonial period but also after independence, from Kenya to Southern Rhodesia, the title of 'chief warden' was almost always held by a foreigner, either from Europe or from North America, who was responsible for all the parks in the country in which he worked. Invariably, or almost always, the 'warden' was also a foreigner allocated to a particular park which he managed sometimes with the help of an 'assistant warden', a role generally filled by a native of the country. Finally, at the bottom of the hierarchy, were the 'guards', often referred to as scouts. These were Kenyans, Tanzanians, Ugandans or Ethiopians and their job was to patrol the parks, keep records of the wild animals and maintain the infrastructures under the supervision of the warden, who was in turn supervised by the chief warden. In each park therefore, a number of different worlds came into contact with each other.

These different worlds were not however peopled only by conservation professionals. Delving into the archives we also find American big game hunters, high-profile African heads of state, Canadian aid workers and volunteers, national and regional officials, anonymous farmers and people expelled from their land. There were also the animals, killed in their thousands or moved around from park to park in their hundreds. I have therefore chosen to make space for all these different actors, whatever their role.

A great many different worlds coexisted and each of them was significant, albeit in its own way. This explains why accounts of the conservation of African nature generally tend to be thematic. Given the scale of the archives and the large numbers of actors and actions referred to in them, historians find themselves forced to focus on an international institution (such as the IUCN for example), on a group of professionals (such as the major experts) or on a particular country. In my case, I decided to limit the chronology in order to be able to 'include everything'. This is because my close study of the African national parks has led me to formulate the following hypothesis. In order to understand the current violence associated with the conservation of African wildlife, the only viable path is to go back to the postcolonial moment and to consider conservation as the product of each of the different worlds involved at that time, from the beginning of the 1950s to the end of the 1970s. These were worlds led by international expert gentlemen, by field experts, by political decision makers and by local people – four groups closely linked to each other but which remained distinctive.

In order to give an intelligible account of the history of this worldwide ecological mission in Africa, my final choice was to apply the same method in each chapter. First of all, each of the four chapters begins with an opening section entitled 'Arusha 1961'. By systematically using the Arusha conference and the African Special Project as a starting point, it becomes apparent that each group had their own particular way of approaching 'African nature'. The next section, always under the title 'History', sketches a rapid overview of the work already produced by other historians – setting out what is already known is ultimately the best way of understanding the unknown. And this pattern is repeated, chapter by chapter. After these two short sections, 'Arusha 1961' and 'History', each chapter will focus on one particular world, and more precisely, on the lives of the men and women who inhabited it, over a period of time spanning a decade before and a decade after the Arusha conference, namely at the time when African countries were in the process of becoming independent.

The first chapter turns its attention to the expert gentlemen. In order to gain a clearer understanding of how the major conservationists of the time perceived Africa, we need to scrutinize their public communications, the records of their conferences and the reports produced after their trips into the continent. At first sight, this material gives a historical overview which is institutional and sometimes bleak. Yet it soon becomes apparent that it is of crucial importance since it demonstrates that between the imperial institutions and the international organizations, what begins as competition gradually transforms into collaboration. The process then appears to be accompanied by a new developmentalist narrative on nature, but also by a portrayal of African ecologies which remain Malthusian and colonialist. And, in this context, the expert gentlemen appeared to be the main drivers of continuity in that they continued to define the problems which threatened nature in Africa, but also the solutions to be implemented in order to resolve these issues.

And at that point the colonial agents now converted into international experts stepped onto the stage, the focus of the second chapter. Thanks to the reports of their field trips, their autobiographies and their private correspondence, their presence throughout Eastern Africa can be tracked. Very quickly a picture emerges which is one both of continuity, since their aim was still to naturalize this 'region', and of division, since they must now work on an equal footing with the very people who had formerly been colonized. In the words of experts working in the East African parks, a conservationist 'dream' began to emerge which would rapidly turn into a 'nightmare'.

A nightmare, because they now found themselves face to face with the leaders of the new African states – a situation indicated in the stories of the national, regional or local employees of the Ethiopian state who are the subject of the third chapter. Here, progress reports, rules and policies, the records kept by park guards and the correspondence between experts and leaders show that in the aftermath of Arusha, a previously unprecedented relationship was taking shape between the expatriates with their considerable power and the government agents determined to create a world-nation, or in other words, a nation where internal change was intrinsically part of its relationship with the outside world. Subsequently, tensions between the two groups became so acute that they seemed to give rise to a profoundly divisive ecological policy on the ground – one which was neither purely national nor fully international.

This policy permeated postcolonial village life and this is the subject of the fourth and final chapter. If the archives tell us little about the day-to-day lives of those who lived in the midst of African nature, some traces of the past can nevertheless be salvaged by studying three relatively small territories: the Awash, the Omo and the Simien – three national parks each home to several thousand inhabitants. Thanks to research conducted in the field, to the administrative records of expatriate wardens or Ethiopian guards and to the confidential notes kept by international institutions or by the Ethiopian government, it first of all becomes apparent that some local people worked with national managers and international experts, sometimes deferring to their authority, sometimes using them for their own advantage. Some opted for the path of rebellion while others concentrated their attention on learning how to get on with their lives in the face of the new conservation laws. But in all cases, the more 'nature' impacted on their daily lives, the more local people sought ways of using it for their own purposes; with the result that nature would soon begin to resemble the experts and leaders who had first made it their preoccupation – simultaneously contradictory, unjust and violent.

A gallery of institutions

African Wildlife Leadership Foundation (AWLF): a non-governmental organization set up in Chicago in 1961 on the initiative of the judge and East African safari aficionado Russell Train, who was convinced that decolonization and the African demographic threatened the future of nature in the African continent.

College of African Wildlife Management (CAWM): set up in Mweka in Tanzania in 1963 by Julius Nyerere and the AWLF for the purpose of training the new African managers in the international conservation norms.

Commission de coopération technique en Afrique au sud du Sahara (CCTA) (Commission for Technical Cooperation in Africa South of the Sahara): an inter-imperial organization created in 1950 by France, Great Britain, Portugal, Belgium, the South African Union and Southern Rhodesia in response to competition from the United Nations who had decided to offer their technical assistance to the colonies.

Conseil scientifique pour l'Afrique au sud du Sahara (CSA): a scientific hub within the CCTA.

Ethiopian Wildlife Conservation Organization (EWCO): a national institution set up in 1969 to develop and manage the Ethiopian national parks (a role previously occupied by a conservation department, established in 1965).

Fauna Preservation Society (FPS): a non-governmental organization working with the colonies of the British Empire. This organization was founded in London, in 1903, under the name of the Society for the Preservation of the Wild Fauna of the Empire. It was renamed the Society for the Preservation of the Fauna of the Empire in 1919, and then FPS in 1950.

Food and Agriculture Organization (FAO): a United Nations agency set up in 1945 and particularly involved, in Africa, with the management of forestry resources.

Institut français d'Afrique noire (IFAN): a colonial institution set up in 1936 in Dakar in French West Africa. Its scientific activity became more intense after 1945 under the leadership of Théodore Monod, particularly in the fields of zoology, agronomy and the management of natural resources.

International Union for Conservation of Nature (IUCN): a non-governmental organization particularly active in Africa. Set up in 1928, under the name of the International Office of Documentation and Correlation for the Protection of Nature, it initially specialized in the *preservation* of fauna and of protected areas. It was then renamed the International Office for the Protection of Nature in 1935 and then the International Union for the Protection of Nature in 1948. Adopting the name of IUCN in 1956, from that date onwards it prioritized the notion of *conservation*.

The Nature Conservancy: a British government institution created in 1949 to further develop natural sciences and in particular biology and to promote the creation of natural parks and reserves both in Britain and in the colonies.

United Nations Educational, Scientific and Cultural Organization (UNESCO): a United Nations agency set up in 1945 and involved, alongside others, in the *conservation* of natural resources (via the *International Biological Program* and subsequently the *Man and Biosphere programme*) and the protection of the Natural World Heritage List created in 1972 in Stockholm.

United Nations Environment Programme (UNEP): a United Nations agency set up on the occasion of the Stockholm conference in 1972 to encourage international cooperation on environmental policies. The UNEP has access to a global fund for the environment, also set up in Stockholm.

World Wildlife Fund (WWF): a bank founded in Switzerland in 1961 by fifteen renowned conservationists (including Jean-Georges Baer, Julian Huxley, Kai Curry-Lindahl, Max Nicholson, Peter Scott and Edgar Worthington) to finance the IUCN.

A gallery of actors

The 'expert gentlemen'

Jean-Georges Baer, the Swiss parasitologist. Highly renowned – he even had a rodent named after him (*Hyplomiscus baeri* or Baer's wood mouse). Baer was the first president of the IUCN to emphasize the urgency of taking a stance, in Africa, against global overpopulation.

Keith Caldwell, the captain in the British Royal Artillery. After his military career he became personal secretary to the governor of Kenya and then chief game warden, first in the Kenyan national parks and then in Uganda He was the first representative of the FPS in East Africa.

Kai Curry-Lindahl, the academic. Ornithologist, professor in the United States, in Canada and then in Sweden, his native country, he was conservation adviser to thirty or so African governments and acted as a consultant for the FAO, the IUCN and UNESCO.

Bernhard Grzimek, the film director with a passion for zebras. Veterinarian, director of the zoo and then the zoological society of Frankfurt, he made several documentaries in the Serengeti and popularized the idea of Africa in its natural state, rich in fauna, but threatened by overpopulation.

Jean-Paul Harroy, the former beer salesman. Heir to a beer import company, doctor in colonial sciences, he would become director of the *Institut des parcs nationaux du Congo Belge* (Institute of the National Parks of Belgian Congo), governor of Ruanda-Urundi and secretary-general of the IUCN.

Julian Huxley, the man in the white suit. A British biologist and confirmed eugenicist, the first director of UNESCO and later the main spokesperson for conservation organizations, he was one of the leading theorists on the subject of overpopulation in Africa.

Edward Max Nicholson, the lobbyist. An ornithologist with a passion for biology and exploration. In his role as head of The Nature Conservancy, he campaigned to persuade the British authorities to support the international conservation institutions.

Peter Scott, the naturalist and all-rounder. Ornithologist, artist, member of the British sailing team in the Berlin Olympics and spokesperson for the FPS, he designed the famous 'panda' logo for the WWF.

Jacques Verschuren, the elephant enthusiast. A zoologist trained in the field in Africa within the Institute of the National Parks of Belgian Congo, he worked for the Belgian government, for the IUCN, UNESCO and the WWF.

Gerald Watterson, the conservation traveller. Bureau chief at the FAO for African forestry and then secretary-general at the IUCN, he oversaw the first stage of the African Special Project, travelling to Africa to meet with the continent's new leaders.

Edgar Barton Worthington, the field ecologist with an aristocratic air. With his extensive professional experience, he worked for various institutions at a national (The Nature Conservancy), imperial (CCTA) and international (IUCN) level.

The 'field experts'

John Blower, the colonial. After studying forestry, he began his career in Tanganyika, was involved in suppressing the Mau Mau uprising in Kenya, became a game warden in Uganda and then, after independence, an expert in Ethiopia, and later in Nepal, Indonesia and Burma.

George Brown, the former police officer. Born in British India, he and his brother Leslie moved to Kenya where he became a district commissioner before being recruited as warden of the Omo Park in imperial Ethiopia.

Leslie Brown, the scientist in the woollen sweater. Ornithologist, agronomist and meteorologist, he worked in Nigeria before moving to Kenya where he became director of the department of agriculture and then, following independence, became an expert based in the East Africa national parks.

Mervyn Cowie, the military man with the bright red kerchief. Born in British Kenya, head of recruitment during the repression of the Mau Mau, he was director of the Royal National Parks of Kenya and then adviser to the Kenyatta government.

Ian Grimwood, the inveterate fighter. Trained as an entomologist, this British soldier, a survivor of Japanese prison camps, became chief game warden of the national parks in Northern Rhodesia and in Kenya, and went on to lead Operation Oryx before becoming an expert and working in Ethiopia and Tanzania and also in North and South America and Asia.

Peter Hay, the Scot with a passion for hunting. An agronomist, he studied the invasion of wild locusts in Somaliland before finding work in the Ugandan national parks and was then recruited, following independence, as chief warden of the Ethiopian park of Awash.

Clive Nicol, the young karateka. A research engineer first in England and then in Japan, where he became a black belt in karate, he worked in the biological station in the Canadian Arctic before going to Ethiopia where he became game warden of the Simien National Park.

John Owen, the pipe smoker. Born in Uganda, district commissioner in the Sudan and then warden of national parks in British East Africa, he was head of the Tanzanian national parks both before and after independence.

The Ethiopian leaders

Abebe Retta, the minister under Haile Selassie. Minister for Agriculture and one of the emperor's closest associates, he appealed for aid from UNESCO in order to set up the country's first national parks.

Berhanu Tessema, the polyglot. A high-ranking official, he spoke Amharic and Tigrinya as well as English, French and German and as a result became the chief representative of the Ethiopian Empire to the international conservation institutions.

Germatchew Tekle Hawariat, the highly regarded Minister for Information. After holding the most prestigious position in the country, he led the council overseeing national and foreign employees of the Ethiopian Wildlife Conservation Organization (EWCO).

Gizaw Gedlegiorgis, the major in a suit adorned with an impressive array of medals. Trained as a pilot, he fought against Italy for the liberation of Ethiopia, and later became head of the Ethiopian Conservation Department where he worked constantly with foreign experts.

Mebratu Fisseha, the general and ambassador. A police officer for over twenty years, a general in the navy and then ambassador to Nigeria, he was the first director of the EWCO.

Nadew Woreta, the Simien fixer. Former imperial official, chief warden of the Simien National Park, he lost his job when foreign experts took over his post. He subsequently became a politician.

Tamrat Yigezu, the captain. Recognized for his military exploits against the Italian invader, which saw him promoted to the rank of captain at the age of nineteen, he was governor of the Begemder region and, in that capacity, in charge of the Simien Park.

Teshome Ashine, the most American of Ethiopians. After studying conservation at the College of African Wildlife Management in Mweka and then in the USA, he became head of the EWCO where he used his diplomatic skills to develop Ethiopian nature policies.

The nameless

Dehaw, the poor one. He lives, for example, in the Simien National Park in Ethiopia. A farmer, or pastoralist, he has few resources and less and less right to exploit them.

Mengest, the powerful one. He lives, for example, in the Omo National Park in Ethiopia. A park guard, trader or former civil servant under the Empire, he does not necessarily have much power. But he has more than his neighbours.

Serateña, the employee. He lives in the Awash National Park in Ethiopia, for example. He looks after his animals or his land but sometimes takes on paid work for the park administration, doing building work or helping to welcome tourists.

Tekelakay, the insubordinate one. He can be found everywhere, in the Awash, in the Omo and in the Simien. One morning he might decide to illegally extend his land. The next day he could refuse to pay a fine. And one day, confronted with the park guards, he might decide to pick up his gun.

Yemiyastekaklew, the resourceful one. Whether poor, powerful, in work or rebelling against the system, he uses his remarkable powers of ingenuity to get round the conservation laws.

Protecting Africa from the Africans
The world of the expert gentlemen

Conservation, according to the principal experts, is an apolitical matter. Not surprisingly, decolonialization resulted in a great many changes. At the end of the 1950s, the expert gentlemen were becoming increasingly aware of these changes with every passing day – the power relations between the home countries and the colonies were changing radically, European empires were on the brink of disappearing and, in the context of the Cold War, action on an international scale was becoming increasingly uncertain. Yet if nature was to be protected in Africa, stability was imperative. Conservation is, after all, a matter of common sense and not of politics. This is how its promoters were eager to define it – as a universal task rather than a western or an African one. Which explains why, throughout the 1960s and 1970s, the African Special Project met with such success.

Arusha 1961. Changing everything in order to keep everything the same

The project was officially launched in Warsaw in June 1960, at the General Assembly of the IUCN. It was an event where everyone was talking about Africa, while carefully avoiding any mention of the decolonization of the continent.

A 'truly international' project

The General Assembly brought together representatives from thirty countries and 136 organizations. Amongst those attending were the most famous conservationists of the time, men like Harold Coolidge, a zoologist and the American vice-president of the Union; Peter Scott, a naturalist and all-rounder, successful artist, member of the British sailing team in the 1936 Olympics and spokesperson for the Fauna Preservation Society (FPS), the oldest non-governmental organization for the protection of nature; Théodore Monod, naturalist and director of the *Institut français d'Afrique noire* (IFAN); Bernhard Grzimek, a German vet and filmmaker whose passion for zebras verged on the obsessional; and Edgar Worthington, the aristocratically dressed ecologist who had travelled extensively around Africa during the 1930s and was now head of The Nature Conservancy, the public agency responsible for the environment in Great Britain. Many other nature professionals were also present in Warsaw. They came from the USSR, from Canada and from Europe, like, for example, Jean-Georges Baer, a Swiss parasitologist so famous that a species of rodent would be named in his honour – Baer's wood mouse (*Hylomyscus baeri*).

Baer, at the time president of the IUCN, immediately raised the crucial question of demographic growth, which he described as 'a worldwide danger'. In order to combat this issue, he insisted, in his opening address, that 'efforts must be ... concentrated on a few problems requiring immediate action and where the degree of urgency is universally acknowledged'. He was referring to Africa, rather than the world:

> The most important of these problems ... is to save African wildlife, the existence of which is threatened as a result of changes which were introduced and which are still in place in the administrative structure of the African states. ... This wildlife symbolizes a heritage of universally recognised scientific value, a genuine treasure which it is incumbent on the entire world to preserve and which, were it to disappear at the hand of mankind would represent for our Union the failure of its activity and the futility of its efforts. No one seeks to deprive local people of a source of protein indispensable to their well-being, but we must put a stop to the shameful waste which is still going on and which has even increased in certain regions, now independent. Independence brings with it responsibility, and the irrational massacre of wildlife must be replaced by its rational exploitation.[1]

For this assembly, the IUCN had brought together 183 participants, but out of these, only two were African. These were M. Medani and M.K. Shawki from Sudan, one of them minister of animal resources, the other a representative from the forestry department. This meant that the delegates from the Union were discussing Africa without having invited any Africans, but they insisted that they wanted to leave the *colonial* past behind them and turn their attention instead to an *international* present.

Initially it was all a matter of rhetoric. No mention was made of colonization, but neither was there any criticism on the subject of independence. There was a problem, the 'irrational massacre of wildlife', and a solution: 'conservation' – a 'universal' principle which was a matter for 'the entire world'. Developing universality also required concrete action and as a result the Union decided to abandon its headquarters in Brussels, where, in 1935, the *Office internationale pour la protection de la nature* (OIPN), the forerunner to the IUCN, had first been established. It would certainly be seen as a positive move to leave Belgium, an imperial nation, for a more 'neutral' location. This move provoked a certain amount of discussion but a consensus began to emerge around the argument put forward by Mervyn Cowie, head of the Royal National Parks in British Kenya, who pointed out that 'if the headquarters of the Union could be in a country whose government had no possession or territories in Africa, it would show that the Union was really an international body'. Following his example, delegates from the Soviet Union and some other countries then suggested a move to Switzerland – a 'neutral' country.

Consequently, it was from there, in the little town of Morges, that the Union found itself overseeing the African Special Project.[2] The aim of this project was to respond to 'the extremely rapid changes' which were threatening the future of 'wild life and of natural habitats' in Africa. What was distinctive about the project was its international focus. It would take place over three stages, all of them coordinated by the IUCN, the FAO, UNESCO and the CCTA. The three stages would consist of a period of 'preparatory work including a field mission', a 'conference in Africa' and then 'an organization for following up the decisions of that conference'.[3]

Helping Africa help itself

The first phase began at the end of 1960. Released from the FAO to work for the IUCN for a period of a few months, Gerald Watterson embarked on his African tour. A forestry officer and indefatigable traveller, this

Englishman reported that, in the sixteen countries he had visited, he was 'accompanied by Africans' whose expenses were funded by the FPS and the New York Zoological Society. These 'Africans' were also present during the second stage of the Project, at the Arusha conference in September 1961. Watterson's report of the event, numbering 373 pages, describes it as a 'success', culminating in the Arusha Manifesto, signed by three representatives of the soon to be independent Tanganyika – the prime minister, Julius Nyerere, the legal affairs minister, Abdallah Said Fundikira, and the lands and surveys minister, Tewa Said Tewa. Their manifesto is short and unequivocal:

> The survival of our wildlife is a matter of grave concern to all of us in Africa. These wild creatures amid the wild places they inhabit are not only important as a source of wonder and inspiration but are an integral part of our natural resources and of our future livelihood and well-being.
>
> In accepting the trusteeship of our wildlife we solemnly declare that we will do everything in our power to make sure that our children's grandchildren will be able to enjoy this rich and precious inheritance.
>
> The conservation of wildlife and wild places calls for specialist knowledge, trained manpower and money and we look to other nations to cooperate in this important task – the success or failure of which not only affects the Continent of Africa but the rest of the world as well.[4]

The time had therefore come for international cooperation. With this in mind, working together, panel by panel, resolution by resolution, the 130 delegates first of all set about defining the problem confronting them, namely 'the accelerated rate of destruction of wild fauna, flora and habitat in Africa'.

From there, they turned their attention to the causes of the problem, also clearly identified: 'these great and unique faunal and floral resources could become exhausted merely because the indigenous people had not had adequately demonstrated to them methods to maintain maximum economic and cultural benefits from them'. Here too, colonization was not mentioned, nor was the ecological devastation associated with it or the failure of its purported education programme. But neither was blame attributed to local people. The proceedings of the conference make a clear distinction between, on the one hand, the threat afflicting the entire planet, notably the 'rapidly advancing tide of human population', and on the other hand, the fact that 'The African is a realist' for whom 'the use of game as a source of food ... is more easily understood than the idea of conserving wild animals for aesthetic, scientific or sentimental reasons'. Furthermore, the report goes on to say, for 'the African ... the use of game as a source of food also fulfils in many instances a strong instinct and a way of life'. This explains why the delegates made little specific reference to nature itself, since in their view, 'The major issues of Governments lie not directly with animals, vegetation or soil, but with people'.[5]

Faced with this practical instinct demonstrated by Africans, the experts present at Arusha could envisage just one solution: 'Only by the planned utilization of wildlife as a renewable natural resource, either for protein or as a recreational attraction, can its conservation and development be economically justified in competition with agriculture, stock ranching and other forms of land use.'[6]

Once the solution had been identified, the next step was to outline practical ways of implementing it. The first of these, according to Scottish ecologist Frank Fraser Darling, was a scientific one, which involved the introduction of a 'human' ecology where the aim was less about the 'preservation' of nature than about its 'conservation'. Rather than overprotecting nature, what was needed was a sustainable exploitation of the environment which took into account all its various components: in other words, one which focused on fauna and flora but also on human beings.[7] After science, it was the turn of economics. In an ever more urban world, explained Bernhard Grzimek, vet, filmmaker and director of Frankfurt Zoo, the tourist industry will serve the conservationist cause. There can be no doubt, he wrote, that Africa would grow richer by offering 'modern man' the opportunity to satisfy 'his desire for contact with animals'. Furthermore, Grzimek went on to point out, thanks to the enthusiasm of the entire planet for its natural heritage, African governments would gain the sense of 'pride' they needed in today's world: while European countries could rely on their monuments and their architectural heritage to be the glory of their nations, the African countries could achieve the same thing with their wildlife and natural environment.[8] This theory was reiterated by many of the delegates at the conference, and summed up by its principal advocate,

Jacques Verschuren. According to this Belgian zoologist who had trained in the *Institut des parcs nationaux du Congo Belge*, where he had learned to know and love African elephants, if 'Europe has its cathedrals, preserved through ages; Africa is proud to show the prestigious natural spectacles which she has helped to save'.[9]

Science, economics and nationalism would therefore come together in a single space – that of the national park. Former director of UNESCO, the biologist Julian Huxley clarified this in his account of his recent stay in East Africa. The wildlife there was 'spectacular' but the agriculture and grazing were causing 'deterioration', he confidently declared. As a result, urged Huxley, sporting his customary white suit, the only solution was to set aside areas to be 'reserved as wild lands', or, in other words, to transform them into parkland.[10] This was where international aid would be needed, an intervention supported by all those attending the conference. Thanks to 'Governmental and private organizations and foundations which are anxious to assist economically underdeveloped countries and regions', there would be many 'individual interested countries of Africa where responsible Government services would be shown how to help themselves', concluded Gerald Watterson.[11] And so began the third stage of the Special Project.

The national park as the only viable solution

The IUCN hoped that any 'aid' given to Africa would be 'channelled in such a way as to avoid wasteful duplication'.[12] And, in concrete terms, this was achieved by sending Thane Riney and Peter Hill to visit the countries requesting that aid. Riney was an ecologist with a particular interest in wild animals and considerable experience in Africa, Australia and North America. Hill was an agronomist specializing in land use and had studied in the department of agriculture at the British University in Ghana. The two men were based in Morges, at the Swiss headquarters of the IUCN, from where they travelled to Africa on two occasions, first in 1961 and then in 1962. Their mission was coordinated by the CCTA and UNESCO, their expenses were covered by the FAO and the FPS, and their task was essentially 'to help governments to help themselves' by integrating the recommendations made at Arusha into their own national policies.[13] And for over a year, this was precisely what the two men did – in Senegal, in Mali and in Nigeria, and then across the whole of East Africa, from Ethiopia to Tanzania, and as far as Uganda and Bechuanaland (the future Botswana).[14]

Like the Arusha conference, the third stage of the Project was a success. At least that was the conclusion reached at the 8th General Assembly of the IUCN which took place in Nairobi, Kenya, in September 1963. The country was not yet fully independent – that would finally come in the month of December – but its future leaders demonstrated that they were already enthusiastic defenders of conservation. In the keynote speech at the start of the conference, government minister Joseph Murumbi praised the action of the western experts, declaring that he and his colleagues in the new Kenyan government were eager to 'learn something … that will assist us to undertake our duties in nature conservation more efficiently and more effectively'.[15]

Murumbi's plea was particularly appreciated by the president of the Union, the Swiss parasitologist Jean-Georges Baer. He reminded the delegates of the message of the Arusha Manifesto, notably, according to the extract he had chosen, the soon to be established international cooperation which would bring to Africa 'specialist knowledge, trained manpower and money'. Baer then emphasized that many African states had 'supported the Arusha Manifesto'. For the first time, said the president of the IUCN, in terms of conservation 'the solidarity of the African Continent with the rest of the world is also recognised'. The resolutions adopted at the end of the General Assembly would therefore reinforce this new 'solidarity'. The IUCN, UNESCO, the FPS, the FAO and the CCTA advocated the introduction of ecological studies on the African savannah, the development of new conservation projects and, in very concrete terms, the creation of new national parks in Kenya, Tanzania[16] and Zanzibar as well as in Northern Rhodesia.[17]

This then was the roadmap which was being put in place in order to protect nature in postcolonial Africa. Preservation must give way to 'conservation' and, from that point on, 'human ecology' must drive the management of natural resources. But behind these new words from the international discourse, the privileged tool for conservationists remained the one they had all agreed on in 1933, at the time of the imperial era, at the 'International Conference for the Protection of the Fauna and Flora of Africa', notably the creation of national parks. It was as though everything was changing so that nothing would really change, except, that is, for just one thing – the colonial domination of Africa would give way to an international cooperation now demanded by Africa. Théodore Monod expressed this clearly: '*mutatis mutandis* [that which should be changed having been changed], will enable those now responsible for taking decisions … to pass from the stage of factual equilibrium imposed from without, towards one of deliberately chosen and organised equilibrium'.[18]

From imperialism to internationalism. History

On the subject of these transformations within a context of continuity, and of these ongoing elements within a context of change, historians have already provided us with many of the tools needed for our investigation. They have written, for example, about the images associated with colonization, about the ideology of development and about overpopulation.

Colonial imaginaries

Let us begin with the images that went hand in hand with colonization at the end of the nineteenth century – images of once lush territories, located in the Middle East, in South East Asia and in Africa and subsequently destroyed by human activity. This is an erroneous vision: humans have been adapting their way of life and utilizing deserts and forests for more than 5,000 years. But the colonialists were steeped in this 'environmental orientalism' which led them to believe in the virgin state of non-European nature.[19] For the more Europe became industrialized and urbanized, the more they believed they could rediscover in the tropics a nature they had lost in their own countries. This belief was all the more widespread amongst botanists, zoologists and foresters because they were able to travel. And that meant that, instinctively, they made comparisons. In their view there was Europe with its environment essentially created by humans, and Africa, where the '"true" and "unspoiled" nature' remained untouched and authentic and had not yet been completely destroyed by its inhabitants.[20]

This continental fantasy spread through the colonies, across the 'Old Continent' of Europe and then throughout the entire world. Since the

1950s, literature and films dedicated to wildlife had proliferated, with the documentary *Savage Splendor* from ethologist Armand Denis, the novel *Born Free* illustrated with Joy Adamson's photos of her lioness Elsa or the film *Signals for Survival* by Niko Tinbergen. Western spectators were therefore invited in their millions to explore Africa as a 'visual refuge of nature', which had survived thanks to the conservation policies put in place there.[21] These texts and images were not necessarily neocolonial. Those responsible for them denounced the imperial ethos of hunting and defended the cause of wildlife across the entire planet.[22] Yet all of them described the same African bestiary in its naturally wild state and, even more significantly, they referred to the protection of African wildlife as a responsibility that must be shouldered by them and by the western world.[23] And it was in this way that they succeeded in turning their fantasized vision of the world into a reality.

The anthropologist Jim Igoe observed this phenomenon in the context, for example, of the Tanzanian Park of Serengeti. In the mid-1950s, the images captured by Bernhard Grzimek and his son were 'true without being accurate', Igoe writes. Although the two men in their zebra-striped planes zoomed in on animals and places which were indeed real, they excluded from the frame any inhabitants of the park, except to show them killing wildlife. By focusing public attention on *one* version of reality, this ended up being perceived as *the* reality. So much so that their images were used to support the criminalization of the Maasai people of the Serengeti which was in force at that time. Initially, the FPS and the Frankfurt Zoological Society had recommended emptying the park in order to protect it from its inhabitants. The images selected on site by the Grzimeks further reinforced the belief that African wildlife was threatened by poachers and herdsmen who were the 'despoilers of African nature'. All this explains why the British authorities were finally able to expel some Maasai groups and to criminalize the use of the land by all other inhabitants, in the name of respect for an environmental order.[24]

Much has been written on the colonial roots of this global movement for the protection of nature. At the end of the nineteenth century, the imperial administrations embraced the myth of an African Eden *once* luxuriant but *now* under threat, since this allowed them to justify the expropriation of colonized populations and to ensure the continuation of colonial capitalism. It was in this context that European hunters were instrumental in the creation of game reserves in which they monopolized the right of access to big game. Then, in 1933, during the International Conference for the Protection of the Fauna and Flora of Africa in London, these hunters transformed themselves into 'penitent butchers'.[25] From that point on, they campaigned for the reserves to be converted into national parks designed either for better regulated trophy hunting, or simply as places for the contemplation of nature. Finally, after the Second World War, nature-based tourism began to replace tourism centred around hunting. The colonial authorities encouraged this new market since it provided them with additional funding for reconstruction work in their home countries. But the movement was also supported by scientific administrators. In the name of nature, they established a trans-imperial cooperation which encouraged the most influential organizations, to which they belonged, to restructure or, at the very least, change their names. So, for example, in 1948 the International *Office* for the Protection of Nature became the International *Union* for the Protection of Nature. And, in 1950, the Society for the Preservation of the Fauna of the Empire was renamed the Fauna Preservation Society (FPS).[26]

Promoting 'development'

This transition from imperialism to internationalism went hand in hand with the growing interest in developmentalist ideology. After 1945, imperial organizations found themselves in competition with the new international institutions, and the British Colonial Office, for example, sought to prevent the FAO from making contact with its foresters. London was keen to retain control over its scientists and to maintain sovereignty within its colonies.[27] Then, during the 1950s, development led to the establishment of a new cooperation. For the FAO or UNESCO, working with colonial powers was not perceived as a problem since the majority of their employees had been trained in the colonies and they too were convinced that 'Africa' lacked the necessary expertise for development. Equally, empires willingly collaborated with international organizations to improve the outcome for their colonies: it was a good way of improving their legitimacy and, as a result, retaining their existing position. A status quo was therefore established, which was then encouraged by the African elites. During their journey towards independence, the latter had increased their popularity by criticizing the lack of development brought by Europe. Once independence had been acquired, they therefore needed to deliver the promised development to their citizens, over whom, like their colonial predecessors, they exercised a 'paternalistic sense of responsibility and power inherent in the making of the postcolonial state'.[28]

Conservationists were also embarking on the developmental path, but, in their case, no mutual agreement on the subject could be reached. Their disagreements finally came to a head in August 1949 at Lake Success, in the USA, on the occasion of two simultaneous conferences, both sponsored by the United Nations. The first of these was supported by heads of state and politicians who were adamant about the need to 'conserve' nature, or in other words, to exploit it in a rational manner in order to prevent an overpopulated and under-resourced world from tipping into a third world war. But the second conference was critical of this economic bias. At this event, non-governmental associations, biologists and ecologists insisted, first of all, that the planet's threatened ecosystems needed to be 'protected'.[29] Consequently, a confrontation ensued between conservationist ideals (in favour of a development which respected nature) and preservationist ideals (calling for nature to be left untouched by development).[30] The debate was all the more heated since other disagreements began to surface. Who should be responsible for managing resources on a worldwide scale? Should this be a task for the new agencies of the United Nations or for the already experienced non-governmental organizations? And what exactly should be protected – human ecosystems or unspoilt nature?

Faced with such questions, the International Union for the Protection of Nature (IUPN) appeared to be the only institution capable of offering a compromise. As historian Raf de Bont makes clear, with ecologists as its leaders and governments as its official members, the Union could claim to be both scientific and political, or in other words, to be capable of 'managing not only (colonial) fauna and flora but also (colonial) popula-tions'. With the IUPN, the 'expert gentlemen' would therefore be able to maintain a continuity between the colonial and the postcolonial eras. Having been preservationists during the inter-war period, during the 1950s, Julian Huxley and Edgar Worthington became the promoters of a systems-based conservation. The two ecologists, already well recognized in all international arenas, were joined by other well-known professionals, like the British ornithologist Max Nicholson or the American biologist Raymond Dasmann. Together, they worked with both the IUPN and UNESCO. They forged links between the two organizations and, through these discussions, a conservationist model began to take shape.[31] From its base within the United Nations, UNESCO became the guarantor of a 'human' and 'universal' ecology, to be applied across the whole world – an approach which, some years later, would lead to the launch of the International Biological Program (IBP), later renamed MAB (Man and Biosphere).[32] The IUCN however, although claiming to be supporting the same global ecology, confined its attention to the protection of animal species and of the national parks – a focus which would later see it obtaining the status of official adviser for UNESCO on the classification of park areas as World Heritage sites.[33]

The division of tasks was therefore a very real one. But the major conservation experts were also working for the continuity of their group by building a consensus around a single entity: the national park.[34] Under the influence of the United States, ever more present in the IUCN, the United Nations and in Africa, the national park became the tool of choice when it came to translating conservationist discourse into action. With its 'List of National Parks and Equivalent Reserves', and subsequently its 'Red List of Threatened Species', the *Red Data Book*, the IUCN provided the United Nations with the norms it needed in order to manage the natural world. The United Nations and the IUCN then jointly organized 'The First World Conference on National Parks' in Seattle in 1962 followed by the 'The United Nations Conference on the Environment' in Stockholm in 1972. The latter acknowledged the existence of a worldwide ecological crisis and the need for international action capable of at least protecting the national parks which now represented World Heritage sites.[35]

Combatting 'overpopulation'

This intersection between global thinking and local action became part of what historian Thomas Robertson called the international 'Malthusian Moment'. This concept first emerged in the United States in 1948 when

William Vogt published *Road to Survival*, which rapidly became a best-seller, with millions of copies sold. Biologist, administrator, ornithologist and member of the IUPN, this specialist in South American conservation declared that overpopulation was now depleting resources. The demographic growth of the countries of the southern hemisphere had previously been regulated by a high mortality rate, Vogt explained, but now improvements in living conditions *down there* were disrupting the balance *everywhere*. His reasoning appeared to be irrefutable: too many people equals a lack of food, and therefore more exploitation and more deterioration, and even less food.[36] Throughout the 1950s, these American preoccupations spread in western scientific and governmental circles, finally finding resonance worldwide at the end of the 1960s. Once again, the impetus came from the United States, where in 1968, biologist Paul R. Ehrlich's book *The Population Bomb*, revitalized Vogt's ideas. The same year, with his theory on the 'tragedy of the commons', ecologist Garrett Hardin called on the major powers to implement a 'mutual coercion mutually agreed upon'. Once again, this idea was founded on mathematical reasoning: demographic growth meant imminent depletion of resources and therefore the inevitable prospect of worldwide conflict. Hence the urgency, according to Hardin, to control birth rates (in order to slow down overpopulation) and to do more to conserve resources (in order to allow the current population to survive).[37]

From a scientific perspective, these debates were clearly by no means impartial. Deforestation, for example, which experts blamed on overpopulation, was in reality an 'endless debate', to use the phrase coined by political analyst Marie-Claude Smouts. No possible conclusion exists since 'estimates ... are based on fairly unreliable data', across the whole world and, even more so, in Africa.[38] Conversely, it is clear that, in the developmentalist era which in Africa began in the 1950s, subsistence agriculture practised by peasant farmers, although frequently singled out for blame, was in reality much less destructive than industries exporting wood, rubber and minerals.[39] Hence the necessity of the myth, as defined by the social sciences: its role was always 'to provide a logical model capable of overcoming a contradiction.[40] For the post-war world is marked by two contradictions – on a worldwide scale, western countries are at one and the same time those destroying resources and those seeking to protect them, and on a continent-wide scale, even in the context of Africa's independence, the colonial scientists transformed into international experts remained convinced that they alone were capable of saving it. Which is why in Africa, western models, like those of Ehrlich or Hardin, found expression in the perpetuation of a myth and the invention of a logical solution.

Africa, a virgin and unspoilt continent but one which was also overpopulated and damaged – the colonial myth endured in the form of a certain 'moral geography of conservation' where practices recognized elsewhere as ethical were declared unethical inside the African national parks. This was the case, for example, with small game hunting, pastoralism and subsistence farming. As in the colonial era, in the period immediately following African independence these practices had been declared illegal. But criminalization of such activities intensified since, from that point on, this was no longer justified on the grounds of colonialism but on the basis of scientific 'reason'. The imperative had now become the global battle for the environment and, in order to be successful in that combat, a new ecological principle had emerged in the form of what was referred to as the 'carrying capacity'. This was a principle which stipulated that any given area of land corresponded to a maximum density of occupation, beyond which it was necessary to expel local people or at least curtail their rights of use.[41] According to the rhetoric of the experts, they were bringing a *local* solution to a *global* disaster. But in practice, they were applying the *African* solution to a disaster caused by a *western* capitalism which was never explicitly challenged.

In this way, the internationalization of African nature was gradually taking shape. Historians have demonstrated that, thanks to the key figures of conservation, from the 1950s to the end of the 1970s an entire postcolonial world was emerging. And it is this world that we must now explore more closely given that it seems to have shaped a certain idea of African nature and the correct way of managing it.

The rise of a conservationist 'International'

Paris, New York, London, Beirut, Bukavu – in the immediate aftermath of the Second World War and from one continent to another, the leading nature professionals came together to organize a common action, on a worldwide scale. These meetings produced such a vast quantity of archives that today's readers can quickly find themselves drowning in a sea of ever more obscure institutional acronyms. But once we accept the inevitability of getting lost in the administrative confusion, it becomes apparent that the major experts were in fact taking advantage of this chaos. It was as though they were deliberately using the ongoing confusion in order to strengthen their mutual links and to consolidate a united front which would gradually enable them to construct an unprecedented international collaboration.

From preservation to conservation

The foundations for this collaboration were laid in 1947, in the town of Brunnen in Switzerland. Prompted by the Swiss League for the Protection of Nature and with representatives from twenty-four European and American countries and organizations such as the FAO and the International Office for the Protection of Nature (IOPN), it was decided that UNESCO would shortly organize in Paris the constitutive congress of a new organization – the International Union for the Protection of Nature (IUPN). The acronyms indicated a certain continuity and yet, in 1947, a change of scale was clearly visible – with the growth in the world population, it was now a *global* threat that took precedence. It was therefore in this context that Africa found itself placed at the centre of attention.

The continent was faced with two major problems. The first of these lay with the local inhabitants who were destroying the 'primeval forest' and hunting in a way that often led to 'cruel massacres'. The second problem was that the colonial governments had failed to 'do away with those errors'. On the ground, the creation of parks remained the solution: for the delegates gathered together at Brunnen, 'Agricultural areas and those suitable for the protection of wild life should be clearly defined'. But they were adamant, that from then onwards, 'international rulings' were the only way to bring an end to this destruction. At that point UNESCO, the young agency of the United Nations, intervened. Those attending the conference were resolute on this point: 'But *it is we* who would found the organization', they insisted, and UNESCO 'would help us to obtain the necessary governmental collaboration'.[42] And the following year this was exactly what happened.

In October 1948, in Fontainebleau, UNESCO invited representatives of twenty-five states and six nature organizations to validate the constitution of the new IUPN (which would replace the IOPN). The Union was de facto an intergovernmental organization – internal governance favoured the interests of member states, who were given two votes, to the detriment of member associations, who only had a single vote. But the birth of the IUPN marked the end for the empires – although Great Britain, France, Belgium, the Netherlands and Portugal were represented, they also had to contend with twenty other states which would now also have their opinions on the protection of nature throughout the world, and therefore in the colonies of Africa and Asia.[43]

Thanks to UNESCO, the IUPN had now been established but, in both these organizations, the hardest work still lay ahead for the 'expert gentlemen'. They needed to prevent representatives from the colonial empires from undermining the IUPN and UNESCO from within and, even more importantly, they needed to convince them that protecting world nature was the responsibility of the two organizations, and no longer a matter for the empires. In order to do so, they took full advantage of a certain amount of institutional confusion. Guided by the diplomatic skills of its director, Julian Huxley, UNESCO was careful to deal sensitively with the empires by emphasizing that it was up to the IUPN, and not to UNESCO, to undertake the task of 'making mankind aware of the relationship of living things with each other and with their environment, or the science of ecology'.[44] And conversely, the IUPN shifted the responsibility onto UNESCO. So, for example, when Roger Heim, the French botanist and vice-president of the Union, announced that 'international control' was essential in order to save wildlife, he was quick to add: 'It is up to UNESCO to take the initiative'.[45] UNESCO and the IUPN were therefore waging a delicate battle over nature – they blended the authority of an international agency with the apolitical legitimacy of a non-governmental association, while taking full advantage of the confusion over their respective roles.

But their objective was well and truly the same – to promote conservation on what was now a worldwide scale. Jean-Paul Harroy made this point very eloquently. Having worked in the family beer import business, this Belgian engineer had studied colonial science at the University of Brussels and, since 1935, had been head of the *Institut des parcs nationaux du Congo Belge.* He became secretary-general of the IUPN after the Fontainebleau conference, at which he had delivered a resounding plea for the 'preparation of a world convention' on the protection of nature.[46]

The argument struck a chord in conservation circles and, in 1949, at Lake Success, it was reaffirmed by the secretary-general of UNESCO, who announced the launch across all five continents of a campaign of 'education in the protection of nature' and a programme of 'ecological surveys'. Since their field of action now extended to the entire world, it was not surprising that the experts remained somewhat vague. In terms of 'education', they were thinking along the lines of literature, films and educational materials which 'would have to be carefully adapted to the mentality ... of different people'. When it came to ecology, the discourse was equally vague. The participants referred to 'methods of conserving soils', the dangers of 'the generalized use of insecticides' or to 'modern methods of protecting plants'. But some interventions were nevertheless more specific and, when this was the case, they referred first and foremost to Africa. Administrators, ecologists and field managers spoke about the 'extinction of big game' or about 'game control'. Their speeches were peppered with real examples, with references to zebras, gorillas, the savannah and the forest, and the proposed solutions referred to specific areas such as Kenya, South Africa and French Equatorial Africa.[47] This switching between global generalities and African cases would be repeated during subsequent conferences, in Brussels and then in Caracas. In fact, the more Africa was seen as the continent where action was needed, the more it became the region from which it appeared possible to build the international cooperation so much desired.

The IUPN set out the international dimension of its activity during its 4th General Assembly, in Copenhagen in 1954. 'In order to avoid possible faux pas', its secretary wrote, the Union would avoid direct negotiations with governments. Instead, it would concentrate on maintaining 'as close contact as possible with the United Nations', so as to retain 'special consultative status' with UNESCO and the FAO. But the IUPN also wanted to take practical action. And that was why they were eager to be present at Bukavu, in the Belgian Congo, in 1953, for the 'Third International Conference for the Protection of the Fauna and Flora of Africa', organized by the CCTA, the Commission for Technical Cooperation in Africa South of the Sahara. The conference had launched an appeal for the definition of 'a general policy of nature conservation in Africa', and subsequently, in order to ensure its involvement, the Union coordinated research programmes which would then be used to offer practical recommendations to any governments interested in them.[48]

Ostensibly, by the mid-1950s, the agenda had therefore changed. Gone was the concept of *preservation*, the idea of placing nature under wraps with the attendant policy of social exclusion. From that point on, the focus switched to the sustainable exploitation of resources and to their *conservation* by, and for, human beings. But all of this was also, essentially, a matter of rhetoric. On the occasion of the 5th General Assembly of the IUPN, organized in the autumn of 1956 in Edinburgh, its new president, Roger Heim, declared his commitment to the 'preservation' of nature. The Union nevertheless needed to attract funding and, in order to do so, Heim continued: 'It must be said that in a great many domains, we have to play somewhat false with public opinion ... put the emphasis on the necessary in order to enable the useful to happen, and on economic imperatives in order to gain acceptance for that which touches only the mind.' In other words, if *conservation* was seen as 'necessary', and was associated with development, its promoters had not lost sight of what was really 'useful', in other words, *preservation*. This strategy was supported by Alain Gille and Gerald Watterson, the representatives of UNESCO and the FAO. In their eyes, 'the change of name proposed by the president will certainly help the organisation's cause' with the United Nations. Consequently, in the autumn of 1956, the IUPN was renamed the IUCN.[49]

Its role was still to protect the 'sanctuaries of natural life', according to the report of its annual general assembly which took place in Athens in 1958. Moreover, as Harold Coolidge, the American zoologist, insisted: 'There was, however, no more efficient form of conservation than setting aside territories as national parks or nature reserves.' The IUCN could therefore stay on course. By deploying a conservationist and developmentalist discourse it even succeeded in obtaining the funding necessary to take action. Still in Athens, Watterson conveyed the congratulations of the FAO for the 'lively' cooperation between the

FAO and the IUCN. Gille promised that UNESCO would increase the value of the subsidies it was providing and Edgar Worthington, the aristocratic ecologist at the head of The Nature Conservancy, announced that the British government would bring its full support to the new IUCN.[50]

At that precise time, in 1958, Worthington had not yet received the approval of his government. But this was the great skill of these expert gentlemen. They were present in each one of the institutions working for nature, including those associated with the colonial powers, the United Nations and non-governmental organizations. And, as a result, they could self-legitimize each other by inviting each other to each of the conferences they organized in the name of the institutions they represented, to the point that they were able to construct an authority which was becoming increasingly recognized, and therefore less and less subject to challenge, even by colonial administrators.

From colonial action to international cooperation

The British archives provide ample evidence of the way these major experts set about organizing the transition between the colonial era and the international era. Take, for example, the hundred or so letters exchanged between 1950 and 1959 by the employees of the Colonial Office, The Nature Conservancy (the government agency for the environment), the British Committee for Nature Conservation at the CCTA (the inter-imperial agency for cooperation in Africa), and finally, the Scientific Council for Africa (CSA) in association with the CCTA. Here too, we need to look beyond the acronyms in order to understand the strategy adopted by the major conservation experts.

In 1950, the CCTA was largely in the hands of the European empires who were afraid of seeing their colonies come under the control of the United States, the USSR or the United Nations.[51] However, in the month of August, the parasitologist Jean-Georges Baer, acting on behalf of the IUPN, decided to engage in direct contact with Keith Caldwell, a former military pilot who had been a game warden in Kenya, then chief correspondent for the Fauna Preservation Society in East Africa, and member of the British Conservation Committee at the CCTA. This man had as much influence in London as in Nairobi, and it was this that led

Baer to personally send him a questionnaire intended to establish all the existing measures in place in the protected areas of Kenya, where Captain Caldwell was based at that time. The senior figures at the Colonial Office were immediately worried. They explained to Caldwell that 'there is no obligation to complete the questionnaire', and made it clear to Baer that 'any communication between the Union and [other] Colonial Governments should come through the Colonial Office'.[52] The warning was unmistakable: the IUPN should not be meddling in British colonial matters. The result would however turn out to be the very opposite of that intended.

After this warning, Caldwell and Baer kept up a regular correspondence. They sent a copy of each of their letters to the Colonial Office, and letter after letter, the two men campaigned for cooperation between their respective employers, the CCTA and the IUPN. Then they decided to include Max Nicholson and Edgar Worthington in their discussions. The former was director of The Nature Conservancy, the latter its deputy director, and – in this capacity – seconded to the CSA.[53] And it was these four men who invited the IUPN to take part in the conference organized by their CCTA colleagues in Bukavu in 1953, where 'A Charter for Nature Protection in Tropical Africa'[54] would be drawn up. Thanks to Caldwell, Baer, Nicholson and Worthington, the IUPN was now very much an official player in the conservation game played out by the British Empire.

With this charter, the imperial powers of Britain, France, Belgium and Portugal hoped, *via* the CCTA, to continue to monopolize control of the protected sites in Africa. But the conservationists were determined to instigate a course of action that would be truly international, rather than simply colonial. With this in mind, Max Nicholson went as far as to engage in a veritable lobbying campaign with the top officials of the Colonial Office: 'The IUPN has reached a point where fuller official support from the United Kingdom would be justified and would be in British interests', he wrote to them in 1956, proudly pointing out his 'close connection with the highest body of experts' which would be of benefit to them if the United Kingdom officially allied itself with the IUPN. But his efforts were in vain. London only agreed to give additional research grants to the Union, and then, in 1957, proposed reforms to the 'Convention Relative to the Preservation of Fauna and

Flora in their Natural State' (a convention dating from 1933). While aware of the demands of the 'African people', the CCTA (and therefore the empires) would consequently remain very much in command of the protection of nature in Africa.[55]

Faced with this initiative, Worthington, who had replaced the lobbyist Nicholson at the head of The Nature Conservancy, decided to present the imperial authorities with a fait accompli. India and Pakistan had just joined the IUCN. Now that they were independent, Ghana and the Sudan were also intending to do so. The USSR was becoming more and more active within the Union. 'Under such circumstances', Worthington urged the Colonial Office in 1958, it was 'crucial' to work with the United Nations and the IUCN if they were to be able to continue the work of protection already in place in the soon to be independent colonies. Thanks to the wave of decolonializations which was rapidly spreading throughout Africa, the argument was finally heard and, in 1959, the Colonial Office asked Worthington to be the United Kingdom's official representative in the IUCN.[56] A role he had, in fact, already taken on.

The end of the empires removed the political obstacles restricting the cooperation of the conservationists. But, if they were to make this cooperation more effective in the field, conservationists still lacked appropriate funding. Max Nicholson and Julian Huxley were the first to tackle the problem head on. In April 1961, in Morges, they brought together the key figures in conservation, including Baer, Worthington, M.K. Shawki from Sudan and Peter Scott, the naturalist and all-rounder and an increasingly active member of the FPS.[57] These men then came up with the idea of setting up a bank of which the primary function would be to finance organizations like the IUCN. The first lines of the Morges Manifesto went straight to the point: 'All over the world today vast numbers of ... wild creatures are losing their lives and their homes, in an orgy of thoughtless and needless destruction.' The text went on to emphasize the need to send 'money' and 'experts' to the continent of Africa. The ambition was still on a worldwide scale but, once again, Africa was the continent where action seemed most urgent, and above all the one where it seemed possible to act quickly.[58] And as a result, on 11 September 1961, the creation of the World Wildlife Fund was announced in Arusha.

WWF, the experts' bank

The establishment of the World Wildlife Fund was officially formalized the following month, in London. Its headquarters were set up in the premises of the IUCN in Switzerland, and its members included all the major figures of post-war conservation: Harold Coolidge, the first vice-president of the IUCN for the United States, the German filmmaker Bernhard Grzimek, who represented the Frankfurt Zoological Society, Gerald Watterson, the itinerant conservationist at the FAO, and Peter Scott of the FPS – the latter used a drawing made by Watterson to provide the new institution with a logo which was destined to go down in history – the famous WWF panda, inspired by Chi-Chi, London Zoo's first giant panda. Thanks to their activism, the Fund had soon accumulated almost 2 million dollars. With the result that, in 1965, like a sort of 'modern Noah's Ark' as Peter Scott put it, the WWF had successfully carried out thirty-nine 'international projects', including twenty-three in Africa. These included projects in South Rhodesia to reintroduce the rhinoceros, in Kenya to construct new nature reserves and in Tanzania to extend the Ngorongoro reserve and to set up the College of African Wildlife Management, an institution which would train the African elite who would one day be called on to replace western conservationists.[59]

These projects were carried out in association with the main organizations involved in international conservation – UNESCO, the FPS and, above all, the IUCN. The latter had only 'a tiny fuel tank', wrote the IUCN, but with the WWF they had 'a new pump to ... refill it'.[60] The Union's quarterly *Bulletin* indicated the strength of the links uniting the two institutions. During the 1960s they jointly led 359 projects in fifty-seven countries[61] and, in 1972, they set up 'joint project operations' focusing on the 'conservation of wild species and biotic communities'.[62] Peter Scott's papers, currently archived in Cambridge, also indicate a close relationship between the WWF and the FPS, represented by one of its leading figures, the ornithologist and botanist Richard Fitter. In 1962, the two men referred to the 'mutual gains' of their collaboration.[63] In 1966, the FPS obtained funding from the WWF to carry out a first project in Zambia (ex-Northern Rhodesia).[64] Then, over the next few years, thanks to the new 'FPS/WWF Revolving Fund', their experts participated in a whole series of international operations, ranging from a survey of wild asses in Somalia with the Frankfurt Zoological Society to the study of gorillas in Gambia, with the IUCN.[65]

During the 1960s, the IUCN took the decisive step to concentrate its attention on wildlife. While the expert gentlemen of the FAO and UNESCO led the International Biological Program (IBP), notably in order to help the southern countries exploit their resources in a sustainable manner, the experts at the IUCN, along with their counterparts at the FPS and the WWF, concentrated their attention on managing large fauna and national parks. Their institutional affiliations were therefore multiple, even to the point that they were sometimes difficult to pin down, but all these expert gentlemen represented a body which was much more united than might have appeared. The end of the empires had enabled them to establish what amounted to a genuine 'International' body of conservationists and, between them, there was more 'complementarity' than there was 'competition'. So, for example, when in 1965 Worthington explicitly drew attention to this complementarity, he was speaking both as a special adviser to UNESCO and as a member of the executive board at the IUCN, where he worked closely with Alain Gille, a UNESCO observer within the Union.[66] And in 1969, thanks to both Gille and Worthington, the United Nations invited the IUCN to join them in preparing the United Nations Conference on the Human Environment scheduled to take place in Stockholm in 1972.[67] Finally, that same year, UNESCO officially commissioned the Union to devise 'a world system of biosphere reserves'.[68]

The major conservation experts had therefore outlasted the empires by strengthening their connections with the most important conservation institutions. Even more importantly, they had taken advantage of the demise of the imperial world to revitalize international cooperation, something they had been trying to establish for so many years.

How to conserve: Globalize on the one hand, Africanize on the other

These conservationists had no intention of leaving Africa, but they were by no means simply nostalgic for colonialism. At the end of the 1950s, the CCTA had appeared in its true guise – an inter-imperial organization which sought to reform the colonial system simply in order to keep it in place.[69] The experts, on the other hand, championed real transformations. They explained these in detail at Arusha in 1961. The recognition of human and dynamic ecologies meant that preservation must be replaced by conservation, they insisted, and, according to them, the process of independence must culminate in the 'Africanization' of protected areas, or in other words, in a situation where these would be managed by 'African' personnel.[70] Given this appetite for change, the question needs to be openly asked: what exactly was it that convinced western conservationists of their right to remain in Africa?

One world, one nature

The first part of the answer touches on ethics and science. When the experts met in May 1962 in Seattle, for the First World Conference on National Parks, they unanimously drew attention to the risk of potential extinction which threatened 'the world's flora and fauna': 'There is no longer any question that threatened species ultimately are an international concern rather than a local one.' UNESCO and the FAO promised to encourage 'scientific studies and research' all over the world and in particular in 'underdeveloped countries' which could then be offered 'technical assistance programmes'. The same spirit had moreover been very much present at the launch of the African Special Project, the IUCN pointed out, for 'the accelerated rate of destruction of wildlife and habitat in Africa was the most urgent problem requiring concerted international effort'.[71]

The Union did not deny the significance of the decolonization process but argued that, 'purely political considerations ... can now be subordinated to the more precise considerations of primary human and animal needs', as it declared in Nairobi in 1963 at the 8th General Assembly. Rather than referring to colonization and the ecological damage it had caused, the IUCN preferred to look to the future: 'The African people themselves now have it in their power ... to rivet on to their natural resources modern methods.'[72] In his role as spokesperson for the United States at the IUCN, Stewart Udall went even further. In front of the African delegates gathered in Nairobi, he spoke of the 'errors' of the American people that had 'laid waste the prairies' in his own country: 'It was a race between conservation and catastrophe with catastrophe

48

winning ... I hope that you will learn from us.'[73] UNESCO took the same view. In August 1964, along with the United Nations and their Economic Commission for Africa, it gathered delegates from forty-two African states in Lagos, Nigeria. Faced with a situation 'where the natural balances are especially precarious' and given the lack of research scientists and science teaching staff, UNESCO undertook to support a 'veritable mobilization of international resources ... to help Africa'.[74] This was the conservationists' role. The Europeans and North Americans had 'destroyed' much of their own nature, and they had 'woken ... too late', declared the resident aristocrat Edgar Worthington, also present at Lagos, before adding that, with ecological science as it was currently defined, 'most countries of Africa could avoid such errors'.[75]

The international institutions and the western conservation experts had the technical power and therefore the moral duty to help Africa escape the destruction which was threatening the planet, a situation that justified maintaining and even reinforcing their presence on the continent. But the argument did not go far enough. Or rather, it only made sense if it also opened the door to a new perception of the world.

This vision of the world is revealed in a striking manner in the archives. Each year, the conservationists left behind them thousands of pages of reports. For 1970 alone, for example, we discover that the IUCN had identified 1,204 'national parks and reserves' currently in existence across the world, in which, along with UNESCO, the WWF or the FAO, it had introduced or was continuing to run, IBP, MAB, SCOPE, INCP, TELM, MAR or AQUA programmes. Under this jumble of baffling acronyms, a few countries nevertheless emerge from the reports – Madagascar and its reserves, India and its parks, Ecuador and its Galapagos Islands. But what stands out above all are the endless programmes dedicated to 'exotic animals', or to 'biome field stations in Isolated areas'.[76] In fact, by the time the archives have been thoroughly analysed, the researcher will know everything about the actions of the IUCN in the world in 1970 but almost nothing about the societies in which it was operating. We must therefore rely on a process of accumulation as the only weapon capable of bringing some meaning to the account the major experts give of themselves. Their version is marked by the absence of reference to any recognizable society, or to any specific people. But isn't that, after all, the very essence of their history – one which involves the dehumanization of the places in which they were active, and the construction of that abstract entity they called the 'world'?

This is certainly suggested by the mass of archives produced, amongst others, by UNESCO. With Baer, Worthington and Nicholson heading the International Biological Program, in 1966 UNESCO laid the foundations for a 'worldwide conservation programme' which would operate according to the principle of 'a chain reaction': collecting data from all over the world, ensuring it is 'comparable' and establishing 'A Trust for the World Heritage' which could provide governments everywhere with advice on the measures to be applied in their countries.[77] The discussion continued from conference to conference and then, in 1970, the United Nations decided to replace the IBP with a new programme called 'Man and the Biosphere'.

UNESCO was still one of the institutions behind the project but, on this occasion, it decided to seek support from the IUCN in order to establish a 'world foundation' which would have responsibility for the conservation of 'World Heritage'.[78] UNESCO and the IUCN were then joined by other experts from the FAO. Ten years after the launch of the African Special Project, the expert gentlemen consequently found themselves part of a task force where, for many months, they would work on drawing up the 'Convention Concerning the Protection of the World Cultural and Natural Heritage'.[79] This convention was ratified during the United Nations Conference on the Human Environment, in Stockholm 1972.

During this same conference, the United Nations also created a world fund for the environment, which would enable UNESCO to define the 'outstanding universal value' of sites to be included on its new World Heritage List.[80] As for the IUCN, it found itself on this occasion 'acting as the world "conscience" in conservation'. As such, its role was to assess the applications for sites that the member states of UNESCO were proposing for World Heritage status. The Union was moreover well placed to do so since the WWF had recently tripled the subsidies it made available to it.[81] As a result, the two institutions were able to implement a number of projects, ranging from Latin America to Africa and, in 1978, they confirmed the registration of the first four natural sites on the World Heritage List: four parks, situated in Canada, the United States, Ecuador and Ethiopia.[82]

This listing is evidence of the consensus which had existed since the 1960s and which was based on the vision of a single 'world'. This representation is reflected in the archives as they continue to accumulate – that of a world whose oneness has been fashioned as a result of a triple movement: the recognition of a worldwide ecological crisis, the belief in the capacity of science to resolve this crisis, and the existence of a universal tool – the national park.

'Africa' as an ecological category

The famous process of the 'Africanization' of the continent's national parks came about as a result of this globalization of nature: if Africanization would soon become a reality, it was purely in order to serve a worldwide (and not continent-wide) objective. Here too we need to take all the archives seriously and not confine ourselves to seeking out only the 'crude' information needed by the historian – this particular expert, this particular country, this particular park. The words used are also highly significant. Yet, since the 1960s, every single report or programme now cites 'Africa' as a significant category. In 1966, for example, when the IUCN wanted to reply to its detractors who were accusing it of being 'a "talking shop" which does not get things done', it referred them to the work it had carried out in the 'Africa area'.[83] In the same way, when in 1968 UNESCO held its first intergovernmental conference of conservation experts in Paris, the event included a total of eighty speeches. All of them were general in scope, with no specific country being mentioned in the titles of the contributions. Yet Africa was mentioned a total of forty-nine times, with experts referring to it in each report of 'overgrazing', 'massive deforestation' and 'hunting by local populations'.[84] This process whereby Africa was reduced to its essential characteristics continued to intensify throughout the 1970s. When the IUCN and UNESCO summarized their shared programmes, they either referred to 'tropical ecologies' and went on to list their research in Ethiopia and Ghana,[85] or they made reference to the 'two regions' where they were particularly active, 'eastern Africa' and 'western and central Africa'.[86]

From being a political category within the context of imperial action, Africa had become an ecological category within that of international action. A transformation which seemed moreover perfectly justified since the conservation institutions had officially declared their support for the 'Africanization' of the personnel in charge of managing the country's national parks. That had been announced by the director of UNESCO in 1964 in Addis Ababa, at the headquarters of the Organisation of African Unity (OAU)[87] where members had requested the IUCN to draft for their consideration an 'African Convention for the Conservation of Nature and Natural Resources', which went on to be approved and signed in 1968, replacing the London Convention of 1933. The empires had promised this new convention eleven years earlier, via the CCTA, and it was the conservationists who had finally succeeded in obtaining it, via the new heads of the African states.[88]

Words shaped this concept of a great 'Africa' in people's minds and the Africanization of nature programmes enabled it to become a reality on the ground. This is particularly evident in the work of the African Forestry Commission. Established in 1960 by the United Nations, this organization was run by representatives of the African states who worked alongside 'experts' from the FAO and 'observers' from UNESCO and the IUCN. In the Commission's first year, delegates from fifteen African states came from Cameroon, Nigeria or Tanganyika amongst others to request 'assistance' from the FAO to help them draw up 'adequate policies on the subject of wildlife'.[89] They received the help they needed and, five years later, by which time they were working with almost all the newly independent African countries, the Commission suggested that, given the economic advantages already gained by nature tourism, 'wildlife management should be considered alongside those of other forms of land use'.[90]

From that point onwards, African leaders and western experts worked closely together to conserve the environment. Two international colleges were set up, in Mweka in Tanzania in 1963 and in Garoua in Cameroon in 1967, with a view to providing training for 'African personnel' working in protected areas, under the supervision of 'senior staff', composed of Europeans or North Americans.[91] Then, between 1969 and 1971, the FAO sent thirty-one 'experts' and three 'associate' experts – in other words, Africans – to study the national parks in Botswana, Congo-Kinshasa, Kenya, Ghana, Madagascar, Mali, Morocco, Nigeria and the Sudan.[92] The FAO moved its 'African bureau' from Rome to Accra[93] and, alongside the Forestry Commission, began work on an 'accurate compilation of wildlife statistics [in Western and Central Africa]'.[94]

The project would be abandoned in 1976 when the FAO decided to concentrate exclusively on its forestry policies and to leave the IUCN and the WWF to set up a 'coordinated network of national parks' in the 'region'.[95] By then however, over and above this new distribution of tasks, the three institutions had already bridged the gap between the colonial period and the postcolonial period. On the one hand, by making nature a worldwide issue and national parks a moral solution, their leaders had succeeded in depoliticizing conservation. And on the other, by supporting a policy of 'Africanization' within the continent, they had enabled it to break free from any colonial associations. And that, in the view of the major experts, made their continued presence in Africa entirely justifiable.

Protect the planet, take action in Africa

It should be pointed out too that, if western conservation of African wildlife seemed legitimate, it was largely because the people who had first come up with the concept had insisted that it was necessary. In this context, in analysing the semantics of the discourse used by the experts, I had already had the opportunity to study two different stories: one recounting the invention of an African Eden which *should* have remained intact but which *in reality* was increasingly deteriorating; and one based on a partnership composed of predator and protector which had led western ecologists to set off for Africa in order to save the natural world they had lost in their own countries. These two versions still seem correct to me but, thanks to the work done by psycho-sociology, I have come to the conclusion that by focusing too closely on the social consequences of a discourse, it is all too easy to forget to look closely at its content, and what it tells us about those who formulated it.[96]

The correspondence that the IUCN and UNESCO make accessible to the public and to their employees enables us to somewhat mitigate this omission. Not only does this source help to clarify the conservationists' idea of Africa, but it also reveals them as men driven by a genuine sense of urgency.

Africa as a 'human time bomb'

Delivered to the doorstep of every UNESCO office in the world, the *UNESCO Courier* reveals first of all the sheer depths of anxiety felt by the professionals of international action. As early as 1949, with the work of an agricultural engineer like Alain Gille, the institution expressed its concerns about 'the gap, which is growing every day between the ever increasing population of the world and its declining resources'.[97] In 1952, it was the turn of a scientific journalist to explain in the same *Courier* that, in one century, a third of the world's forests had become deserts. 'It is time', he wrote, 'we put an end to our indiscriminate waste, not only of this natural resource but of natural resources generally.'[98] But years went by and nothing changed. 'Are we headed for catastrophe?' asked Roger Heim, the president of the IUCN, in 1958, in a special edition of the *Courier* where he pointed out that it was now a case of 'man against nature' since 'world population is rapidly growing', a situation that has led to 'the deterioration of the soil, the dryness and the irresistible progress of semi-deserts and deserts'. Two years after Roger Heim first raised the issue, we read in the *Courier* that 'this epidemic of devastated soil seems to be a contagious one'.[99] The drought which devastated India and Africa confirmed this situation in 1966, causing food shortages and then famines.[100] As the secretary-general of the United Nations pointed out in 1970, 'the need to provide food, water, minerals, fuel and other necessities ... will place pressure on virtually all areas of the earth and demand the most careful planning and management of natural resources'.[101] A situation which led to the creation of the World Environment Fund in 1972. At a time when the most recent space voyage had, that same year, brought back the first photograph of the Earth seen from the sky, the Fund needed to demonstrate an 'international political awareness of the world environment', that of 'our solitary blue planet, the Earth-space ship'.[102] But addressing the problem was not enough to resolve it. And UNESCO was becoming increasingly concerned, drawing attention once again in 1976 to the 'population bomb' and the 'ecological disaster' which represented 'the roots of a growing world crisis'.[103]

UNESCO drew attention to the threat menacing the entire world and, on a different scale, it also saw Africa through the totalizing perspective of deterioration. In 1958, in an issue entitled 'Man Against Nature', the institution described how in Africa hunting sometimes more closely resembled 'slaughter'. Clearly, British naturalists wrote, it was time to act. In the *Courier* they explained that the popularity of both 'wild animals' and 'travel' 'arises from the feeling that here is something that must be enjoyed before it is too late'.[104] For if 'Africa's nature reserves' are indeed the 'last refuge' of the modern world, if the Serengeti National Park in Tanzania is, for example, still an earthly paradise, Eden was still under threat.[105] From the north to the south of Africa, they insisted: 'The day of primitive agriculture ... is drawing to an end' as the result of 'the impact of modern life' which was 'sending birth rates up and death rates down'. Modernity had led to 'an increase in population, poaching, an expansion of industrial and food production industries, economic exploitation ... and a deterioration in soil quality'.[106] And, since then, the problem had got worse, both in Africa and in the rest of the world.

That said, the authors writing in the columns of the UNESCO journal were keen to point out that Africa did not represent the world. Many of its lands were 'marginal' wrote the vice-president of the IUCN in 1961, describing the 'poverty of ... soil' which 'cannot support intensive agriculture and stock farming'.[107] In the same year, after three months spent in Africa, Julian Huxley described this African ecology in more detail. Whether in Rhodesia, Mozambique, Uganda, Western Congo, Rwanda or Tanganyika, in 'more than half of its one-and-a-half million square miles', the former director of UNESCO pointed out, there were 'vast areas of wild and marginal land ... too arid for agriculture or domestic stock'. A good reason, he went on, to have parks full of wild animals everywhere. In each of these, 'game cropping' of small numbers of wild animals would provide Africans with the meat they lacked; and the protection of the majority of the animals would attract tourists and therefore capital. For Huxley, what was at stake was the survival of 'Africa's wildlife', destroyed as the result of the 'illegal killing' of animals by 'poachers' who killed in order to sell ivory and skins. And what was also at stake, according to the biologist, were the lives of Africans: tourism offered them a considerable source of revenue since 'as long as western prosperity continues ... more and more people will want to escape further and further from it and its concomitants in the shape of over-large or over-crowded cities … and general over-mechanization of existence'. And finally, also at stake were the interests of the westerners and the 'sense of … wonder and deep emotion' provoked by the sight of 'large animals going about their natural business in their own natural way'. For all these reasons, African conservation should be a shared battle, Huxley concluded, before going on to deplore the fact that conservation projects were either 'subject to provisos about "human interests" or "utility"'. For him 'the constant use of these phrases betrays a misconception of the real situation'. It was therefore a matter of urgency, he declared, 'to educate and rouse local opinion in favour of conserving the heritage of wild life'.[108]

Huxley based this argument on anecdotes rather than on research. On the subject of poaching, for example, he resorts to vague expressions – 'A reliable informant in Kenya', for example. His argument is also rooted in a certain incoherence which can be found in much of the rhetoric of that era. For François Bourlière of the IUCN, as for Julian Huxley of UNESCO, the presence of so many wild animals in Africa is thanks to 'the existence of vast areas of wild and marginal land, unutilized …'. But the two men also claim that the fauna was close to extinction because 'cultivation has been permitted in large areas and has often led to their deterioration and to the reduction of their wild life on too much land' which, as a result, has been 'misutilized'.[109] For Huxley, there was, on the one hand, African nature as it *should* be ('unutilized'), and, on the other as it '*would*' in fact be ('misutilized').

Saving what can still be saved

As I observed in my previous research, colonial scientists had drawn attention to this natural and denatured Africa as early as the 1880s. Yet our focus in this book is the early 1960s, which means that, for almost a century, western specialists in African wildlife had been describing areas which were both untouched and cultivated, and a fauna which was both abundant and on the verge of disappearing. From a scientific point of view the argument was flawed. Nevertheless, and this is something I had failed to notice previously, from a moral standpoint, it held good. Coal, oil, waste material, pesticides, deforestation, the disappearance of whales – the *UNESCO Courier* could not be clearer: 'Man' had become 'the killer of nature'.[110] The *IUCN Bulletin* was no less adamant: 'The toll is appalling. In terms of pollution, plant and animal extinction, degradation ... it seems that nature is down for the count.'[111] The sheer scale of destruction plunged the experts into a state of dismay which was all the more alarming given that they were powerless against the world's industrialists and the governments which supported them. In this context, therefore, Africa seemed to them to be the only continent where the catastrophe *must* be halted. For, in their eyes, it was only in Africa that it *could* still be avoided.

This was reflected in the *IUCN Bulletin*: in the minds of the major experts, Africa was seen as the priority. As early as 1961, while vaunting the 'magnificence of Africa', the Union drew attention to the danger which was threatening its 'big game species'.[112] More than any other continent, the Union reiterated, Africa needed 'international efforts' to 'assist in stabilizing' its population. For, as we read in its 1965 Bulletin under the subtitle 'Population Explosion', birth rates were out of control in Africa, as demonstrated in these few lines: 'One of Kenya's oldest inhabitants, Mzee Atambamala, has died at the age of 140 in the North Kabras Location of Kakamega District. He had ten wives who had 103 children, 87 of whom are now married (*Daily Nation*, Nairobi).'[113] The IUCN and the WWF seemed in no doubt about this 'African' irrationality, and throughout the 1960s the two institutions attempted to counter it with a campaign of 'conservation education'. But when they celebrated the tenth anniversary of the Morges Manifesto in 1971, the two organizations expressed their regret that the message was still so difficult to get across in Africa, where 'the vital need for conservation of the limited natural resources of the world is not understood or is ignored'.[114]

The Union nevertheless claimed 'considerable success'.[115] During the third stage of the Special Project, launched at the beginning of the winter in 1961, ecologist Thane Riney and agronomist Peter Hill were successful in 'assisting governments' in West and East Africa with the latter integrating the 'long-term wildlife potential' of their country into their new political programmes.[116] Subsequently, other projects were set up, for example the 'Elsa Wild Animal Appeal', named after the tame lioness subsequently released back into the wild by Joy and George Adamson. This project took place in Kenya in 1965. With the aid of 'two

European wardens' and 'six African assistants', the IUCN and the Kenya Game Department organized the capture of a number of species of wild animals and their transfer to national parks, thereby saving giraffes and antelopes before 'the whole of the natural range of that species ... was rendered inaccessible by Somai Shifta operations'.[117] The Union subsequently scored a continent-wide victory in 1968 by helping to draw up 'The African Convention for Conservation of Nature and Natural Resources'. Subsequently ratified in Algiers by thirty-eight member states of the OAU, its goal was to promote 'the extension and establishment of conservation areas'[118] across the entire continent. Finally, in 1972, after the adoption by the United Nations of the 'Convention on International Trade in Endangered Species of Wild Fauna and Flora' (CITES), the IUCN launched its 'Save Africa's Elephants' programme. With the support of the WWF, 'antipoaching' operations were carried out as part of 'drastic measures' introduced in Botswana, Ethiopia, Kenya, Tanzania and Zambia.[119]

A turning point would come at the end of the 1970s with the 'World Conservation Strategy'. Experts from the IUCN and from the WWF were involved in drawing up this strategy, but they now found themselves having to work with the new 'consultants' of the United Nations. These were professionals in the fields of law, economics and management who had graduated from leading universities rather than being simply trained in the field. Their role was to lay the foundations for a new era, that of a 'community conservation' which would combine economic profitability and social equity.[120] Now facing competition from the new management professionals, the major conservation experts found themselves on the point of losing their monopoly on the global policies of African wildlife, a monopoly they had enjoyed for thirty years. They were therefore determined to defend their record. The president of the IUCN reminded readers that thanks to their efforts 'new and often drastic laws are being enacted', explaining that they had brought their 'unequivocal support' to 'conservation-minded' leaders, whilst 'systematically and sometimes violently attacking [those official and private institutions] that did not follow suit'.[121] In other words, the expert gentlemen had successfully encouraged the African states to introduce the measures which needed to be adopted throughout the world in order to combat the ecological emergency.

The experts' (a)political quest

This was where the real change lay. In its globalized, developmentalist and Africanized form, the new conservation as defined at Arusha could be seen as simply a matter of discourse, a rhetorical tool designed to smooth out the contradiction which saw the former colonial managers of African wildlife continuing to exert their influence on societies only recently freed from colonialization. A tempting interpretation, but one which does not go far enough.

Not only did the conservationists obtain the right to stay in Africa but they also succeeded in making African governments apply the policies that colonial administrations had been reluctant to set in place. The leading conservation experts saw the continent of Africa as a homogeneous whole and they drew up policies which could be applied across the whole continent. For them, the end of the colonies was, in fact, an opportunity to pursue their dream of an ecological government in Africa. The problem for us is that in their thousands and thousands of pages of archives, 'Africans' simply did not exist, except in the form of large numbers of unskilled peasants, motivated only by the need to survive from one day to the next. If we are to understand an 'African' history from the perspective of the expert gentlemen, we must continue to explore their written contributions in order to observe their commitment to Africa and, in the background, the construction of an African absence, or, as we might put it, an abstraction.

Science: A tool for shaping the Empire

Ecology must take precedence over politics – that was the cause pleaded as early as 1944 by Jean-Paul Harroy, director of the Institute of the National Parks of Belgian Congo.[122] In his doctoral thesis on colonial science, *Afrique, Terre qui meurt*, the beer importer turned colonial administrator accused the Europeans of devastating Africa. Harroy was not questioning their presence on the continent, but simply deploring their 'ignorance'. Faced with the fragile soils of Africa, he wrote, 'the white man ... exacerbated the disequilibrium, a process which was then finished off by local communities'. Harroy therefore called for a cautious exploitation of nature, at the same time emphasizing that 'between the laboratory of African soil scientists and the office of those who oversee the "planning" of the colonial policies of the continent, a bridge is needed'. A 'bridge' which should be built by 'liaison agents' capable of bringing together specialists and politicians. These would be the people, Harroy concluded, for whom 'the role of leadership should be reserved'.[123]

Most of the great experts seemed to share this philosophy. This was the case, for example, of Edgar Worthington, an ecologist who studied zoology in Britain and Africa before working as a scientific adviser to the British government during the war and then as secretary-general of the Scientific Council for Africa South of the Sahara. In the mid-1950s, the CCTA and the CSA asked him to draw up a report on the progress of scientific research on Africa and he in turn took the opportunity to advocate the strengthening of 'contacts … between science and administration, between planning and politics, between black and white'.[124]

Worthington wrote this plea in 1958, when the influence he was attributing to the experts had already been transformed into policies. Evidence of this can be found in the 'faunal survey' carried out eleven years previously in 'Eastern and Central Africa' by Captain Keith Caldwell. A former national park warden in Kenya and correspondent of the FPS in East Africa, Caldwell claimed in 1947 that in that region 'the game areas have been reduced by half, and the game within many of those left by 75%'. In 1948, under the influence of Arthur Creech Jones, the secretary of state for the colonies, the British government ordered its governors in East and Central Africa to put a stop to this '75%' destruction rate. The carnage was attributed to 'Africans', and the figure was not supported by reference to any specific regions or species. But in 1950 Worthington declared the assessment to be 'fair', insisting that across 'the whole of Africa south of the Sahara' the empire should implement a system for managing nature based on 'carrying capacity', an innovative concept according to which an area of land can only tolerate a certain level of human occupation.[125] And Worthington's suggestion was transformed into a reality throughout the 1950s, in the course of what geographer Roderick Neumann described as a 'veritable conservation boom'. From Sudan to Nyasaland, the number of protected areas increased, the powers of those managing them were reinforced, the occupation of certain areas hitherto restricted was forbidden altogether, and recalcitrant farmers and pastoralists were increasingly punished, and, most importantly, expelled from their land in their thousands.[126]

Neumann was right, I believe, in seeing in this story one of the most extreme manifestations of 'the imperialism of knowledge'[127] which was rife in Africa after 1945. By extending the investigation to other archives produced by the major conservation experts, it becomes clear just how hard they had to fight to ensure their message was heard by the colonial governments. In 1950, for example, a hundred experts responded to the appeal put out by the IUPN to assess 'The Position of Nature Protection Throughout the World in 1950'. Théodore Monod, director of the *Institut français d'Afrique noire* (IFAN) in Dakar, said that efforts were being stepped up to ensure conservation was no longer an 'unpopular cause' in the French Empire. Further east, his Belgian colleagues were trying to convince their government to prohibit 'bush fires' in the areas adjoining the national parks of Belgian Congo. In Southern Rhodesia, the Wild Life Protection Society attempted to strengthen its links with the imperial authorities so that they could demonstrate an 'enlightened attitude towards the protection of nature'.[128] Finally, in Kenya, while Keith Caldwell described a 'satisfactory' situation, citing twelve protected areas and 134 game wardens, he was sorry to see it restricted by a 'conflict between those interested in preserving nature and those whose objective is to exploit more and more land for agriculture'.[129] Caldwell repeated more or less the same argument three years later in Bukavu, in the Congo, at the conference organized by the CCTA in 1953. He expressed his delight with the continent's new laws limiting the sale of arms to Africans but, in the name of the FPS, he called on conservationists from all empires to unite in applying pressure on their governments, which were still showing 'great reluctance to take any steps to put an end to, or even to curtail seriously, what they have held to be native hunting "rights"'.[130]

From then on, experts continued to urge the empires to allow themselves to be guided by science. Head of the office of the FAO for forestry in Africa, in 1957 Gerald Watterson tried to explain to all colonial decision makers that while waiting for ecologists to determine the carrying capacity of nature reserves, they should continue to organize the displacement of local people.[131] And in the same year, in his role as head of The Nature Conservancy, the lobbyist Max Nicholson stated that the colonial administrators should agree to defer to the conservationists: 'As we understand the processes we may hope to guide and at times even to control them.'[132]

National parks – the way forward for Africa

As followers of the new human ecology movement founded in Oxford in the 1930s, all these scientists were thinking on a global scale. According to them, ecology was the only means of 'achieving global control through planning the social system and the ecosystem'.[133] But these great minds of conservation were also what historian Anna-Katharina Wöbse defines as *park people*.[134] They were intent on consolidating their ecological vision of the world inside clearly delineated park areas, and no matter what they might say, they were in this respect taking a political stance since, ultimately, they were constantly dealing with individuals. This is clearly demonstrated in a 'confidential note' kept with Peter Scott's papers in Cambridge.

Entitled 'The problem of influencing African native opinion on conservation', this note was written by Edgar Worthington in April 1960, at a time when he still had one foot in the empire and one foot on the international stage, since he represented the British crown in both the CCTA and the IUCN. In this dual role, he had recently organized two London 'dinners' with Jean-Georges Baer, Julian Huxley, Max Nicholson, Victor Van Straelen representing the Belgian Congo Parks and Lieutenant-Colonel Charles Boyle, then secretary of the FPS. For all of these individuals, this was an opportunity, as Worthington wrote, to discuss one 'problem' in particular, notably the fact that 'popular leaders' were promising freedom to their citizens, a pledge which was 'sometimes translated as freedom to graze cattle or cultivate in National Parks'. If the expert gentlemen wanted to succeed in conserving wildlife in Africa, they would therefore need to 'establish "contacts"' with the future leaders of independent Africa and emphasize to them, on the one hand, the 'economic aspect of wild Africa' and, on the other, the 'emotional pride of possession' it could bring. Consequently, they were planning 'to establish a small group of people within Africa ... to seek out and talk to leaders individually'. 'However this group should preferably be composed of men with black skins', Worthington continued, before citing three names: David Wasawo, a Kenyan close to the Tanzanian prime minister Julius Nyerere, and 'who is set fair to become the first African zoologist of real standing'; Jean-Marie Kititwa, a Congolese 'known to Professor Van Straelen'; and Leki Mani, member of the Kenyan Council of National Parks and close to president Jomo Kenyatta. The list was a provisional one but 'whatever the group of Africans which might be collected', Worthington insisted, 'it is most important to have one white man connected with them'. Worthington then declared: 'And I am sure that the right person if obtainable is Watterson.' Watterson represented the FAO, which had 'an excellent standing with most African Governments' on the continent, and moreover he had already told Worthington he was ready to take on the role. All of which enabled the latter to conclude his note by 'suggesting' first of all, 'that the IUCN should apply to the FAO ... for part-time service of Watterson', and then, 'square this matter with UNESCO', and finally organize 'a meeting of popular leaders'.[135] Two months before its official launch by the IUCN in Poland, the African Special Project had therefore been defined by this little network of expert gentlemen.

UNESCO arrived on the scene in July 1960. It appointed Julian Huxley to undertake a mission to East Africa and, three months later, he confirmed that in twenty years' time wild fauna would have disappeared from the continent. 'We must learn to control the process if it is not to lead to disaster', Huxley wrote, adding: 'The situation can still be saved, provided that the conservationists can induce African governments and the African public to understand and follow an ecological approach.' He went on to say: 'Most tribal Africans regard wild animals either as a pest to be destroyed or simply as meat on the hoof to be killed and eaten.' In practical terms, he recommended 'helping' the African states to set up national parks in order to raise wild animals (as a source of food for the Africans) and to attract tourists (a source of revenue)[136] an operation which had in fact already begun.

Firstly, at the end of 1960, Worthington drew attention to the farming and culling of thousands of elephants and hippopotami in two national parks – the Tsavo in Kenya and the Queen Elizabeth Park in Uganda.[137] Watterson then undertook his tour of Africa with the help of contacts provided by Jean-Marie Kititwa in Central Africa and by David Wasawo in East Africa.[138] This was followed by the Arusha conference, where, represented by the Tanzanian Julius Nyerere, the so-called popular leaders called for 'specialist knowledge' from other nations[139] – knowledge which quickly materialized with the IUCN's publication of the booklet *Our Mother Nature*. Written for use by secondary teachers by the staff of the IFAN in Dakar, this little guide makes no mention of either 'Africans' or 'Europeans' but only of the 'slaughter' of fauna by 'hunters' or 'herdsmen' and, in order to combat this, the need to establish protected areas.[140] Finally, during the third stage of the Special Project, the research undertaken by Thane Riney and Peter Hill finally contributed to the dissemination of expert knowledge. Visiting nineteen countries in less than a year, they noted that 'there was little time for quantitative observations of any kind'. None of which prevented the two men reaching the conclusion that competition between the fauna and agriculture had, from the north to the south of Africa, led to 'increasing soil degradation'.[141]

This finding sparked an acceleration in conservation projects led by experts who seemed to be ever more closely connected. This was the case, for example, of Leslie Brown, a British ornithologist and an active member of the FPS. We find him at Arusha in 1961 and then in Nairobi in September 1963, on the occasion of the 8th General Assembly of the IUCN. Kenya's independence would not be finalized for another two months so Brown was still head of the Kenyan agricultural department. In this role he worked with the new government of Jomo Kenyatta setting up additional national parks where, in order to conform to the carrying capacity of the areas in question, it would be necessary 'to limit the human population'.[142] The British ornithologist was still adamant about this 'carrying capacity' in 1965. Except that by then he was in Addis Ababa and it was there, in his role of UNESCO expert, that he adapted the conservation guide published by the IFAN for the Ethiopian government.[143]

Subsequently, other well-connected men facilitated the creation of other parks, all over Africa. These included men like John Morton Boyd, a leading figure in The Nature Conservancy in London. His archives indicate that, in 1967, he sent two biologists, one to support the Tanzanian and Kenyan authorities and the other to provide similar support to the Rwandan and then Zambian governments. The following year, Boyd organized the return from Tanzania of a forester named John Procter, who, from his base in the British capital, acted in his capacity of 'continental ecologist' to coordinate the sending of 'conservation assistants' to the former British colonies in Africa. Then, in 1969, in partnership with the Rockefeller Foundation based in New York, Boyd sent a dozen or so experts to work with 'African' managers in the parks of Sudan, Malawi (ex-Nyasaland) and Botswana (ex-Bechuanaland).[144]

Conservation – a way of offsetting decolonization

As a result of all this activity, by the end of the 1960s the expert gentlemen had therefore successfully strengthened their involvement in African nature while carefully avoiding any reference to decolonization. This can be seen, for example, in the case of the Swedish zoologist and academic Kai Curry-Lindahl. Member of the management committee of the IUCN, and with a significant reputation in North America, Europe and Central Africa, in 1969 Curry-Lindahl praised the 'modernisation' of the African national parks which was in his view 'very desirable'. But he attributed that process to one moment in particular: '[T]he turning point came in 1961 with the Arusha conference', a turning point which, he said, led the FAO, UNESCO and the IUCN to intensify their collaboration in order to produce new conservation legislation, 'in accordance with the wishes expressed by the African States themselves'.[145]

UNESCO also congratulated itself on this 'modernization', whilst pointing out that 'foreigners are still largely responsible for the ecology of conservation in Africa'.[146] The institution continued to call for training to provide qualified African personnel but, in the meantime, western experts were asserting their right to work in the African parks. Furthermore, they were adamant that it was incumbent on the political leaders of the continent to use their services. Ecologist Thane Riney made this clear to the FAO in 1972. Only 'trained staff' were capable of 'realistically contributing to the improvement of the management of the resource', wrote Riney, who considered that, in this field, nationality did not count. What was needed were 'already confirmed' scientists and these simply happened to be westerners.[147] None of which represented a problem since the new African leaders shared the westerners' vision of conservation. As demonstrated in 1972 at Yellowstone, on the occasion of the 'Second World Conference on National Parks', in his role of director of the national parks of Kenya, Perez Olindo himself stressed the need to respect the 'carrying capacity' of nature and the principle according to which, in Africa, 'within a national park the interests of animals and plants must be paramount and, as far as possible, these areas should be kept free of any human settlement'.[148]

Within a short time, a few voices could be heard calling for space to be made for 'ecosystem people', a term used in 1975 by American ecologist Raymond Dasmann in contrast to 'biosphere people'. According to Dasmann, in their developed nations, the latter were destroying the nature which they insisted underdeveloped countries should protect in their own countries, in areas inhabited by 'ecosystem people'.[149] But the era of community conservation and its challenges had not yet arrived and would not do so until the beginning of the 1980s. For the time being, the very essence of African conservation was to protect nature from the Africans.

Amongst the expert gentlemen defending this conservation-fortress, some were motivated by racist ideas. Russell Train was an example of this. A judge in the US tax court and an enthusiastic big game hunter, he was involved in founding the African Wildlife Leadership Foundation in Washington in 1961. The AWLF existed notably in order to finance the establishment in Tanzania of the College of African Wildlife Management, the first international training centre established in order to educate the new African elites in conservation. And Train's interest in this college was particularly acute given his deepfelt anxiety at seeing 'the native races assuming more and more control over the destiny of the African continent'.[150]

Other leading figures in conservation brought with them the ethos of colonial superiority. This was the case, amongst others, of Jean-Paul Harroy. Director of the Belgian Congo parks in the 1930s, secretary-general of the IUPN in 1948 and then vice-governor of Ruanda-Urundi from 1955, Harroy made his return to the conservation arena immediately after independence. After 1962, he worked for the Council of Europe, the United Nations and the major international conservation agencies. And, in 1972, the colonial administrator-turned-expert was once again calling for Africans to be made 'more conscious' of a nature about which they sometimes remained 'uncomprehending and even, for the time being, uneducable'.[151]

The conservation 'International' was therefore clearly tinged with racism, and of course with paternalism. But if it had survived the decolonization process, if the major experts had managed to go further than the colonial governments had done, it was primarily because they succeeded in sharing their faith in an ecological science capable of steering the world in general and Africa in particular. Max Nicholson, an emblematic figure of The Nature Conservancy, architect of the International Biological Program in UNESCO, member of the FPS and one of the most successfully lobbyists of the WWF, summed up the situation perfectly in his book, *The Environmental Revolution: A Guide for the New Masters of the World*, a best-seller published in 1970 in the United States and translated all over the world. Because of the 'humiliation of having gone so far towards making a slum of our own native planet', he wrote 'conservationists are ... less backward than others in moving towards recognition of this problem in terms of possible action'.[152] It was a message he was to repeat again in 1972 at Yellowstone. In contrast to those who wanted to manage nature according to 'romantic values', Nicholson strongly declared that it was instead 'the scientific pragmatists' who should be given the task 'of winning, defending and operating the parks'.[153]

The world of the expert gentlemen was therefore shaped by the sense of superiority conferred on them by their ecological knowledge and as a result of the managerial power they had monopolized since the 1950s. They failed to see individuals because, quite simply, they did not notice them. They had eyes only for the system, for the whole rather than for the parts: 'Africa' and not the 'Africans'.

Faces and people of Africa

If the 'Africans' remained an abstract concept for the expert gentlemen, the vast 'Africa' in which they operated was, in contrast, very real. It existed because it was tangibly present. Their Africa was synonymous with the iconic species they recorded on the IUCN's red list, and, above all, with the iconic spaces where these could be saved, notably the nature reserves and the national parks.

Africans continue the colonial task

The first national park within the continent, and the best known, was the Albert National Park. Created in 1925 in the eastern Kivu region of the Belgian Congo, it was run first by Victor Van Straelen and then by Jean-Paul Harroy. In accordance with their original vision of the park in the 1920s, this space represented nature freed from human presence, a world which still belonged to gorillas, elephants, lions and okapis, just as it might have been in its original state. The Albert Park was initially created for scientific purposes and then, in the 1930s, under the impetus of Jean-Paul Harroy, it also became a tourist attraction. So much so that when, at the beginning of the 1950s, the colonial authorities proposed relaxing conservation restrictions, the Belgian, European and North American experts launched an extensive protest campaign in favour of wildlife tourism. Working with the IUPN, they produced and distributed postcards, brochures, documentaries and films extolling the wildlife that had existed for centuries and was being preserved in Albert Park. According to the experts from the IUCN, the presence of too many people threatened to upset the balance but conservationists were battling to preserve the original equilibrium. By disseminating this rhetoric, the campaign achieved its objective and the integrity of the park was preserved.[154]

The same discourse could be heard in the immediate aftermath of Congolese independence, a period marked by insurrection. In 1961, the IUCN launched an international appeal to support the park guards.[155] Belgium, Germany and the United States were quick to send funds and then, in 1966, the Union sent Kai Curry-Lindahl to meet the new president, Mobutu Sese Seko. Already known for his knowledge of 'Africa', the Swedish zoologist and academic acknowledged what he described as an 'excellent' situation, drawing attention to 'the evacuation of all the fishing villages illegally established' and reporting that 'all cattle, goats and poultry ... were slaughtered or otherwise removed'.[156] But in 1967 everything collapsed. Citing a second report made by Curry-Lindahl, the IUCN reported that there had been 'massive intrusions ... by Rwanda pastoralists and their cattle, as well as by Rwanda rebels and by dissident soldiers of the Congolese Military Forces (ANC)' in the park. This invasion, the Union reports, was followed by the 'large scale slaughter' of wildlife by hunters and poachers who had transformed park buildings into 'abattoirs', and the killing of twenty-two guards. The 'immediate evacuation of Rwanda herdsmen' was a matter of urgency and the *IUCN Bulletin* described a park 'facing total disintegration'.[157]

Curry-Lindahl nevertheless mitigated this dramatic representation of the situation in the same IUCN bulletin in 1969. Guards had indeed been killed, he wrote, but there had been 'no destruction of … gorillas by direct slaughter'. In the Virunga Park, the new name for the Albert Park, any loss of gorillas was due to 'the spoilation of the habitat, starvation and incessant disturbance' as a result of the presence in the area of 'Rwanda pastoralists'.[158] The park was however 'intact', Curry-Lindahl noted, once again praising the 'evacuation' of several villages by the Mobutu administration.[159] Autocratic and authoritarian, Curry-Lindahl was, in the eyes of the Union, first and foremost an ardent conservationist, a role he himself drew attention to with a certain pride during the opening session of the 12th General Assembly of the IUCN in Kinshasa in 1975, stating that: 'In ten years, we have established more national parks and nature reserves than our colonisers did in eighty years.'[160]

A fervent nationalist, Mobutu was quick to point out that he was working in partnership with the IUCN, the WWF and the United Nations. This was also the case of several other African leaders singled out by the conservationists. Ever since 1961, they had frequently cited the Arusha Manifesto, in which Nyerere announced his commitment to entrust the protection of wildlife to foreigners. Moreover, in 1963, Jomo Kenyatta published a new Manifesto, in which he wrote: 'to provide the specialist staff and money which are necessary', Kenya needed the help of 'lovers of nature throughout the world'.[161] Then, in 1964, the Zambian president, Kenneth Kaunda, followed suit. One month before the independence of Zambia (at that time still Northern Rhodesia) he was adamant that members of his government should prioritize conservation. Until then, killing big game had been a way of opposing the colonial regime and its unfair laws, but in future the protection of wildlife would be in the interests of the nation.[162] The expert gentlemen – Curry-Lindahl, Harroy, Huxley, Monod and Worthington – remained silent in response to this African strategy of dependence which allowed the independent states to avoid confrontation with the former empires and to develop their tourist industries and, as a result, their own countries. The fact nevertheless remained that in the course of this opportune cooperation, African faces did indeed begin to appear in the conservationist narrative which continued to promote a great 'Africa' by associating the entire continent with a few major wildlife sites.

African wildlife still very much alive

After the Virunga, the Serengeti was the best known of these sites. Situated in the extreme north of Tanzania, the hunting reserve was converted into a national park in 1940. The British first became involved in the site in 1948 and from 1951 onwards, they began to expel the Maasai people and subsequently to impose sanctions on anyone entering the park illegally. Consequently, in 1956, the park offered 'the most spectacular assembly of wild animals still remaining in the world', particularly in the area of the Ngorongoro crater, the 'chief attraction' of the Serengeti according to Lieutenant-Colonel Charles Boyle, secretary of the Fauna Preservation Society. His report to the FPS was made at a critical moment in that from 1955 onwards, the Crown had planned to exclude the Ngorongoro from the park in order to allow the Maasai to graze their cattle in that area. For the colonial authorities this was a way of preventing the wave of protests, already present within the country, from degenerating into a full-scale popular uprising, as had happened in neighbouring Kenya which had been in the grip of the so-called 'Mau Mau' revolt for the previous four years. But the experts disapproved of this plan. If the fauna of Serengeti was so rich, Boyle explained, it was because local people rarely hunted it. Nevertheless, 'the Masai, like everything else in this world, are changing', he pointed out. Better therefore to remain cautious: 'Can it be considered likely that even in, say, ten years' time the Masai will not eat game meat?' Pointing out that the land is already 'steadily overgrazed' by their livestock, the British author of the report considered that prevention was better than cure and called on the international institutions for their support.[163]

Bernhard Grzimek was then commissioned to conduct a census of the park's wildlife. The film director-vet was not able to establish precise figures. Nor did he succeed in preventing the British from transforming the Ngorongoro into a 'mixed use' zone, open to the Maasai.[164] However, thanks to the documentaries he and his son made by flying over the park area in their zebra-striped planes, the German filmmaker promoted African wildlife in an unprecedented way. Thanks to *No Room for Wild Animals* and then *Serengeti Shall Not Die!*, awarded the Oscar for the best documentary film in 1960, the western public discovered the work carried out by conservationists in 'One of the most magnificent reserves of wild life in Africa'. As UNESCO stated in 1961, 'in a setting almost untouched by man, of limitless horizons, beauty and grandeur, dwell remarkable species of animals and birds which have drawn to this unrivalled corner of East Africa nature lovers, tourists, hunters and photographers'.[165]

This was the narrative proposed by Grzimek and the institutions which supported him, including UNESCO, and also the IUCN and the FPS, all of whom unanimously argued in favour of preserving the balance within the Serengeti. If, they pointed out, the area still remained 'almost untouched by man', caution was nevertheless advised. In 1961, Huxley drew attention to 'nature's fight for life at Ngorongoro Crater'. The wildlife might indeed be living in an 'unrivalled corner' but, according to the former director of UNESCO, there was extensive 'poaching' which meant that were the crater to be excluded from the park, this would 'spell certain death' to much of its fauna.[166] On the very threshold of decolonization, the fear of upsetting the existing balance was therefore very much on everyone's mind. But, on the ground, such fears were quickly assuaged. In 1965, the IUCN and the WWF praised the Tanzanian authorities for their work within the park. In the Serengeti, 'one of the country's most outstanding assets' was still very much alive.[167]

With his films and his TV programme, *A Place for Animals*, each broadcast of which attracted 35 million European viewers, Bernhard Grzimek was fighting neither for the Cold War between the Americans and the Soviets, nor for the survival of the British or French empires. For him, as for all his conservation colleagues, the combat was an apolitical one. Indeed, the conservationists offered their wholehearted support to the African states, who were in the process of displacing 'whole villages' in order to save wildlife, 'something that was never proposed under European rule, let alone done', according to Grzimek. It was by deploying rhetoric of this kind, historian Thomas Lekan tells us, that the conservationists managed to remain so powerful within Africa.[168] But, more than revealing the story of *their* presence, this narrative reveals the story of *their* Africa. For the expert gentlemen who opted to save them, the national parks represented the original essence of the continent, and even of the entire world. The national park encapsulated Africa; and Africa represented the world in its original state, before the arrival of modern humankind.

Africa, or an example of the world as it once was

All of this explains why, in Kenya in 1963, conservationists were encouraging the government to impose a complete ban on rhinoceros hunting. 'For the simple reason', declared the IUCN, 'that it is difficult to persuade the Africans not to kill them when foreign hunters have the right to do so.' After all, the Union continued, this was an area where it was enough simply to concentrate on the beauties of nature, in a zone which included the Mount Kenya National Park 'with its glaciers, its small lakes, its rugged gorges', the Tsavo Park and 'its volcanic landscapes', and Nakuru Lake where 'vast flocks of pink flamingos are made up of more than a million birds'.[169] The same was true for neighbouring Uganda, which, in 1963, decided to preserve the 'animal sanctuaries' it had inherited from the British announcing that 'no human presence would be authorized there'.[170] In 1966, Uganda even accepted to follow the Union's advice and abandon its project for a hydroelectric power station in the Murchison Falls Park, a gesture that Bernhard Grzimek and the Frankfurt Zoological Society were quick to reward, presenting the park managers with 'a light aircraft to be used primarily for anti-poaching work'.[171] Conservation before development, animals before men – in the African national parks nature was at last increasingly given precedence.

Yet, in the eyes of the expert gentlemen, wildlife was becoming more and more threatened. This was the conclusion they reached in every country they visited, like Ethiopia, for example, visited by Julian Huxley, Edgar Worthington, Théodore Monod and Alain Gille in 1963, just after the 8th General Assembly of the IUCN in Nairobi. Sent on a mission by UNESCO, the leading figures of this new international conservation movement suggested that Haile Selassie I should consider creating national parks in order to save his country's 'rich' wildlife, including 'certain species found only in this country – such as the Walia Ibex and the mountain nyala'.[172] The emperor followed their advice, and three parks were created over the course of the following four years, in partnership with experts from UNESCO, the IUCN and the WWF. While it was clearly their intention to make Haile Selassie more aware of the rich fauna of his own country, the expert gentlemen also acknowledged their 'ignorance' of Ethiopian wildlife. 'We know little about the current situation', they declared, citing the example of the Nubian ibex. But that did not prevent them from claiming that 'this species has undoubtedly been seriously reduced in number over the last few years as a result of poaching'.[173] The argument was taken quite literally by the Ethiopian authorities, who, in 1969, set about expelling the inhabitants from the parks in order to conserve the 'already much depleted wildlife resources' as drawn to their attention by Worthington, Gille, Huxley and Monod.[174]

For these men who had struggled to persuade the colonial administrations to apply their conservationist measures in full, success was finally within reach. Thanks to a postcolonial moment that they had successfully navigated ever since the 1960s, the expert gentlemen continued to pursue their goals, which they were now voicing with increasing clarity. 'The national parks' would have a new role, namely 'to serve as ecological sample areas for our guidance in managing the world's renewable nature resources', stated for example Kai Curry-Lindahl in 1972, in front of an audience of colleagues gathered together in Yellowstone.[175] And the expert gentlemen were convinced that the original sample area was to be found in Africa. Lions, wildebeests, antelopes, leopards, elephants and gorillas had been the living evidence of this during colonization, and this was still very much the case since independence: African nature had survived. Now it was time to save it from men.

2

Saving the East African stronghold
The world of those who stayed

Conservation happens first and foremost on the ground. Regardless of
the big speeches and the rhetoric, without the park wardens, big game in
Africa would die. 'In this action what I want are bullets and shells', said
John Owen, director of Tanzanian National Parks, addressing the Arusha
delegates in 1961. As was his custom, the British conservationist clutched
his still smoking pipe in one hand while with the other, in the manner
of a preacher, he pointed a finger at the sky and, after a short pause,
concluded: 'I want money that I can deploy in the fastest possible time.'
His compatriot Mervyn Cowie was the next speaker. Sporting a meticulously trimmed moustache and dressed in a tweed jacket with a bright
red kerchief knotted at his neck, he spoke on behalf of the department of
the Royal National Parks of Kenya, pursuing much the same argument.
In a calm and almost icy tone, Cowie condemned what he described as
a 'disastrous situation'. He had been working to protect nature in Kenya
for fifteen years and, in his view, 'the Kenyan government has betrayed
the cause of conservation. It amounts to a gigantic hoax. On the one
hand there have been government statements. ... But on the other hand
there have been no effective steps taken to implement this policy.'[1]

Arusha 1961. Working in a liberated Africa

Mervyn Cowie[2] and John Owen[3] were born in Africa, the former in
Kenya in 1909 and the latter in Uganda, in 1912. The sons of British
colonialists, they had studied natural history at Oxford in England
before returning to East Africa. Both of them had been keen hunters
until, at the end of the 1930s, they began to advocate the transformation
of hunting reserves into national parks. They had also held positions of
responsibility both before and after the war, Owen as district commissioner in the Sudan and Cowie as head of recruitment during the Mau

Mau uprising in Kenya. Since then, they had been in charge of the national parks that the British authorities were counting on to attract tourists. And it was indeed to the British leaders that their criticisms were addressed. In Arusha, in September 1961, John Owen and Mervyn Cowie asked their government to do more for the nature they were striving to save in East Africa. Yet the two men knew very well that, in a few months' time, or at the very most, in a few years, the people in charge of the region would no longer be British.

The new independentist order

In Tanganyika, Julian Nyerere's TANU (Tanganyika African National Union) had already obtained independence and this would be officially inaugurated three months later. In Uganda, Milton Obote's UPC (Uganda People's Congress) was in the process of gaining the upper hand over Benedicto Kiwanuka's Democratic Party and independence would come in October 1962. In Kenya, after eight years of repression throughout the entire country, Jomo Kenyatta had been released from prison, and the KANU (Kenya African National Union) was already dominating the negotiations which would lead to independence in December 1963. Finally, in the Federation of Rhodesia and Nyasaland, uprisings were becoming ever more frequent and, here too, attempts to crush these failed to prevent the independence process. Independence was then declared in 1964 in Malawi (former Nyasaland) and in Zambia (former Northern Rhodesia), countries governed respectively by Hastings Banda and Kenneth Kaunda, and then in 1965 in Southern Rhodesia, a country which would be independent but would continue to be governed by Ian Smith's colonialists.[4] Out of Nyerere, Obote, Kenyatta, Banda and Kaunda, only Nyerere was present at Arusha, but John Owen, Mervyn Cowie and all the colonial conservationists who had come from Eastern Africa to attend the conference were addressing all of them when they spoke.

What exactly did they tell them? First of all, that African nature was putting up a fight in 'eastern Africa'. In the special edition devoted to the conference, the *UNESCO Courier* described the region as '"The stronghold of the wild" ... where 28,000 square miles of territory have been declared as National parks or Reserves'.[5] Moreover, in this region, as American Lee Talbot pointed out at Arusha, 'the truly indigenous livestock, are the wild animals'. We know now that goats were widespread across the continent six to seven thousand years ago, followed a short time later by beef cattle.[6] But Talbot had another theory. An ecologist working for the IUCN and the FPS, he studied the behaviour of East African wildlife with the help of funding from the New York Zoological Society. And he claimed that cattle and goats had been imported into the region in 'relatively recent' times. Which, in his view, was why only wild animals were truly adapted to the East African environment. In the competition between wild animals and domestic livestock, Talbot concluded, there was therefore every interest in seeing zebu cattle, sheep and goats being replaced by lions, zebras and elephants.[7]

Leslie Brown confirmed his colleague's conclusion. Director of the agricultural department in Kenya, Brown was an experienced conservationist in the field. He had travelled widely in India, Nigeria and Kenya, always, as his fellow travellers liked to point out, wearing the same rather worn woollen jumper, and he was as well-versed in ornithology as he was in the study of rainfall. It was the latter area of expertise that he focused on at Arusha.[8] In East Africa, the low levels of rainfall found across the whole region explained, in his view, why most soils were 'unsuited to intensive agriculture'. Then Brown took his argument further by pointing out that, if nothing were done, all those who cultivated the land would remain in poverty, trapped by the inevitably low levels of 'production at this miserable level' and that if, as a result of demography, other people moved into the area, they too would descend into poverty, whilst continuing to damage the habitat for wildlife, since 'in such country' Brown pointed out, 'African pastoral usage ... is almost invariably destructive and usually results in destruction'. All of which, Brown added, explained why, in Eastern Africa, conservation was 'clearly a far more valuable form of land use'. He concluded his argument with a plea 'for increasing and restoring the wild life resource'. By doing so, the soil and the wildlife would therefore be protected, local populations would be able to eat meat obtained from the animals and the new governments would benefit from income derived from tourism.[9]

The goal was still very much focused on nature but, from that time onwards, its protection must also serve the interests of 'Africans'. This was implied in Leslie Brown's comments, and certain conservationists stated it in more explicit terms. John Owen was one of these. With his pipe always at the ready and his perennially lively tone, he suggested making a clean break with the past in Tanzania:

> In the original Serengeti National Park, human interests co-existed and conflicted with those of the animals. As fervid protagonists of the latter, the National Parks came to be regarded by local opinion as being antagonistic to African interests. Because the Parks were used almost entirely by Europeans, they were regarded as being run exclusively in the interests of the white man.
>
> Now there are, of course, perfectly understandable reasons for much, if not all, of what has happened. But, I for one, doubt the advisability, at this stage, of any sustained effort to argue the rights and wrongs of the past. As the Arabs say, *el fat mat* – the past is dead. Let us concentrate on the future recognising that what has gone before casts its shadow along the path ahead – that we have not only to awaken public opinion, but to change it.[10]

The colonial past was dead: what was now needed was to rally the Tanzanians to the conservationist cause. In order to achieve this, Owen suggested launching a media campaign centred around the 'pride' and the 'profit' that could arise from nature. The minister Tewa Said Tewa spoke along very similar lines, declaring unequivocally that as a 'poor country', Tanzania needed a 'tourist industry which will ... make a better life for our own people'. Tewa then appropriated the metaphor used by the Belgian zoologist Jacques Verschuren who had just stepped down from the podium. According to Verschuren, deeply passionate about the Congo and its elephants, if 'Europe has its cathedrals preserved through the ages; Africa is proud to show the prodigious natural spectacles which she has helped to save'.[11] The Tanzanian minister agreed, but he brought a touch of national pride to the picture: 'It is the lion, the elephant, the rhino and the herds of other game which ... we can set against the cathedrals and art galleries of other countries as our special tourist attraction.'[12]

The conservationist success

Following Tewa, it was the turn of Ian Grimwood to extol the exceptional qualities of the region. This man, frail-looking and slightly built, was highly respected by all his colleagues. An escapee from Japanese prison camps during the war, he was capable of tracking wild animals for days on end in the middle of the desert and even when suffering from several broken ribs.[13] This reputation had led to him being recruited as chief game warden of the Kenyan National Parks in 1960 and it was in this capacity that he was speaking at Arusha. He interspersed his speech with scientific arguments pointing out that eleven of the sixteen 'major types' of vegetation found in the African continent occurred in East Africa, as well as fifty-two of its 'more spectacular animals'. But the latter were victims of 'predation', which Grimwood claimed to have 'studied personally'. In the coastal zones of East Africa, the 'tribes' cultivating the land were all the more 'antipathetic to game' in that they were themselves victims of the elephants who frequently raided their fields. From the south of Tanzania to Angola, he continued, deterioration was caused by 'hunting both legal and illegal' practised by 'many tribes'. Around Lake Victoria, that is to say, in western Tanzania, south Kenya and most of Uganda, 'increased settlement' represented 'the greatest threat'. Finally, in Kenya, Grimwood stated that 'the greatest danger' came from 'the trespass of domestic stock' which resulted in 'the destruction of forests'.[14]

Like most of the experts gathered in Arusha, when Grimwood described 'African' wildlife, the British expert was in fact referring to East Africa. And although he insisted that wildlife must be protected with the help of Africans, like his colleagues, he considered that it was still necessary to put up a fight against the Africans who were destroying it. This was the message conveyed by the experts in Arusha. It may have seemed contradictory but, after reading it from the pen of first one expert, and then another, and another, it ended up making sense.

John Blower made this clear. Tall and thick-set and with a penetrating stare and a confident and authoritarian manner, this British man was chief game warden of the Ugandan National Parks. And it was in Uganda that, over the previous three years, he had coordinated one of the first 'game cropping' projects, developed in the hope that eventually the Africans would give up eating cattle and goats in favour of wild animals which it would then be in their interest to 'conserve'. In practical terms, this would mean replacing zebus, goats and sheep with zebras, wildebeests, elephants and lions which would be reared and killed and subsequently form an integral part of the African diet. In front of the Arusha delegates, Blower explained the project in the following terms:

The African is a realist; if he and his family are short of meat, no amount of conservation propaganda will bring him to think of the fat eland which he sees out on the plains other than in terms of food. Nor are you likely to convince him that the herd of elephant which flattens his banana plantation should be left unmolested on account of their potential value as a tourist attraction. It must be recognised that though governments, politicians and conservationists may play an important part, the survival of African wild life … must depend ultimately on the cooperation of the peasant farmer in the 'bush'. We shall only achieve his cooperation provided that we are prepared to accept his utilitarian view of wildlife as a source of food to be harvested, like fish, fruits, wild honey and other natural produce of the countryside. … The ideal to be aimed at from many points of view would be a series of management units each consisting of a National Park surrounded by buffer zones within which game would be utilised either through controlled hunting or cropping.[15]

This then was the goal of this utilitarian conservation: big game which would be admired in the confines of a park, therefore generating tourist income, and which would also be hunted as a food source in the surrounding areas. As for the 'Africans', they would ostensibly benefit from an unequal exchange whereby they would obtain food, while the conservationists would have control over animals which would no longer be *poached* by other people but instead *hunted* by themselves. For the conservationists would be in sole charge of the 'management units' mentioned by Blower. The delegates from Northern Rhodesia confirmed this view. They were planning to introduce similar projects, and were adamant that 'a management scheme involving the use of the village hunter … would fail' and that only the 'meticulous methods' of the conservationists would bring success. Conversely, 'the African Governments' would be required to organize 'resettlement' of local people and the local farmers would be employed during the 'annual burn' which would serve to encourage the savannah to grow back before the tourist season.[16]

Brown, Grimwood and Blower, the field experts, would never fully achieve their goals for, across Africa, they found themselves having to adapt in the context of countries which had now become independent. Adapting did not however mean failing. So, in 1963, when the IUCN gathered in the same auditorium in Nairobi and Mervyn Cowie once again addressed the assembly, there was a radical change of tone. Whereas in Arusha the man with the bright red kerchief had denounced a 'hoax' and criticized the 'apathy' of the British authorities, in Nairobi he declared himself 'glad to report that there has been a marked change of attitude', adding: 'I would like to pay … particular tribute to our Prime Minister [Mr Jomo Kenyatta]. Here in Kenya the pendulum is now swinging the other way and we are on the threshold of formulating a sound policy for the conservation of … our wildlife, scenery and attractive climate.'[17]

Mervyn Cowie had been involved in the repression of the Mau Mau revolt which had led to Kenyatta spending seven years in prison, yet there he was, in 1963, congratulating his former enemy. That the British citizen should consider Kenya as 'his' country is understandable, but to go from that to referring to Kenyatta as 'his' prime minister must surely have led to a certain number of questions. It was difficult to believe that in the space of scarcely two years John Owen could declare that 'the past is dead'. What man could so quickly abandon the sense of superiority conferred on him by his status of colonialist-leader in the context of a community of settlers? That said, it is even more difficult to imagine that the conservation experts could have succeeded in establishing themselves so easily after colonization, as though independence were just another 'hoax' which must not be mentioned. Surely no one could be sufficiently strong to emerge unscathed from such an overturning of the balance of power. What then was Mervyn Cowie saying exactly? What was he telling us about these field experts who like him continued to live in this now postcolonial East Africa?

Being part of the transition to independence. History

As in the case of the great Africa of the expert gentlemen, a considerable amount of research is available to help us find the best route from which to pursue our investigations in East Africa. The authors of the existing research tell us about development and conservation, and about the narrowing of the gap between these two spheres of international action since the 1950s.

The colonialists transformed into experts

The sociology of science was the first to demonstrate that to be an 'expert' you must first of all be able to justify the title by proving that you have acquired a sufficient body of knowledge, then by demonstrating that you are in possession of certain technical aptitudes, and finally, by showing that you are sufficiently impartial to be able to offer reliable advice. These prerogatives are so subjective that anyone could claim to be an expert, which is why, so the sociologists of science tell us, being an expert is first and foremost a matter of being identified as one: you need to be *known* to have experienced a certain problem, and *recognized* as having attempted to resolve it.[18] This applies to expertise in general as well as to the expertise which emerged in Africa after 1945, during the course of what historians refer to as the 'second colonial occupation' – a period during which the European empires would claim to be 'developing' Africa in order to be able to remain there.

The British were the first to instigate this curious occupation. Anxious to remain in the colonies but seeing their legitimacy challenged, the leaders of the Colonial Office defined the problem – the lack of 'development' – and, in order to resolve it, they sent increasing numbers of scientists with training in forestry, animal health or ecology to work in Africa. But by thinking too much along the lines of a 'model', and by being too anxious to define a single form of maximum and rational exploitation of the empire's resources, these scientific-administrators ended up producing a 'conventional wisdom', or in other words, a knowledge which corresponded less to the facts being examined and more to the anticipated results. They believed that development would only be achieved by controlling overpopulation, deforestation and soil erosion and it was on this basis that, at the beginning of the 1950s, across the whole of British Africa, a 'technocratic imperial state' began to take shape.[19] This thinking determined the norms of colonial intervention during the last years of the empire, and, from that point on, these norms would remain in place thanks to the joint action of the international institutions and the independent African administrations. These former colonial managers were in the process of transforming themselves into international 'experts' not any longer in order to govern Africa but to help it.[20]

Agronomists, foresters or field ecologists, these men formed a professional group in their own right and, as such, bridged the gap between before-independence and after-independence. Yet they never completely dissociated themselves from the societies in which they had pursued their careers. Before the 1960s some of them thought of themselves as 'scientists in the colonies' and not as 'colonial scientists' – employed *by* the empire, they did not necessarily see themselves as working *for* the empire. Which, on a day-to-day basis, meant that they were capable of working at one and the same time with the representatives of the imperial system, the agents of the colonial state and the colonized elites.[21] And then, along came independence.

Half of the 25,000 men employed by Great Britain before independence continued their careers in Africa or in Asia. Some became 'planning officers' in the Foreign and Commonwealth Office. Others became 'experts' at UNESCO or at the World Bank, or 'advisers' for the new postcolonial states such as Kenya, Tanzania or Zambia (formerly Northern Rhodesia).[22] Here too, any attempt to analyse their work requires a certain element of nuance. For example, amongst the British agronomists who remained in East Africa as employees of the Commonwealth, not all of them advocated the same methods. While many of them focused their attention on mechanization and the use of artificial fertilizers, some favoured models based on practices they saw being used on the ground – in one place, monoculture with long fallowing practices; in another, polyculture aimed at maintaining fertility in fragile soils.[23] Whether from the British, Belgian or Italian empires, these former colonialists who had subsequently reconverted within the international organizations were therefore by no means cut off from the environment in which they found themselves working. Instead, they represented a 'nebula' of experts rubbing shoulders with African heads of state, government officials and regional or local actors who together represented the world of postcolonial expertise.[24]

Historians have demonstrated the complexity of this new professional body of 'postcolonial experts', but that has not prevented them from identifying the salient traits that characterized them. The first observation to be made is that they got together on a regular basis at the various conferences and congresses organized with increasing regularity by their employers, so much so that, at the beginning of the

1960s, these experts were responsible for crafting 'a real production line of international knowledge'.[25] Nevertheless, when it came to Africa, their knowledge was generally distorted by what anthropologists call the 'illusion of tradition', in which they were convinced of 'the irrationality of peasants ... who do not understand where their interests lie and who cannot grasp the logic of the structures put in place, ostensibly to help them'.[26] It was precisely this belief which explained why, at the time of independence, for many experts the disappearance of the colonies in no sense diminished the vital nature of their mission. The historian Frederick Cooper explains this with such clarity that his words deserve to be cited directly: 'planners were saying that while Africans, like anyone else, could become actors in labour unions and legislatures, officials themselves had the essential knowledge to build the stage and write the script. Modernizers were asserting the right to govern Africa for a time, and they did so on the basis that they knew what Africa should be like, even if it eventually governed itself.' [27]

The postcolonial moment

This faith in social engineering was one of the cornerstones of the postcolonial moment. Society represented a structure which the experts could reorganize, improve and enhance – an attitude that had prevailed since the 1950s in all areas of public intervention. As a result, East Africa saw first the convergence of developmental and conservationist policies and then the transition between the colonial and postcolonial eras.

Between the imperial leaders and the conservationists of East Africa, history took a serious turn when, in 1946, Arthur Creech Jones was appointed secretary of state for the colonies. Jones was neither a conservationist nor a big game enthusiast. But, in 1940 he was one of the founders of the Fabian Colonial Bureau, the institution set up to promote imperial development. For Jones this was the pressing issue. According to him, 'Much of what is wrong in under-developed societies comes because of the poverty of nature and the backwardness of people.' In his view, planned development was therefore a lifeline for the African colonies. Accordingly, in 1947, he decided to support the conservationists by promoting the organization in Nairobi of a conference for the head game wardens of British East Africa. In 1948, it was once again Jones who provided the region's governors with the famous figure of '75%' with reference to the amount of fauna destroyed by 'natives'. Then, at the beginning of the 1950s, he supported the creation of national parks and, with them, the abolition of 'primitive' hunting practices, the relocation of self-sufficient rural communities into urban centres and the development of a tourist industry. Jones was convinced that the use of such practices would enable conservationists to play a part in the building of developmentalist colonial societies, governed by an authoritarian control over their citizens. This was the empire's goal for the whole of East Africa and it would also be that of the leaders who, ten years later, found themselves being advised by the same experts.[28]

It should be pointed out that in the meanwhile the latter had succeeded in sharing their knowledge and their methods with the East African elites who had recently come to power or were on the point of doing so. The historian Raf de Bont was one of the first to highlight this phenomenon in his work on the practice of game cropping.

A figurehead of the African ecologists, the Scotsman Frank Fraser Darling was the person behind this theory. He was supported by the major experts, men like the elegant Huxley and the even more distinguished Worthington and then by American ecologists like Raymond Dasmann or Thane Riney. The latter introduced their first project in 1958 in the Queen Elizabeth National Park in Uganda. In order to reduce the hippopotamus population to the level of what was esteemed to be the 'carrying capacity' of the park, and to supply the regional market with animal meat, park staff killed more than a thousand specimens during the first year of the project. In Kenya, it was the surplus of elephants that needed to be brought under control and, in 1960, 3,000 pachyderms were shot in the Tsavo National Park. The conservationists then extended their projects beyond the national parks. They worked with ranch owners and concluded that the rearing of wild ungulates could prove more profitable than the rearing of livestock. Yet they failed to organize the transport of meat, to generate income and to stimulate the enthusiasm of investors, and, even more significantly, of potential consumers. These projects would come to an end between the 1960s and 1970s. Their impact was however significant. By seeking to transform the food economy of East Africa, the experts disseminated their idea of conservation and of the 'sociotechnical imaginaries' which went with it – that is to say, they shared their vision of the desirable future for the region. Yet, in this Africa of the future ruled by science and by the state, Africans had only a subordinate role. In Uganda, even if the park managers employed traders to sell the harvested meat, they still made no steps to reverse the recent expulsion of Basangora pastoralists. Similarly, in Kenya, although Waliangulu hunters were employed to kill elephants in the Tsavo Park, they stood to gain nothing from selling the meat they had themselves hunted, since this was purely destined for the regional market.[29]

Each change of direction brings its own continuity

These projects encourage us to see the 1960s as the pivotal decade of the postcolonial moment. But how should that moment be interpreted? How can we make sense of a period which brought with it both continuity and abrupt changes of direction?

First of all, the killing frenzy had come to an end. In the East African reserves the 1930s had seen a period of abundance. A relative abundance, certainly, since colonization had already begun to trigger the disappearance of big game, but nevertheless European chief wardens could still slaughter as many wild animals as they considered necessary. To ensure the sound economic development of the colony, their duty was to 'control' the wild animals which could devastate crops or contaminate cattle by introducing the tsetse fly. Consequently, as soon as it was necessary, they killed the fauna – wild boar, hyenas or baboons, zebras, gazelles, elephants or rhinoceros.

But the 'hunter-wardens' did not survive the new conservationist doctrine which emerged in the 1950s. With men like John Blower in Uganda, or Mervyn Cowie in Kenya, the wardens stopped killing everything in sight. Like the world's natural resources, wildlife was now perceived as being a limited resource with the result that in the national parks and in the areas surrounding these, every action should contribute to their survival. The change of direction was an unmistakable one. But 'game cropping' and controlled hunting also represented a sense of continuity. Visitors with a permit could still kill big game, and the park wardens could still pick up their guns, climb into a jeep, take aim, kill an elephant and then give the carcass to a local butcher who would pay back 50 per cent of the proceeds from the sale to the managers of the local park. Game continued therefore to be exploited, but from then on, that exploitation was defined as a protective measure.

The scientific nature of conservation constituted the second major change of direction. In this respect, according to historian Simone Schleper, the Serengeti National Park can be seen as a textbook case. At the end of the 1950s, prior to reducing the overall area of this Tanzanian park inhabited by the Maasai, the British had closely studied the movements of the thousands of wildebeests in the area. The first studies carried out in the Serengeti indicated that the migratory journeys of these wildebeests changed from one season to another. This discovery was confirmed in the mid-1960s by the chief warden of the park and Murray Watson, a young British researcher, who tracked ungulates from the air in real time. And the two men also noticed that the Maasai were constantly adapting to the presence of wildlife so that, season after season, when the wildebeests arrived the pastoralists would abandon their grazing areas, and when the animals left, they would set up new areas of pastureland. Watson and the chief warden therefore advised John Owen to take note of this cohabitation between men and animals. In spite of independence, Owen, the British conservationist, was still there, with his perennial pipe in his hand and his determined approach. He was still in charge of the Tanzanian national parks, then managed by a national institution called TANAPA (Tanzania National Parks). And Owen decided to encourage the mixed use of the Serengeti land, which would be shared by pastoralists, livestock and wild animals.

The experiment came to an end however at the beginning of the 1970s, at the instigation of the European conservationists from the Serengeti Research Institute, founded in the mid-1960s and fully operational in 1971. The institute focused primarily on fundamental rather than applied research and, very quickly, the observation of migration patterns in real time was replaced by aerial photography. But a photo simply captures a single moment within the park area. Instead of observing the seasonal alternation between wildlife zones and pasture zones, and the cohabitation of humans and animals, conservationists were only seeing the immediate moment the photo was taken so that, for example, where they saw signs of the Maasai, they claimed that the fauna had been wiped out. The result was that the TANAPA, in the absence of any international recognition, limited, and then sanctioned, human presence in the area.[30] In this way changes of direction and continuity were interwoven. Conservation always took a stand against the Africans, but it was no longer a matter of colonization. Instead, conservation was now purely driven by rational considerations. Quixotic percentages were wiped out by reductive aerial photographs, and with them the exclusion of local people was seen to be 'fair' because it was scientifically justified.

This led to the emergence of the third example of continuity within the context of a change of direction, notably the practice of exclusion. The colonial managers now transformed into international experts claimed to be replacing preservation by conservation – placing nature without any human presence in a protective bubble was giving way to the rational management of human and non-human ecologies. Historians have however pointed out that in the immediate aftermath of independence, in most of East Africa's national parks, protecting nature still involved the exclusion of the people who lived there.

This was evident in Uganda at the end of the 1950s when British chief game warden Bruce Kinloch allowed American biologist Helmut Buechner to fine-tune his concept of 'biological territoriality' in the field. According to Buechner, the survival of the large mammals depended on 'territorial systems of reproduction'. The biologist developed his theory by studying the Ugandan kob, a species of African antelope, and Kinloch implemented it by introducing projects for game cropping in the colony and then, in the 1960s, in Botswana and Malawi. These projects failed but the concept of territoriality remained. The more 'biological' conservation became, the more the park managers set aside entire areas for wild animals where they could reproduce and be observed by tourists. However, in order to achieve these objectives, they banished, or at least sanctioned human habitation and the exploitation of these areas.[31]

At the same moment, in 1964 to be precise, the same legislation was introduced in Zambia, former Northern Rhodesia. Prior to independence, Kenneth Kaunda, the leader of the United National Independence Party (UNIP), had promised his citizens that he would end the restrictions imposed on the colony's national parks, which covered 40 per cent of the surface area of Northern Rhodesia. However, once independence was declared and Kaunda came to power in 1964, the UNIP continued to impose the British laws. And, a few years later, the government ordered the creation of eighteen new national parks and thirty-two 'game management areas'. In reality, these protected areas effectively sustained the patronage system which was an essential part of political life in Zambia. In each of the country's electoral divisions, the UNIP nominated officials who had the right to be elected locally and, as a result, the right to vote on a national level. In order to guarantee their support, the party needed to offer them certain guarantees – it had to reward all its 'clients' for example by providing employment in the parks, by allocating percentages on the revenues obtained from tourism and even by offering meat and trophies to those who wanted them. In this way, the perpetuation of a 'colonial' conservation policy generated more benefits than costs for the Zambian government.[32]

In Tanzania too, from 1961 onwards, Julius Nyerere had tightened the laws previously introduced by the German and then British authorities. From the Selous Game Reserve in the south to the Arusha National Park in the north, the TANU were 'imposing wilderness', to use Roderick Neumann's phrase. Ten years after independence, the Tanzanian authorities had doubled the surface area of the country's protected areas, quadrupled the public budgets allocated to them and, in each of those areas, the British wardens and the Tanzanian guards had driven out local people, or at least restricted and criminalized their access to the resources contained within them.[33]

The same story was repeated in Kenya, where the presence of European experts led to higher levels of violence than elsewhere. Historians have demonstrated this by comparing the archives of conservationists working in the field with those covering the Mau Mau uprising, a rebellion which struck terror in the colonists between 1952 and 1960. Yet, during this period of insurrection and repression, park wardens such as Mervyn Cowie, Noel Simon or brothers Leslie and George Brown were very much present on the ground at the forefront of these events. All these men had met, at one time or another, in the Kenya Regiment African Trackers. Originally intended to track the Mau Mau insurgents, this unit ended up training an entire generation of British wardens in post in Kenya between 1950 and 1960.[34] These were men who, until the end of the 1970s, were also responsible for promoting the internationalization of Kenyan wildlife. By mobilizing networks and funding from the IUCN and UNESCO they helped to support both the creation of new parks managed in the rational way demanded by the new conservation movement, and the introduction of a policy which was as dehumanizing as the previous policy of preservation.[35]

This was, I believe, the real rift which characterized this postcolonial moment. For the expert gentlemen of conservation like Curry-Lindahl, Fitter, Harroy, Huxley, Monod, Verschuren or Worthington, internationalization was primarily a strategy. Their goal was to control nature by setting up a model of expertise which claimed to be politically neutral.[36] This was achieved, on the one hand, by the Africanization of conservation with the training of African ecologists like Perez Olindo and David Wasawo,[37] and, on the other, by the growing importance of figures such as Kenyatta or Nyerere. But for these African heads of state too, the internationalization of nature quickly proved to be a sound strategy. Like the colonial government before them, their goal was to build developmentalist societies, governed through an authoritarian control of their citizens. And to achieve that goal, they relied on the experts who were already in office – men like John Blower, Leslie Brown, Ian Grimwood, Mervyn Cowie and John Owen, who could therefore continue to live in East Africa thanks to this project of internationalization.

From preservation to conservation, from the colonial era to the postcolonial era, these experts were part of the new independentist change of direction. But how did they themselves experience that change? As we have seen, from Ethiopia to Southern Rhodesia and including Kenya and Tanzania, historians have had much to say on the subject. We must however continue to sift through the archives in search of clues which will enable us to look beyond the strategies and to immerse ourselves in the depths of these experts' lives.

The East Africa 'International'

The first thing we discover from a comparative perusal of the archives was that conservation was perceived on a regional scale.

East Africa, or 'the best of Africa'

In 1960, when the American biologists George Petrides and Wendell Swank summarized the research they had been conducting for the last seven years, under the Fulbright research programme in the United

States, they confirmed that they had concentrated their attention on the 'eastern half of Africa'. The two men mention first of all Kenya and Uganda. On the subject of Kenya, they praise the merits of Mervyn Cowie, who had 'undertaken all out poaching control efforts' and 'overpowered organized game destruction'. In Uganda, they described how the chief game warden Bruce Kinloch had devoted all his energies to the protection of hippopotamus and elephants: if the latter should one day disappear, the national parks would become sanctuaries where these animals could make 'their last stands'. Petrides and Swank then turned their attention to the role of the Tanganyika Wildlife Society and of its president Noel Simon, a former member of the British airforce, trained in conservation in Kenya and at that time lobbying the British authorities in Tanganyika to force them to strengthen conservation laws. The researchers emphasized the need to coordinate the work of the region's parks since, as they pointed out, 'East Africa is some of the best of Africa from the tourist viewpoint', adding that 'much of its character … will be lost if further wildlife depletion occurs'.[38]

This regional vision owes much to the British Empire, which ruled over almost all of East Africa with the exception of Ethiopia and the colonies of Djibouti, Somalia and Ruanda-Urundi. And decolonization did not prevent the Fauna Preservation Society from organizing what it called 'East African safaris'. The first of these took place in 1965. On that occasion the participants were provided with the services of two famous guides, Richard Fitter, the secretary of the FPS, and Charles Pitman, its vice-president, a former park warden in Northern Rhodesia and Uganda. With their help, the participants were able to see 'staggering' quantities of wildlife. In Tanzania and in Kenya, the FPS reported, 'Photographers … were given a feast such as they could never have expected in their wildest dreams.'[39] The safari met with such success that a second one was organized in 1966, this time led by Hugh Elliott and Leslie Brown. At the time of colonization, Elliott was in charge of the Tanzanian Ministry of Natural Resources and Brown was head of the Kenyan department for agriculture. Since then, the two men had worked for the IUCN, in Elliott's case, and for UNESCO, in Brown's, but they both declared themselves very much 'at home'. Thanks to their contacts with employees in the national parks of their former colonies, they were able to provide those participating in the trip with the opportunity to see 'some 420 species of birds and 55 of other vertebrate animals', 'a rate which it would be hard to beat anywhere in the world', wrote Elliott, with reference to 'East Africa'.[40] He would make a further reference to the region in Yellowstone in 1972, on the occasion of the Second World Conference on National Parks.

With Elliott acting as official spokesperson, during the conference conservationists called for the establishment of 'regional groupings of nations' which would be responsible for protecting 'representative samples' of 'natural ecosystems'.[41] The appeal was made public, and in 1974, the FAO, the IUCN, the WWF and the United Nations Environment Programme (UNEP) organized a major conference devoted to the creation of 'a coordinated system of National Parks and Reserves in Eastern Africa'. This took place in Serengeti, Tanzania. It was presided over by Hugh Lamprey, a former warden of the colony who had since become a consultant for the IUCN. Lamprey had just visited 'the nine African countries of the region' where he had met the leading figures in conservation. His task was now to group these together in pairs so that each nation was represented by 'a national [African] body' and a '[western] advisor'. Experts and leaders concluded that in all areas 'some wildlife populations have been greatly reduced'. Nevertheless, they observed that 'over very large areas the habitat has survived'. From Ethiopia to Zambia, they were therefore determined to preserve 'ecosystems in as natural a state as possible'.[42]

The conservation of African wildlife was not therefore simply a concept formulated in East Africa. It was also going to be *put in practice* on this regional scale. This is the second lesson we learn from a comparative perusal of the archives.

A 'regional mission'

During the 1950s, in all the East African national parks, hierarchy was very much determined by skin colour. In Kenya, for example, in 1960, the Royal National Parks Service employed a director, a deputy director and four wardens, all Europeans, supported by five assistant wardens and between 180 and 200 scouts (or guards), all of whom were African. The chief wardens had been trained in their home countries and the assistant wardens in the Ugandan College of Makerere, or at the

University College of Rhodesia and Nyasaland, in Salisbury (the future Harare, in Zimbabwe).[43] But, as the experts pointed out, independence 'must come soon'. In 1961 – in other words, two years before Kenya's official independence – they participated in the conversion of 'National Reserves' into 'African District Council Reserves'. In practical terms, that meant that those protected areas were now managed not by Kenyan settlers, of European origin, but by Kenyans from... Kenya itself.

Preferring to retain control of this 'Africanization' rather than have it imposed on them, the expert gentlemen of conservation were keen to 'select Higher School Certificate boys and send them on fellowships to selected universities in the U.S.A.'.[44] The field experts did not however agree. During the Arusha conference, the British zoologist Leonard Clayton Beadle, a professor at Makerere, was adamant that the 'training' of 'Africans for senior posts' should take place in 'Tropical Africa'.[45] His American colleague Helmut Buechner agreed with him. At Arusha, the biologist insisted that 'the major training effort should be developed in Africa'. In order for that to happen, Buechner added, the conservationists could get support from the association recently founded by the judge and safari enthusiast Russell Train in the United States – the African Wildlife Leadership Foundation.[46] And indeed, in 1963, thanks to a donation from the AWLF, the Tanzanian college of Mweka opened its doors for the first time.[47]

The success of the operation owed as much to Julius Nyerere as it did to Bruce Kinloch. Nyerere had promised the world to protect the national parks his country had inherited from the British and he had made a commitment to his citizens to Africanize the country's public services. As for Kinloch, who had left his post in Uganda in order to take up the role of chief warden of the Tanzanian parks in 1960, he was known for his faith in science, the only guarantee, as he saw it, of an efficient conservation.[48] And the chief warden seemed determined to stay in East Africa, even if it meant working under the very people he had himself supervised prior to independence. This was how the College of African Wildlife Management came into being. With Kinloch and Nyerere as its instigators, the establishment was a compromise between Africanization and expatriation.[49]

The motto of the college was moreover very clear. Thanks to foreign instructors, the college set out to 'help Africans obtain the knowledge to preserve and manage their unique wildlife resource'. [50] It was to this end that, in 1963, the college welcomed thirty students from Tanzania, Kenya and Uganda and subsequently, over the course of the next ten years, the majority of students were from Botswana, Ethiopia, Sudan and Zambia. As for the teaching staff, like Anthony Mence, Leslie Robinette and Patrick Hemingway, second son of the famous writer, they switched from being 'colonialists' to becoming 'expatriates', with their salaries now paid by the AWLF, the Ford Foundation, the Frankfurt Zoological Society and UNEP.[51] Originally from Great Britain or North America, they delivered lessons on mammal anatomy, the use of firearms in the prevention of poaching, the compilation of wildlife surveys, the management of hunting for tourists and the killing of dangerous animals.[52] Each of these subject areas was focused on East Africa and, as a result, the conservation of African wildlife took on an East African face.

The college ostensibly fulfilled a 'regional mission' as confirmed by its management committee, which, along with representatives from the IUCN, UNESCO and the WWF, included delegates from Kenya, Tanzania, Uganda and the East African Community, an organization created in 1967 to strengthen political cooperation in the former British colonies.[53] But this regional focus also applied to the students and teachers. When the former returned to their respective countries to work on the conservation of protected areas, they took with them the same norms – learned, over the course of one or two years, in this ostensibly East African training centre. As for the teaching staff, when they arrived in Mweka, they generally came from Tanzania or Kenya. And when they left, they were often heading to Ethiopia, Uganda or Zambia.[54]

This is the third lesson to be found in the archives of these field experts: from the 1950s to the 1970s, from one British colony to another and then from one independent country to another, experts travelled extensively throughout the whole of East Africa.

Genuine 'circulatory regimes'

These travel patterns were already apparent in the colonial era, for example in the correspondence exchanged in 1959 between members of the Fauna Preservation Society. On 3 November, Lord Willingdon, president of the FPS and member of parliament representing the old nobility which still governed England, decided to write personally to the secretary of state for the British colonies. He went straight to the point: 'Does the Secretary of State appreciate that African poachers are destroying thousands of wild animals in many parts of East Africa?' Willingdon asked. 'Is the Secretary of State aware that there has been no substantive Chief Game Warden in Kenya for most of this year, that there is now a similar vacancy in Tanganyika, that the Game Department of Northern Rhodesia has virtually disintegrated?' The archives fail to reveal whether Willingdon received a reply. They do however contain a letter sent ten days later by a certain R.A. Whittle, of the FPS, to Mr Woolverton, at the Colonial Office. The two men mention the nominations currently under discussion in East Africa with Ian Grimwood leaving Northern Rhodesia to take up the post of chief game warden of Kenya and Kinloch being transferred from Uganda to Tanganyika, pointing out that there were already several candidates available to fill the posts freed by those two.[55] Far from being part of a fixed or even strictly controlled system, 'our' experts were therefore the drivers of a genuine 'circulatory regime', or in other words, a 'practical mechanism for intervention' according to the definition given by historian Pierre-Yves Saunier.[56]

This phenomenon had begun to manifest itself in the colonial era and the postcolonial moment saw it become even more evident. Take, for example, the itinerary of John Morton Boyd, a Scottish zoologist and friend of the ecologist Frank Fraser Darling. In 1964, he worked as part of the Nuffield Project where British conservationists were attempting to improve game cropping programmes. Boyd did not take part in these experiments but his mission was to 'assess the current state of the wild fauna' in the Middle East and in East Africa. And, in the course of a three-month journey which took him from Jordan to Uganda, via Egypt, Kenya and Tanzania, he produced a weighty report in which the spectre of the degradation of nature caused by 'natives' once again raised its head. But the report also features names which appear in many other archives. In Kenya, Boyd encountered the Brown brothers, George and Leslie, first seen at the Arusha conference and then reappearing in Ethiopia in 1966, two years after the publication of the report. And it was in Ethiopia that he came across Peter Hay, a Scottish agronomist and experienced hunter, currently working in Uganda. Boyd met him a few weeks before continuing his journey to Tanzania where he encountered

Hugh Elliott, former director of natural resources in Tanganyika, and, in 1964, employed by the IUCN.[57]

Field experts therefore also contributed to the construction of this conservationist 'International'. This did not detract from the leadership of the expert gentlemen who were strengthening the conservationist network by travelling between New York, London, Brussels, Morges and a handful of African capitals, where they would come across men such as the biologist Julian Huxley from UNESCO, the American zoologist Harold Coolidge from the IUCN, and ecologists Edgar Worthington and Max Nicholson from the FPS and the WWF. But the work of these expert gentlemen was nevertheless intrinsically bound up with that of the field experts for whom the conservationist 'International' was first and foremost centred in East Africa.

The archives of the Ethiopian Wildlife Conservation Authority (EWCA) also provide evidence of this phenomenon, for example in a file labelled 'J.B.', abbreviation for John Blower, head game warden of Uganda who moved to Ethiopia in 1965. This file opens with three letters. The first, dated February 1966 and signed by Thane Riney of the FAO, acted as an official introduction between the German minister of agriculture and John Blower. Germany, at the time about to send funding to help with the establishment of the first Ethiopian national parks, left it up to Blower to decide which parks it should finance.[58] Then, in May 1967, whilst based in Nairobi in Kenya, agronomist Alain Gille forwarded to Blower a questionnaire drawn up by the United Nations Development Programme (UNDP) and UNESCO. In the name of these two institutions, Gille was in fact addressing all the chief wardens of East Africa with a view to finding out how fauna was being managed across 'the region'.[59] Finally, in June 1968, in a report carefully preserved and annotated by Blower, Leslie Brown stated that he had just left Kenya for two exploratory trips to Ethiopia, on behalf of UNESCO and the WWF. On that occasion Brown reported that in the Ethiopian parks 'just as in East Africa', 'livestock is beginning to be banned' by 'expatriate wardens' assisted by 'American biologists from Peace corps'.[60]

In this way, as far as the field experts were concerned, the conservation world was conceived, set up and *put into operation* in East Africa. The stronger the connections between them became and the more involvement they had in the national parks of each of the region's states, the easier it was to intervene within those states and the more they found themselves travelling around within the region.

In the name of the last stronghold of nature

This approach centred on circulatory regimes encourages a rethinking of conventional chronologies,[61] notably, in this case, those associated with colonization–decolonization. It also enables a certain amount of confusion to be tolerated. The historian may well seek broad explanations, as Pierre-Yves Saunier writes, but when confronted with the experts he finds himself contemplating a 'maelstrom of communications' which can never be thoroughly pinned down.[62] There is no alternative but to accept the confusion and then attempt to identify, in this postcolonial moment, the rationale which governed the battle for conservation in East Africa.

Killing to protect

In this respect, we must first of all address the contradiction which consisted in saving animals by killing them. This was particularly flagrant in Uganda where, at times, European wardens felt utterly helpless. Like the incident in the Murchison Falls Park, in 1957, where four buffalos were discovered trapped in a pit dug by local inhabitants. Using the winch mechanism on their truck the wardens tried to haul the animals to the surface, first once and then a second time, but the animals struggled, the rope broke and they fell back into the trap. It took an entire day to finally free three of the buffalo. The fourth animal died from its injuries but, as the wardens reported, 'honour had been sustained and the ideals of the National Parks maintained'.[63] None of which prevented them, later in the same year, from raising the issue of 'overprotection'. This could be as fatal as 'over-hunting' given that if there were too many animals for the same habitat, it would end up being destroyed and the wildlife would not survive, warned George Petrides, biologist with the Fulbright programme. The wardens therefore had a duty to authorize trophy hunting, and they did exactly that. But in order to keep it under control, from 1958 onwards, they also introduced 'game cropping programmes'.[64]

John Blower coordinated these game cropping operations in Uganda. From 1960 onwards he was assisted by Richard Laws, zoologist and director of the Nuffield Unit of Tropical Animal Ecology (NUTAE), set up by Nuffield College in Cambridge. In the Queen Elizabeth Park, surveys carried out by these experts indicated the presence of some 15,000 hippo in the area. This number was considered excessive and was causing serious deterioration of the grass cover as well as soil erosion. Each year therefore, the wardens killed a thousand hippopotamus, with the meat being sold by an 'African butcher' who then paid half of his earnings back to the park. This was a viable system in the view of the British authorities, and, in 1961, they decided to extend this policy to the other protected areas of the colony.

In the Toro Reserve, Ugandan kob were shot by a 'European' game ranger, and their meat sold by 'local' butchers. In the area near the Murchison Falls National Park around a thousand elephants were shot each year and their ivory sold on the markets of Kampala. Ninety per cent of profits from these sales went to the central government, with the remainder being paid to the provincial governments. The managers of the Ugandan parks went on to designate 'controlled hunting areas' in each of these protected areas. These were a source of revenue and, it was claimed, resulted in a more efficient 'management' of wildlife,[65] an aim which could also be achieved by moving animals. In 1961, John Savidge, warden of the Murchison Falls National Park, made reference to the imminent 'introduction' of thirty white rhino, currently living in the west of Uganda with no protected area to ensure their survival. Ken Randall and Pat O'Connell, two professional game trappers working in the south of Kenya, were employed to capture them. They pursued their targets in jeeps, captured them using a rope noose and then tied their legs together before transporting them in crates to the Murchison Park. John Savidge expressed regret that two rhinos had died during the process, 'probably from the after effects of bruising during capture', but, as he told the FPS, he also recalled 'the excitement of my first view of those rhino'.[66]

Tracking, forced displacement, killing – conservation was not without its contradictions and this did not change after independence. As is evident, for example, in the case of a man like R.J. Wheater. Successor to Savidge at the Murchison Falls Park, in 1969 he was still making a strong distinction between the people he welcomed to the park and those he was often in conflict with – in other words, the tourists who had come for 'controlled hunting' and the local people guilty of 'poaching'.[67]

Controlling in order to conserve

The problem was not therefore predation but how to control it. This was starkly evident in Kenya. In 1955, Mervyn Cowie, director of national parks, asked the question: should conservationists 'preserve or destroy'? The British civil servant acknowledged that 'there must be food for millions of human mouths'. Some form of exploitation was therefore inevitable. He added, however, that Africa represented 'the last stronghold of wild nature'. As a result, Cowie continued: 'We must set aside suitable areas for total protection'. Yet to achieve this, at least in Kenya, Cowie did not necessarily intend to forcibly exclude the local, colonized populations.[68] The Maasai 'have not been killers and poachers', he informed his superiors in 1956, urging that they should be allowed to hunt where authorized, and be involved in the management of national parks where any human presence was banned.[69] The British authorities initially ignored his advice. Then, in 1961, as independence drew closer, they found themselves obliged to hand over certain protected areas to the African district councils. The decolonization process was therefore favourable to Cowie. On the one hand, he encouraged enforced management of nature by 'local' authorities – in Amboseli for example, where drought had resulted in famine, the Maasai, who had killed eleven of the forty rhinoceros in the reserve were brought to justice by the district council. But, on the other hand, Cowie also launched the Galana River game cropping scheme, to be carried out with the involvement, subordinate but very real, of local people.[70] Cowie, the British expert, therefore provided his own answer to the question he had asked in 1955 – conserving meant both preserving *and* destroying.

This policy would be contradictory if some preserved whilst others destroyed. But this is not what the experts in the field wanted – like the expert gentlemen, they wanted to control *all* uses of natural resources. The British warden Ian Parker spelled this out almost explicitly in 1969. Still in post in Nairobi, the former colonist and now Kenyan citizen campaigned for the cropping schemes to be reinstated. This was, according to him, the only way of responding to the 'need for ... aesthetic stimulation' experienced by the visitors and to the 'basic requirements' of those who lived in proximity to the animals.[71] His colleague and fellow park warden R.K. Davis took a similar approach, urging that 'development' and 'preservation' could be compatible, on condition that the Kenyan authorities left the task of managing both of these to the conservationists.[72] Finally, Patrick Hemingway defended the same cause as his colleagues, with yet different words. If people really wanted to see the 'tribes' abandoning their pastoral activities and nature being truly protected, it would be necessary to 'redesign' trophy hunting for the benefit of those people, said Hemingway. Not stopped, but redesigned.[73]

For these field experts, conserving meant keeping nature intact, controlling its development and, even more importantly, shaping it – to the extent that conservation was sometimes synonymous with creation. This was the case all over Africa, and perhaps even more so in Tanzania. Here, in 1966, in the Arusha Park, chief game warden David Anstey even envisaged altering the course of the river which ran as far as the Mkomasi reserve. Thanks to the help of the East African Wild Life Society, the park was doing well, Anstey said. The tourist infrastructures were well maintained, the environment was protected. But upstream from the park, local people grazed their animals and, with drought threatening the region, it was highly likely that at some point the water would no longer reach Amboseli. So, through the intermediary of the highly influential Peter Scott, the British naturalist who had designed the Panda logo for the WWF, Anstey asked the FPS to finance the construction of a dam which would divert the water needed by the park's wildlife.[74] The project would not come to fruition until the 1970s, but the archives indicate the extent to which, as early as the 1960s, the protection of nature and territorial engineering could easily be confused.

The same preoccupation was also evident in the context of 'the elephant problem in the Serengeti'. In 1968, in response to the damage resulting from excessive numbers of pachyderms, the managers of the Tanzanian park envisaged killing several hundred elephants, even if only in order to preserve the trees which were also a food source for antelope, eland, buffalos and giraffes.[75] But subsequently they had begun to have doubts about the scheme as Hugh Lamprey admitted in 1972. At the time head of the Serengeti Research Institute, Lamprey, the former warden of Tanganyika, left no stone unturned. From killing elephants, marking out areas where the ground trampled by the elephants provided grazing areas suited for ungulates and regular burning of the land to encourage tree growth, Lamprey and his staff experimented with all possible solutions[76] – except the one which consisted in no longer interfering with nature. For inaction was unthinkable for these field experts convinced that, without their presence, wildlife would simply disappear.

Naturalizing, by every means possible

Killing, displacing people, attracting tourists, providing a source of animal proteins – the policies varied depending on the different contexts across the whole of East Africa, yet these men nevertheless seemed to be in pursuit of the same goal: that of giving a certain 'margin' to nature. The expression comes not from them but from the writer Romain Gary. Gary used it in his novel *The Roots of Heaven* in 1956. It is the motto adopted by Morel, the hero of his book, a French expatriate who takes up arms to defend elephants against the people who are killing them, whether colonizers or colonized: 'I don't care a damn whether they are Communists, Titoists, Nationalists, Arabs, or Czechoslovaks … What I'm defending is a margin – in which their – and our – natural right to live and roam freely would be preserved and respected. I'm asking the nations, the parties, the political systems, to draw together a bit and leave a little room for something that must never be threatened … We're doing a well-defined job here – the protection of a certain natural splendour, beginning with the elephants … No need to look further.' This was the rationale adopted by Morel and by the French men who joined him in his crusade. According to another character in the novel, the Sudanese Waitari, they were simply pursuing an 'opium dream'. Waitari accused them of trying to 'take refuge … in the heart of "magic" Africa, … among the herds which help you to dream of Biblical times, and you'll never forgive us for trying to deprive you of your opium dream'.[77] The metaphor of opium is perhaps not the most appropriate to describe the state of mind of the East African experts. But this determination to see animals rather than humans, or even more precisely, this obstinacy to humanize African wildlife and to dehumanize the Africans underlies much of what they wrote on the subject of East Africa.

As early as 1951, for example, in his short account of his recent trip to East Africa, Captain Keith Caldwell, the first representative of the FPS to visit the region, devoted more than a page to the Tsavo National Park. Elephants were at the heart of his narrative: 'Up to fifty or sixty can be seen drinking together with numbers of others waiting their turn … fathers, mothers, and their young. … A few elephant … lie down to a real bath. Now and again a rhino tries to join the party.' It is for their sake, Captain Caldwell writes, that in the East African parks 'the meat hunter has been faithfully dealt with', a reference to this anonymous figure who gets only a single mention in his report on the Tsavo. Unlike the elephants he was threatening, this individual had neither father nor mother, he would never have children and would not be attending 'drinking parties' with his friends and family. The elephant therefore has all the characteristics of a human being, since he/she thinks, feels and lives. As for the African, he is no more than an obscure 'poacher'.[78]

The same attraction to animals, seen as more endearing than humans, explains why, at the beginning of the 1960s, experts welcomed the end of campaigns to eradicate the tsetse fly, a programme which involved killing wild animals to prevent them from contaminating cattle. Conservationists were delighted to see the end of this policy which had been responsible for the deaths of thousands of warthogs, buffalos and elephants. But they now insisted that action be taken against the effects of the policy. 'For Tsetse fly control … nevertheless ends in a transfer of wild lands to livestock pastures', noted the two Fulbright programme biologists, Georges Petrides and Wendell Swank. In order to save 'East Africa's magnificent and unique wildlife displays' they asked the managers of the parks to address the problem of 'over-utilized tribal grazing areas'.[79] And they also recommended the use of another practice increasingly common in the region – the 'translocation' of animals. This method had been devised by the British veterinary scientist Antonie Harthoorn ten years earlier and, in 1961, he was able to put it into action in Kenya and Uganda, capturing antelope, rhinoceros and giraffes in one area and reinstating them in a national park.[80] The procedure was repeated in 1962 and 1963. Financed by the Zoological Society of London, several British experts were involved in this operation in Uganda and Kenya and then in Tanzania and Northern Rhodesia. Wild animals were moved not only from areas outside parks to those inside them, but also even within protected areas. In the Kafue National Park for example, in Zambia (former Northern Rhodesia), when the park's antelope population was threatened by a surplus of lions, the wardens killed several of these before capturing those left alive and transferring them into zones well out of reach of their prey.[81]

The question raised by Mervyn Cowie was clearly still a pertinent one – did the conservation of nature mean protecting it or destroying it? The field experts no longer expressed it in those terms but the question still continued to preoccupy them. Especially since in 1969 the Fauna Preservation Society had asked them to draw up a strategy to ensure the 'management of the herds' in order 'to bring population stability' to the 'elephant populations' in East Africa. Encouraged by his experiments in translocation in Uganda and Kenya, Harthoorn proposed setting aside areas which would be exclusively populated by elephants, and then monitoring their reproduction and the increase in their numbers, thereby favouring the creation of grassland areas which would provide an attractive habitat for zebras, oryx and buffalo. 'And if in a national park the desirable aim is the greatest variety of fauna then this may be no bad thing', the veterinary scientist concluded. But zoologist Richard Laws and warden Ian Parker disagreed. Based in the Kenyan national parks of Tsavo and the Murchison Falls, they suggested instead that human intervention was needed in order 'to accelerate the population crash'. They argued that since these parks were surrounded by people, their livestock and their fields, the elephants could no longer extend their territory any further, and, since there were too many of them to survive on the same area of land, it was preferable to kill some of them today in order to prevent the entire species becoming 'extinct in these parks' tomorrow.[82]

Whether encouraging an increase in the number of animals, if necessary by controlling reproduction in an entire species, or stabilizing their numbers, even if that meant killing some animals, there was scope for disagreement between the field experts. Whether to protect or to preserve remained the key question. On the other hand, they appeared never to challenge the somewhat artificial, or put another way, human dimension of nature which was being ever more organized, ordered, improved and shaped on all sides. For East Africa was the last stronghold of African nature and that was all that mattered. And the experts were determined to save it, even if it meant resorting to human intervention which was, of course, anything but natural.

With the 'Africans', against the 'Africans'

In order to continue saving nature, the expert gentlemen needed to be able to control it, and maintaining that control meant being part of the transition to independence. With this in mind, they involved 'Africans' in their Special Project – leaders like Julius Nyerere, young scholars like the Kenyan Perez Olindo and newly qualified ecologists like his compatriot David Wasawo. But what of the field experts themselves? What did they do, in practical terms, to ensure they were still actively involved with nature in the context of independence?

Cooperation on the one hand, repression on the other

In Southern Rhodesia, the future Zimbabwe, in October 1960, the field experts handed over previously unprecedented responsibilities to the people once subject to colonial control. The Sebungwe operation was one of the last campaigns to eradicate fauna carrying the tsetse fly and, for the first time, European head wardens employed around fifty 'Africans' to hunt down the animals. By way of rations, they gave them a share of the meat from any animals slaughtered. But they never allowed them to sell any excess meat.[83]

At the same time, as part of a series of 'cropping schemes', the Galana project was set up in south-east Kenya. Chief game warden Ian Grimwood coordinated the operation from the capital and, on the ground, having ascertained their 'submission', warden Ian Parker employed Waliangulu to hunt the animals and sell the meat.[84] The Waliangulu were however denied access to any neighbouring national parks – just like the Maasai, their neighbours in Tsavo. When the Maasai herds were decimated by drought, the British authorities offered to buy all their stocks of surviving cattle – on condition that they left the Tsavo Park, which needed to be entirely consecrated to wildlife and to wildlife alone.[85]

With the postcolonial era fast approaching, it seemed therefore that the experts did not want to get rid of 'Africans' because they were 'Africans', as they called them, regardless of which country the people concerned were from. They wanted to get rid of Africans because they were inhabiting and destroying *their* nature, that is to say the nature which belonged to the experts, the one they were conserving, preserving or cropping – the words mattered little – the nature they wanted to keep in its natural state and therefore empty of any human presence. Although difficult, until the beginning of the 1960s, their mission was possible because the colonial administrations shared their need to exert control over the colonized populations. The problem was how to continue their work in the aftermath of independence. From Sudan to Malawi (ex-Nyasaland), foreign experts still needed to carry on working *against* the Africans – they simply had no choice since, when it came to nature, the Africans were increasingly numerous and ever more destructive. But from that time on, the experts also had to work *with* them. Once again, they had no choice but to adapt.

The transition sometimes happened quite naturally, as though nothing had really changed. In Zambia, former Northern Rhodesia, for example, where in 1961 they had introduced lechwe captured in Uganda,[86] the European experts from the Wildlife Conservation Society of Zambia continued to repeat the same declinist discourse they had proclaimed in the colonial era. With reference to this African antelope, they stated that 'the 1966 population stood at 4,500 – to be compared with the million or so in the early days'. In order to put a stop to the 'poaching' which threatened the survival of the species, the following year they successfully obtained funding from a South African mining company, the Anglo-American Corporation, as well as benefiting from the experience of a former British army officer, Colonel Ronald Critchley. Using helicopters and light aircraft, Critchley led a number of 'anti-poacher' missions and, in 1969, with the official backing of the UNIP, the clientelist party of Kenneth Kaunda, the Wildlife Conservation Society launched a project to rehabilitate the lechwe. According to the conservationists, now that the African 'poachers' had been brought under control, they would be able to 'build up the herd' bringing it 'to an optimum figure of about 150,000 head' and guaranteeing 'a sustained yield of 30,000 head a year, the equivalent of 750 tons of meat'.[87] In this way, the experts continued to protect wildlife from certain Africans (those living in the national parks), while killing animals to provide food for other Africans (those living outside the parks and who were supposed to benefit from the meat available as a result of cropping programmes).

Independence – threatening but beneficial

The experts were not however immune to changes of policy. This was something they encountered, for example, in Uganda. In 1966, on the advice of the IUCN, Milton Obote's UPC agreed to abandon the idea of constructing a hydroelectric plant in the heart of the Murchison Falls Park. In a gesture of gratitude towards the authorities and on behalf of the Frankfurt Zoological Society, the veterinarian-filmmaker Bernhard Grzimek presented the park managers with a donation enabling them to buy 'a light aircraft to be used primarily for anti-poaching work'.[88] But Obote revived the hydroelectric project in 1968 and Lord Willingdon wrote to him personally, 'as President of the Fauna Preservation Society and as an Honorary Trustee of the Uganda National Parks'. After informing him that the number of foreign tourists to the park brought in almost $10 million per year to his country, Willingdon went on to 'urge the Ugandan Government to think hard' before giving permission to such a scheme. Obote replied ten days later. The positioning of the dam had been 'immediately' modified, he wrote: 'it will be sited at a distance far away from what is called the "Hippo Walk"'. But, with a touch of irony, the Ugandan president added: 'When my colleague, the President of Kenya went to open the Kenyan Power Station [at Kindaruma] the Game Wardens had to use their guns against the animals to allow him to perform the Opening Ceremony. We do not think the animals in the Murchison National Park would behave differently.' Obote's determination continued to cause alarm at the FPS over a period of several months, as is evident from the correspondence between the administrators of the London society and their experts stationed in Kampala. The latter thought that the World Bank could put pressure on the Ugandan authorities, by 'suggesting' in their turn that a national park could generate a lot more revenue than a hydroelectric plant.[89] The correspondence ended at that point, or at least it is no longer included in the archives and it is impossible to say whether the FPS followed the strategy recommended by its field experts. Nevertheless, no plant was ever built in the Murchison National Park.

Navigating continuity, backlashes and political manoeuvres in East Africa, the experts seemed in fact to be living in a constant state of uncertainty. The more we read of what they wrote, the more we sense the deep anxiety they felt, their fear of seeing wildlife disappear and their dread, above all, of at some point finding themselves deprived of the mission to protect nature bestowed on them by colonization. Like anyone else living in a situation of constant uncertainty they veered between delight and dejection. The life of George Dudley Hayes provides a good illustration of this.

Having left England in 1925 to cultivate tobacco in Nyasaland, the future Malawi, Hayes became a hunter, defender of nature, park warden and, after the war, founder of the Nyasaland branch of the Fauna Preservation Society. On that occasion, Hayes became friends with Lieutenant-Colonel Charles Boyle, secretary of the FPS. It was to Boyle that he wrote in December 1960, when independence was imminent. 'My Dear Boyle, I think you should know that our politician friend – Dr Hastings Banda – … is, in the course of his many virulent speeches, made all over the country, advocating the abuse of wild life conservation laws of all kinds.' Then, in April 1961, Hayes asked a colleague to alert the authorities back home. Failure to do so, he assured Boyle, would mean 'every single head of "game" will shortly be exterminated'. Boyle immediately forwarded the letter to those in charge at the FPS, including Lord Willingdon.[90]

Independence would come three years later, but the predicted extermination did not happen. In 1967, Hayes conceded that 'the preconceived notions regarding the African attitude towards wildlife conservation proved to be completely erroneous'. Malawi was proof of this, he went on, pointing out how, 'under the enlightened leadership of Dr. Banda', plans for a sugar development project were abandoned, a rest camp for tourists was constructed, former European wardens came from all over East Africa to help manage the country's protected areas and, each day, 'patrols' ensured the parks were protected from the 'farmers', 'pastoralists' and 'poachers' who lived there. In this case, concluded George Dudley Hayes, or 'G.D.' as his colleagues called him, 'independence saved an African reserve'.[91] He had assumed that the advent of a Malawian government would be a catastrophe, but Banda enabled him to finally follow his dream – with good (African) leaders, nature could be freed of its (African) inhabitants.

An impossible dream

G.D. emphasized that once they had become independent, the 'indigenous inhabitants' had shown that they could be 'sensitive' to the task of protection. But, as he pointed out in 1972, the end of colonization had not brought an end to the real problem: 'human overpopulation' always implied 'destruction' of 'nature'.[92] This applied to the entire 'stronghold' of East Africa, as UNESCO called it,[93] since it was here that it was deemed still possible to save 'Pleistocene' Africa, the era before humans first appeared. This was the mission taken up by the British experts who were in charge of the national parks of Kenya and of the entire region from the 1950s right up until the end of the 1970s. 'An impossible dream', as they would admit many years later.[94] But, for that moment, this dream would shape their lives and guide their steps.

Scientists in power

Amongst these experts, one typical representative of colonial expertise can be identified – that of the scientist. Leslie Brown is an example among many others who perfectly epitomizes this type. Born in England in 1917, he grew up in India and returned to his home country to study ornithology and agronomy. After a period working in Nigeria, Brown arrived in Kenya in 1946 and joined the department of agriculture. It was there that he first began to wear the famous woollen sweaters that would be affectionately mocked by his colleagues. He became deputy director and then director of agriculture, a post he held until the end of colonization.[95] Independence was declared in 1963, but already in the spring of 1962, in a letter to a colleague in London, he observed: 'things are crumbling slowly down here'. The administration is 'being Africanized' and, in the streets, 'some people are attacked from time to time … but no one pays any attention to that'. 'They are white after all, and deserve it', bemoaned Brown. 'I fortunately have a lion on my plot from time to time and I treat him very carefully as he is a great thug deterrent.'[96] As a colonial official, he was therefore preparing for his inevitable future downgrading and, as a man of science, he had every intention of bouncing back. At the end of 1962, he set off on a trip to Lake Magadi, on the Tanzanian border, an opportunity to see the region's flamingos and to assess the 'danger' potentially represented by vultures and by the men likely to hunt these birds.[97]

Brown made numerous trips between Nairobi and Lake Magadi over the course of a year, during the period before Kenya celebrated its independence in December 1963. Rather than attending the celebrations, he set off to explore the high plateaux of Ethiopia, where Huxley, Gille, Monod and Worthington had undertaken a preliminary mission a few months earlier. Following in their footsteps, Brown set about tracking the walia ibex, a wild goat endemic to the Simien Mountains in northern Ethiopia. On his return to Nairobi after a four-week trip, he wrote to his friend and colleague Noel Simon, the former pilot with whom in the mid-1950s he had tracked down Mau Mau rebels in the Kenyan Aberdare Mountains. Simon was at that time working for the IUCN in Morges and, thanks to him, the Union had employed Brown to go to Ethiopia and meet its people. 'They are without exception the most destructive human beings I have ever seen', he reported to his colleague. They are 'industrious to boot, so that they do more damage per head than would an entire people'. The proof, wrote Brown, who had conducted surveys of animal numbers in the Simien Mountains, was that in this region 'there are no longer more than 150 to 200 walia left'. Simon replied within a week: 'It was so good to receive your letter and to know that you have returned from Darkest Ethiopia with all your parts intact.' And he suggested that his friend should 'apply' for the new projects financed by the IUCN and the WWF. Which is exactly what Brown did, in January 1964.[98] The scientist was in the process of becoming an 'field expert'.

Leslie Brown then embarked on another trip to Ethiopia in 1965. On that occasion, he spent a total of four months there. He identified three areas which merited being transformed into national parks and met with staff from the new Ethiopian Conservation Department. Brown even suggested they introduce legislation which would enable them to save their natural resources, since at that time, as he pointed out, 'the whole picture of Ethiopian conservation is one of the most depressing in Africa'. According to him, deforestation had been happening 'for many centuries' but had 'accelerated in recent years' and he predicted that 'forest will be gone from Ethiopia in 25 years or so', unless the authorities curbed 'demographic growth', '[the] spread of agriculture', 'overgrazing' and 'poaching'.[99] The account of his trip, written during the time he spent in Ethiopia and published under the title *Ethiopian Episode*, was commended by Hugh Elliott, himself a former stalwart of the British East African empire, who had spent twenty years in the national parks of Tanganyika. Elliott had started working for the IUCN in 1961 as 'liaison officer' in Africa, and it was in this role that he informed the Fauna Preservation Society of the merits of his colleague at a time when '[F]ew naturalists have penetrated far into the wide and attractive spaces between Ethiopia's main lines of communication'.[100]

Leslie Brown returned to Ethiopia on several occasions but continued to live in Nairobi. From Karen, the expatriate district of the capital, he made trips to Kenya, Uganda, Tanzania and Ethiopia, working for both the IUCN and the WWF as well as for the FPS and the World Meteorological Organization (WMO).[101] His expertise extended over the whole of East Africa. 'The damage pastoral tribes do to the environment … is almost universal', he wrote in 1969, reiterating the argument he had already put forward eight years earlier at the Arusha conference – since rainfall in East African was too low to allow the soil to support domestic animals, the conservation of wild fauna was the only reasonable way of using much of the land in the region.[102] In the same year, at the Pan-African Ornithological Congress organized in South Africa, the expert emphasized the role of 'field staff' in the planning of this regional conservation.[103] These should form a 'conservation army' he declared in 1971, speaking at the University of Addis Ababa, where he was invited to open a national conference on the protection of nature in Ethiopia.[104] In certain countries, it was indeed a matter of 'survival' urged Brown, addressing the representatives of the Ethiopian government who had come to listen to him. And for all the international institutions this had to be a matter of common sense.[105]

He would reiterate the message to Peter Scott in 1973, at the moment when, in Kenya, the East African Wild Life Society learned that the WWF and the IUCN would place their future projects under the official sponsorship of the United Nations. Brown was aware of the financial stakes behind this decision. But, as he told Scott, 'United Nations agencies can be admitted to be almost ineffective'. He asked Scott to emphasize to the WWF and to the IUCN the need to defer to 'people who are directly engaged with wildlife conservation', namely, the scientists and field experts who had remained in place and who, it seemed, were concerned that nature could not be conserved without them.[106]

The trailblazing administrators.

Where Brown had prioritized science, others insisted on the importance of experience. Ian Grimwood is the most perfect example of this second incarnation of postcolonial expertise – the trailblazer. Before arriving in Northern Rhodesia – the future Zambia – in 1948, Major Grimwood had studied entomology in London, served as a soldier in the Indian Imperial Army and been a prisoner in Japanese camps during the war. He was a key figure in the wildlife rescue scheme Operation Noah. In order to construct a huge hydroelectric dam on the border between the two Rhodesias, the British planned to create an artificial lake, the Kariba. But in the process of doing so, and on the instigation of the FPS and the IUPN, they undertook to rescue the region's wildlife. More than 6,000 animals including elephants, antelope, rhinoceros, leopards and zebras were captured and transferred to the national parks of Northern Rhodesia. Like a modern-day Noah's Ark, the operation took place over a ten-year period. Grimwood was involved in the scheme in his role as game warden and then chief game warden for the wildlife department.[107] Then, in 1959, he went to Kenya, where he met Mervyn Cowie, who was planning to involve the Maasai in the game cropping projects currently in operation in the colony's parks. Grimwood made no attempt to hide his reticence at the idea of sharing their budget with 'indigenous people', but in 1962 Operation Oryx put an end to any such debate.[108]

This operation was carried out on the other side of the Red Sea, in the eastern Aden Protectorate where hunters had just slaughtered at least forty Arabian oryx. Already under threat, the antelope was at that point on the very brink of extinction. In order to prevent this happening, the FPS decided to send Grimwood and a team of experts to the south-east of the protectorate, in the sultanate of Qu'aiti de Shihr and Mukalla. Their mission was to identify the whereabouts of the last surviving oryx, capture them and dispatch them to Kenya. In Nairobi, Grimwood immediately set about constructing a 'special car' equipped with hoists designed to lift the antelope from traps. He then set about assembling his team – a biologist from the wildlife department, a former warden

from Northern Rhodesia, a veterinary surgeon from Tanganyika and an
administrator based in Aden. In April 1962, the five men set off together
to comb the desert for a month in the course of a mission which they
described as epic and which included a number of memorable incidents
such as customs officers blocking their strange vehicle in the port,
encounters with Bedouins who wanted to know if they had seen any
rain in the course of their travels, the excitement of the first sighting
of an oryx, consternation when their vehicle broke down in the middle
of the dunes when they were in full pursuit, being woken up at dawn
by their aides de camp (of whom it was said 'one of the chief attributes
of the Bedu is his cheerfulness'), the capture of first one oryx and then
another, the death of the first in its carrying crate, and more dunes,
desert and captures. Exhausted but victorious, they returned to Kenya
with three oryx.[109]

Grimwood was careful to keep the 'special car' used by the team and
he would make use of it again in 1963 in a new 'rescue operation', on the
Somalian border. The Hunter's antelope was under threat in the region:
not from poaching, Grimwood insisted, but because 'no area had been
set aside specifically for their preservation'. This meant that 'any change
in land use could result in their extermination' – a reference to the
danger represented, in his view, by the recent independence of Kenya
and Somalia. But, once again, the worst was avoided, thanks to funding
from the WWF, to Alistair Graham the biologist from the Kenyan
wildlife department, to wardens David McGabe and David Sheldrick,
and above all to the pilots of the East African Wild Life Society who used
their helicopters to drive the antelope towards the experts waiting on the
ground. Together, around twenty were captured and then transported to
the Tsavo National Park.[110]

The operation was the last undertaken by Grimwood in Kenya. The
country became independent in December 1963 and, shortly afterwards,
the chief game warden was given notice by the Kenyan administration,
who had taken offence over his refusal to allow the former Mau Mau
generals the right to sell ivory acquired by the national parks department.[111] Once a colonial administrator, British-born Grimwood now
found himself expatriated. We come across him again in 1964 in Kuwait
and in Saudi Arabia, where sheikh Jabir Abdullah Al-Sabah and King
Saud had agreed to present the WWF and the FPS with a gift of five

oryx from the zoo in the palace gardens. Once again funded by the WWF, Grimwood supervised the transport of these animals from Riyad, to Beirut, Rome, Naples and to Arizona, where the antelope joined the herd captured two years earlier and placed in the Phoenix Zoo in the USA as part of a breeding programme.[112] The expert was then employed by UNESCO for a mission to Ethiopia, one month prior to that undertaken by Leslie Brown. Grimwood recommended the creation of three national parks in Ethiopia – the Awash, the Omo and the Simien – and advised they should be staffed with either 'suitably qualified Wardens … who have recently been retired as a result of Africanization programmes',[113] or professional hunters like Ted Shatto, an 'American …, objective in his reports on faunal matter, despite his schizophrenic character'.[114]

Grimwood subsequently headed for new horizons. Sent to Peru by the Commonwealth Office, he suggested to the authorities that the areas selected for national parks 'should be in a virgin state, uninhabited and unaffected'.[115] Advice he also gave to the governments of Colombia and later Pakistan at the beginning of the 1970s.[116] We encounter him next in the FAO, conducting 'ecological surveys' in Swaziland in 1974,[117] in the Philippines in 1975 and in Malaysia in 1976. And then, in 1979, the IUCN sent him to conduct a survey of black rhino, then threatened with extinction in Malawi, Zambia and Tanzania.[118] Ian Grimwood's career ended where it had begun – at the heart of the East African stronghold that he had sought so vigorously to defend, an area extending from Zimbabwe to Ethiopia.

The colonialists versus the incapable

Part scientists, part trailblazers but above all administrators and men in the field, many experts in the end distinguished themselves by their capacity to perpetuate the imperial ethos they had imposed on East Africa. This was the final typical incarnation of postcolonial expertise – the colonial. However hard we try to avoid the trap of oversimplification, when we come face to face with men like John Blower, there is no mistaking the fact that the ideas and practices of these 'international' experts generally remained firmly anchored in the colonial era into which they had been born.

After serving in West Africa during the war, Blower obtained a degree in forestry from Edinburgh University in 1947. He then went to Tanganyika where, as 'assistant conservator of forests' and then warden in the Liwale National Park, he described how he had spent time 'exploring some of the wildest and most sparsely inhabited country in East Africa'.[119] From there, Blower went to Kenya. The Mau Mau uprising had been raging in the country since 1952 and, the following year, the British authorities provided him with 'a small tracker team to go after the terrorist gangs based in the forest'. From being an explorer, he had now become a conqueror. In 1954, he took part in the hunting down and execution of the famous Kago, one of the generals of the Kenya Land Freedom Army, known by the colonialists as the 'Mau Mau'.[120] Two years later, Blower arrived in Uganda. In his role as chief game warden, he supervised game cropping projects with a utilitarian vision of African wild nature and a racist view of 'the African', whom he described as a 'realist' who would never be able to see big game 'other than in terms of food'.[121]

Out of a job as a consequence of independence, Blower then headed for Ethiopia. In December 1965 he became adviser to the emperor on wildlife conservation and, over a period of five years, his work continued to be guided by stereotypes with racist and paternalistic overtones. He explained, for example, to the FPS that 'hunting big game' was seen as 'a manly pursuit', given that the Ethiopians have always been 'a warlike people' who considered that 'the slaying of an elephant was accounted equivalent to killing 40 men'.[122] The practice was all the more shocking, the expert insisted, since big game hunting had been banned in Ethiopia since 1944. That said, this legislation did not prevent Blower from hunting himself. There was, for example, a red lechwe from which he had 'collected quite a good head,' as he proudly wrote in a letter to David Maddox, an American friend he had met in Uganda and who he subsequently invited to 'enjoy the controlled hunting areas' of Ethiopia. Maddox accepted the invitation at the beginning of the summer of 1966. He hunted in eastern Ethiopia for a week and, on his return, like Grimwood before him, he wrote to Blower in enthusiastic terms describing the service provided by the company Safaris International and its founder, Ted Shatto, 'a guide and hunter based in Addis Ababa who likes his beer but seems quite capable of holding it'.[123]

The anecdote is comical but it shows us that Blower was a well-connected man. And there is further evidence of this in 1966, when Hugh Elliott and the IUCN 'send' him a former warden from British Kenya to run the Ethiopian Awash National Park.[124] Or, in 1967, when Richard Fitter and the FPS would 'entrust' him with several of their zoologists to study Ethiopian wildlife,[125] or again in 1968, when Blower invited veterinarian-filmmaker Bernhard Grzimek to visit the country's first national parks.[126] And when the expert complained in 1969 about 'the repeat failures' of his Ethiopian employers and about practices worthy of a 'medieval empire',[127] he was addressing conservationists from UNESCO whom he knew personally.[128] That prestigious institution subsequently employed him directly to 'remedy' this situation, a move which enabled Blower to write to Abebe Retta, the Ethiopian minister of agriculture, with the tone of someone who holds authority: 'If Ethiopia intends to host parks recognised as such', he urged ministers close to Haile Selassie, it needed to 'endorse' the measures he had been recommending for the last four years in order to demonstrate their intention of 'punishing local farmers [who] are slaughtering the wild fauna'.[129]

This was the common thread in the mission he would pursue throughout his entire life. Explorer, conqueror, hunter, somewhat racist or very paternalistic, John Blower was first and foremost a man who was passionate about nature in its wildest form, and who was convinced that the responsibility of managing it should be left to him. In Tanganyika, as an 'incurable romantic', he was determined to protect the fauna from 'bush fires', 'cultivation' and 'poaching'.[130] In Uganda, he claimed to be working for 'one of the most spectacular views in East Africa'.[131] In Ethiopia he wanted to save 'the most extensive areas of high mountains in the entire continent'[132] where local people were 'decimating' nature.[133] Then, in 1970, when Blower went to work for the FAO in Nepal, the same mantra continued to guide his work. With rhinoceros, elephant or snow leopard, he told the FPS, the fauna is 'diverse' but was being 'greatly depleted ... following the enormous spread of human settlement'.[134] The same was true in Indonesia, where he went to work for the FAO and the WWF in 1974. Nature was 'still surviving', he reported, despite 'the enormous pressures of human population'.[135] The situation was not much better in Burma, where Blower discovered 'outstanding' islands and 'lost valleys' but these landscapes were under threat and, more importantly, were compromised by the country's leaders, who seemed incapable of conserving them and who had even been heard 'remarking that national parks were "a foreign idea", and Burma didn't need them'.[136]

According to John Blower, these problems remained unresolved, a situation he himself had suffered the consequences of over a period of twenty years. Moreover, in the early days of the postcolonial era, he had already warned his colleagues about the situation: for example, in Ethiopia, when he had been forced to recruit a new expatriate for the Simien Park, after the dramatic resignation of the previous game warden. This park 'obviously represents a dream for any naturalist', he wrote to John Morton Boyd, who, at that time, had been working for The Nature Conservancy since 1966. 'But I do not want to disguise the fact', Blower had added, 'that it is also a conservationist's nightmare.'[137]

A nightmare

Many years later, the park wardens would acknowledge that turning an area into a national park, emptying it of its inhabitants or banning them from hunting, farming or grazing amounted to an 'impossible' dream. Not surprisingly the dream often turned into a nightmare. This is clear when we observe the daily lives of these men, for example, in the three areas selected by UNESCO in 1965 to become the first national parks in Ethiopia.

'A park warden with no official park'

The creation of the first park began on the low-lying land of the Awash, a semi-arid region where local people alternated grazing their cattle with cultivating the land. In 1966, with the help of funding and engineers from the UNDP and the USSR, the first tourist trails were laid out and several buildings were erected to house the administrative staff. Work continued for a year and, in the summer of 1967, the park opened its gates to visitors. The trails allowed them to observe 'game in sufficient number and variety' and, according to Blower, thanks to the construction of small huts with thatched roofs, which the Ethiopians call *tukul*, tourists were able to experience 'a genuine African safari atmosphere'.[138] But the hardest task still remained to be tackled, he added, addressing the members of the Ethiopian Conservation Department. This included 'removal of the local people', described by Blower as men who were 'well armed and very truculent', adding that 'it will not be possible to move these people without an adequate show of force (Police or Military)'.[139] This was a task easier said than done when, on the ground, the chief warden of the park, Scotsman Peter Hay, had neither policemen nor soldiers at his disposal. Trained in Somaliland and in Uganda where he studied locusts and devoted all his free time to hunting,[140] Hay was supported only by an Ethiopian assistant warden, Tadesse Mikaël, an American biologist from the Peace Corps, along with a German mechanic and twenty-four Ethiopian scouts.

Adopting his habitually jaunty tone, in his 1998 annual report Peter Hay nevertheless referred to some 'fantastic' progress. In the areas adjoining the park, the FAO had introduced a programme of irrigation and established a sugar industry which was developing rapidly. 'Several thousand hectares have already been carefully cleared', he wrote to Blower. Inside the park, Hay reported, 'daily work' was producing results. He regularly spotted zebra, antelope, leopards and a few hippos. He had already catalogued more than 438 species of birds. Several leopards and three lionesses had been captured in east Ethiopia and then introduced into the park. With the exception of two lionesses, one of whom had had to be put down and the other moved elsewhere after attacking some of the park's inhabitants, 'lions now seem well established' in this park where, Hay added, 'poaching is practically negligible'. This was a situation which, according to him, made it easier to welcome visitors who came to observe or hunt big game. On that subject, the warden also reported a similarly 'satisfactory' state of affairs, which he insisted was largely due to Ted Shatto's 'talent' in negotiating with local inhabitants over the price of the livestock he bought from them in order to provide food for the tourists.[141]

Ultimately Peter Hay was faced with just 'two problems'. The first of these concerned the Ethiopian scouts placed under his command. 'Were they efficient and hard working, the situation would then be tolerable, but the materials [sic] given to me is of such a low standard that most of it is superfluous', he confided to Blower. Hay did however admit that '[his] scouts' had helped him 'address the stock issue'. Together they had confronted the 'tribes within the park', the Karayu and the Ittu, who survived on a subsistence agro-pastoral economy; they had successfully 'rounded them up' and 'with their stock put across the river ... about 1,000 people and 6,000 head of livestock'. But the Karayu and the Ittu kept repeatedly returning, with the result that, 'instead of having a Park practically clear of all stock, the warden declared, we reverted overnight to a Park full of nomads and their animals'. 'I thus find myself in a unique position', he wrote, concluding his report on a note which was now one of disillusionment as he described himself as 'a Park Warden with no official Park'.[142]

'Once is enough, thank you'

Peter Hay, nicknamed 'Ibex 2' by his expatriate colleagues in Ethiopia, was not the only one to suffer as a result of the situation. In the Omo Park, 700 kilometres south-west of the Awash, George Brown was also struggling to carry out his duties as park warden. Brown, or 'Ibex 3', had only recently arrived from Kenya. A former soldier turned policeman and another passionate hunter, he had worked for the British colonial government as a district commissioner for fifteen years. Then independence had come along, and in 1966, after a brief period of inactivity, on the recommendation of his brother Leslie, he was taken on by John Blower as warden of the Omo National Park, created a few months earlier. In this sub-desert terrain, most people were agro-pastoralists, like those in the Awash; although in the Omo, pastoralism took precedence over agriculture for the Surma and Mursi people. In contrast with the Awash, given the absence of a tarmacked road linking the park with the capital city, the construction of buildings destined for tourists was particularly challenging. As a result, Brown spent most of his time surveying the fauna, marking out the park boundaries and, above all, fighting to impose the regulations necessary for the smooth running of the park.

In the western area of the park, the warden and his 'men' attempted to drive back the Mursi before they could enter the Omo area with their cattle. And, in the eastern area, they tried to prevent the Surma from carrying out their seasonal burning programme. But here, as in the Awash, each morning could represent a small victory and each evening a defeat. A situation which George Brown, clearly a man with a somewhat different temperament than Peter Hay, found exasperating. His feelings can be sensed in the letter he sent to Blower in May 1969. 'Beware of one thing', he told his British compatriot, 'the expression "right to search a building" in existing Ethiopian practice seems to mean only, in effect, "right to search a building if furnished with a warrant from a court to do so".' Faced with what he perceived as an absurd denial of authority, the former colonial commissioner asked his chief warden to obtain for him: '(I) the right to enter any houses or camps without a warrant from the court … ; (II) the right to used armed force … ; (III) the right to remove huts and crops'. And Brown concluded his letter by emphasizing the urgency of his request. He was aware that his case was not an isolated one, he told Blower referring to the Awash and the Simien, but nevertheless, he had been 'shot at' and so, as far as he was concerned, it was a case of 'once is enough, thank you'.[143]

George Brown would certainly have appreciated the 31st edition of the Ethiopian *Negarit Gazeta*, the government gazette, in which the empire declared that 'No person shall reside, hunt, cultivate, graze cattle or livestock, fell trees, burn vegetation or exploit natural reserves in any manner within a National Park.'[144] But the law arrived too late and when it was published, on 19 January 1972, more than a year had gone by since the archives had provided any news of Brown, who had no doubt returned to join his brother Leslie, in Kenya.

'If only the government would support us!'

By that time, it was also too late for Clive Nicol, nicknamed 'Ibex 1', the warden of the Simien Park. Nicol had resigned from his post in July 1969 after two and a half years spent in the north of Ethiopia, in the midst of a mountain range with altitudes of between 2,800 and 4,600 metres, an area where local people made their living from subsistence farming which they increasingly supplemented by pastoral activities.

In the course of my last research on the Simien, in 2019, I found some letters bearing Clive Nicol's signature in the boxes marked John Blower. These few archives first of all trace the transnational itinerary of this British citizen, who had arrived in Ethiopia at the age of twenty-six. A research engineer in England, he had worked in Japan at the beginning of the 1960s, then in the Arctic Biological Station in Canada and, in

1967, accompanied by his wife Sonako, the young Japanese woman who had helped him gain his black belt in karate in Tokyo, he set up home in the Simien Mountains. From the correspondence he exchanged at that time with Blower and Abebe Retta, the Ethiopian minister for agriculture, I had come to the conclusion that the creation of the Simien Park had been chaotic. Nicol described himself as being 'harassed' by Nadew Woreta, a guard, whom he described as 'very clever to intrigue' and much appreciated by the local inhabitants. The latter, for their part, were 'obstructive, and sometimes hostile'. The scouts he was 'provided with' by the local government were 'the worst imaginable quality', 'illiterate', and 'accused of bribery, theft, violence and libel'. All of which led to Nicol's resignation in 1969. Powerless to expel the inhabitants from the Simien and helpless as they continued to 'overexploit' their lands, the game warden packed his bags, accusing the Ethiopian government of failing to support the *farenji* or, in other words, foreigners like him.[145] It is therefore all too easy to understand why Blower spoke of a conservationist nightmare. But when we turn to Clive Nicol's book *From the Roof of Africa*, written in the year following his departure, we discover even more about those experts who played such a significant part in the postcolonial moment.

The first thing to come out of this narrative is perhaps an obvious one. While these men received three-quarters of their salary from the international conservation institutions, the IUCN, the WWF or the African Wildlife Foundation, which paid them an 'expatriation allowance', Blower, Hay, Brown and Nicol were however employed by the Ethiopian Conservation Department. They were therefore working for the public sector and, in that context, they naturally complained about their administration – its slowness, its inefficiency, its Kafkaesque procedures. All of this was apparent from the moment Clive Nicol arrived in Addis Ababa.

In February 1967, before he left for the Simien, John Blower sent him to the Awash so he could familiarize himself with the country. Once there, Nicol met up with Peter Hay, who decided to call George Brown by radio. From the Omo, the latter asked him if the laws supposedly officially formalizing the Awash Park had finally been passed, and if they could therefore at last begin to apply the necessary legislation. Hay said 'he understood that the draft was completed and was now with the Minister of Pen (one of the highest dignitaries of the empire)'. 'The

Minister of Pen?' Brown repeated. 'Roger on that', Hay confirmed. 'There seems to be some slight delay over the signing.' Then, alone in the depths of the Omo and in his most serious voice, Brown replied: 'Ibex three to Ibex two. Well, the trouble is the Minister of Pen is having a quarrel with the Minister of Ink, because the Minister of Ink stole the Minister of Pen's rubber.' The two men then burst into laughter and this continued for several minutes, under the perplexed gaze of the Ethiopian scouts. As for Nicol, as he wrote in his memoirs, if he had heard this joke two years later, he too would have laughed until he cried. For, like many civil servants and government agents, these experts seemed to think that their employer was the first obstacle to the success of their mission. Yet it was a mission they had to accomplish, come what may. It was not something they owed to the administration of a country, but rather something they owed to nature across an entire continent.[146]

Nicol's memoirs bring with them another lesson. In them the karateka engineer refers at length to the emotion he experienced in the face of 'African nature'. 'Of themselves', he wrote, recalling his early days in the Simien, 'the Walia … are too close to goats to induce that special sense, that strange feeling of recall, way back in the long-ago mists of our innocence'. Then he observed how the animals 'moved with such easy grace on those terrible cliffs … fit for eagles … and not for walking, hooved animals'. At that point he found himself suddenly overwhelmed with emotion: 'I knew it before, but now I felt it. The Walia and the cliffs, the birds, plants, streams, and all living things here were part of a pattern that was unique, a pattern that must be kept and nurtured, and perhaps eventually understood.'[147]

Like him, most wardens felt they understood the nature they were protecting throughout East Africa. But they were confronted with Africans who failed to understand it, who were, as Nicol described the Simien villagers, 'so different'. A few pages later, he goes on to define 'the biggest problem for a game warden here', which was, in his view, 'the destruction of the habitat and the inability of the peasants to see what they were doing'. These lines could have been written by many other experts. As could the following: 'Disaster was surely inevitable', 'They had raped the land', 'the soil was impoverished and eroded away', 'the people were barely surviving on what they raised', 'By destroying what remained, they could not last more than fifty years', 'Surely it was better to have the people moved away now, while there was still time', 'A national park would benefit the country', 'If only the government would truly back us!'[148]

This narrative reflects those of all European wardens working in the East African parks. Except, that is, in one respect: before arriving in the Simien, Nicol had never set foot in the region or even on the continent of Africa. And he would never go back there – his career as a warden and an expert ended there. The difference is a significant one. The majority of experts in East African nature appeared to see exactly the same nature as their British colleague but they undoubtedly did not see the same governments or the same Africans. For Nicol, East Africa was a temporary journey; for them it was the day-to-day world, *their* world, *their* stronghold of nature. Yesterday they were in charge of it, managing its parks and its inhabitants, and even today they should still be authorized to govern them successfully. At least that was their dream, even if it was a dream that sometimes turned into a nightmare.

Governing Ethiopia
The world-nation of African leaders

Conservation is a political matter. The expert gentlemen theorized about overpopulation in Africa, the field experts fought against it in the East African parks, but ultimately, it was up to the African leaders to take action. These included heads of state, ministers, senior officials, directors of the national conservation department, regional administrators and local officials, and it was their responsibility to prevent farmers and pastoralists exploiting nature. They could, of course, choose not to do so. They could also try to keep everyone happy – the director of UNESCO, the representatives from the IUCN, the Maasai authorities and the inhabitants of the Serengeti. But for them, conservation was always a matter of politics, or in other words, it meant taking account of what Hannah Arendt called 'human plurality': these were people in a position to discuss the lives of other people, people over whom they had the power to act.[1]

Arusha 1961. Protecting nature, playing politics

During the Arusha conference in September 1961, five African delegates were invited to speak.

Nature for Africans

The Kenyan Thomas Odhiambo was the first to come to the rostrum. He had studied entomology at Makerere College in Uganda, and was currently pursuing his studies at Queen's College, Cambridge, in England. His chosen field was animal biology, but at Arusha he had decided to discuss 'human factors as barriers to conservation'. He began by reminding his audience of the fundamental problem – the growth in population, the resultant increase in livestock numbers and the impossibility for 'a peasant and pastoral community' to continue to operate 'a highly complex system of land use'. Odhiambo went on to refer to the task of 'scientists' who were determined 'to preserve the magnificent collection of Pleistocene mammals so well preserved in Africa – such as the elephant, hippopotamus and rhinoceros'. Such intentions were, Odhiambo continued, 'admirable', but 'cannot be expected to weigh much with a people fighting for their very existence. For it must be borne in mind that these communities have a long tradition of farming and animal husbandry, and that they have to work extremely hard for the meagre living they get.' Consequently, he concluded, if the people concerned were to be convinced that with conservation, they had everything to gain and very little to lose, they needed to be provided with 'an unusually convincing demonstration of tangible benefits' – or put in practical terms, they needed to be informed about the controlled cropping of game and the meat that would be made available as a result, about tourism and the potential income associated with it.[2]

After the Kenyan entomologist had spoken, the Tanzanian H.S. Mahinda highlighted the need to educate 'indigenous people'. An assistant warden in the Tanganyika game division, he had worked in the colony's national parks for ten years and, in his opinion, in these areas, only the use of an effective propaganda would enable local people to 'see the value' of conservation rather than be forced to 'accept the imposition of regulations'.[3] The next speaker was M.K. Shawki, director of forests in the Sudan, who put the case for an integrated programme of development and conservation, which would benefit both nature and the economy.[4] The Tanzanian minister Tewa Said Tewa pursued a similar theme. A close associate of Julius Nyerere, co-founder of TANU (Tanganyika African National Union) during colonization and subsequently minister of lands and surveys, Tewa extolled 'the value of the tourist industry', which he defined as a source of income for both the national economy and for those living in the natural environments which could be made accessible to tourists.[5]

Finally, it was the turn of David Wasawo. Born in Kenya in 1923, like Odhiambo, he had studied biology at Makerere College, in Uganda. He had then specialized in zoology, first at Oxford and then in London where he obtained a PhD, an achievement which led Edgar Worthington to describe him as 'the first African of real standing'.[6] After joining the teaching staff at Makerere, Wasawo accompanied Gerald Watterson, the travelling representative of the FAO and the IUCN, during the first stage of the African Special Project. Since then, he had become one of the most favoured contacts in East Africa for the international conservation institutions. It was in this role that he had been invited to speak at Arusha. Like his colleagues, he talked about projects for controlled game cropping, tourism, protection and development. The Kenyan was however keen to draw attention to the 'cultural' dimension of conservation. It all began, he insisted, with the beauty of nature:

> One day in late February this year I stood for the first time on the edge of the Ngorongoro Crater. The scenery in front of me engendered such a feeling of the greatness and sublimity of nature that I had only once before had in my life, and that is when I beheld the face of the Matterhorn, in the moonlight, from a hotel window in that delightful town of Zermatt in Switzerland. It is an undefinable feeling – akin to the feeling that one has when one listens to great music, looks at a superb work of art, or even gazes at a historical ruin such as the Coliseum in Rome. Such feelings, I believe, elevate the human spirit. To provide opportunity for our youth, and even our older men and women to have such experiences should be one of the aims of the New Africa. It will never be possible if our flora and fauna and our physical environment are wantonly destroyed.[7]

Nature could therefore elevate the spirits of the 'Africans', Wasawo affirmed, before turning his attention to the inhabitants of 'marginal areas'. According to him, if these people represent a threat to animals, plants and soil, it was 'because the great majority of the people do not know of the cultural and economic benefits [of conservation]'. Consequently, they needed to be educated, the zoologist went on, adding that he was all too aware that, for this to happen, Africa needed 'trained personnel'. In the future this would mean Africans but, in the interim it would be composed of Europeans or North Americans. Wasawo ended his speech on a note which, this time, differed from the contributions of the expert gentlemen and the western field experts:

> The rest of the world has an interest in the wild fauna and flora of Africa because of its uniqueness; because it provides for them an opportunity for having experiences which they cannot have in any other part of the world;

and because of that urge to preserve for posterity something which in many ways is of immense value. The banding together of the people of Africa with those of the rest of the world for the preservation of this resource should therefore be a natural and a happy common effort.

The rest of the world, however, should always remember that new nations are very jealous of their newly acquired independence – and that they have to be very careful as to how their advice or help is given. This is why the conference at Arusha is particularly welcome, because experts from various parts of the world are sitting together with Africans to see what can be done as a joint effort.[8]

The Africans versus the experts

Wasawo had stated it publicly: foreigners were not there to *continue* their conservation work with the help of those they had formerly colonized; they were there to *help* countries which were now independent and firmly intended to remain so. He may indeed have said it, but he would never repeat it, as was clearly evident a year later. In July 1962, the Kenyan zoologist took part in the First World Conference on National Parks, organized by the IUCN, UNESCO and the FAO. On that occasion, he declared that 'Africa is the only place left in the world where a wide variety of wild animals can still be found in their natural settings.' He then went on to share his own memories, recalling, once more, how he felt 'when he beheld that vast creation of nature' while visiting the Ngorongoro crater for the first time, and the 'experience which imprinted itself on my mind' at the sight of the Matterhorn 'bathed in moonlight', seen very early one morning during his stay in the 'delightful' town of Zermatt. Wasawo emphasized the immense 'pride' felt by the African leaders in the abundance of wildlife their countries possessed. But, this time, he did not urge the external world to be careful.[9]

The expert was clearly not troubled by his repetition. It is more of a problem for historians who find themselves confronted with the same ideas or the same expressions, often repeated word for word, in all the official speeches made by Kenyan, Ugandan or Tanzanian officials. The Ethiopian conservation archives allowed me to discover this art of repetition, and the difficulties involved in interpreting it. What, for example, should be made of Wasawo's speech in Seattle? It was certainly an exact copy of the one given in 1961 in Arusha, minus the reference to foreign arrogance. But the disappearance of certain words does not necessarily imply the disappearance of what they referred to, as is clear from the visit to Ethiopia in 1963 made by Alain Gille, Julian Huxley, Théodore Monod and Edgar Worthington.

One year after Seattle, UNESCO sent these four men to Ethiopia to 'help' Haile Selassie draw up his conservation policy. Travelling from Nairobi, in Kenya, where they had attended the 8th General Assembly of the IUCN, the expert gentlemen spent a week in Ethiopia. They concluded that nature was 'deteriorating as a result of agriculture and over-grazing', and advised the emperor to set up a Conservation Office which would be managed by 'an expatriate'. For, as they told him, they doubted there would be 'anyone in the Ethiopian public sector capable of taking on the job of director of the Conservation Office'.[10] In reply to which, according to Worthington, the emperor replied: 'You should recognise the fact that my country suffers from the disadvantage of never having been a British colony.'[11] Clearly in 1963, the need to be 'very careful' urged by Wasawo no longer applied.

Ethiopia was, by then, fully involved in the African Special Project. It had not sent any delegates to Arusha in September 1961, but Gerald Watterson went to Addis Ababa in January, and, in November, the FAO instructed H.P. Huffnagel, one of its experts, to visit Ethiopia in order to assess the state of its forests.[12] Then, in 1962, the Ethiopian minister of agriculture, Akelework Habtewold, travelled to Paris where he asked for assistance from UNESCO to set up the first national parks in his country.[13] The minister subsequently sent some of his staff to Nairobi in 1963 where the IUCN was holding its 8th General Assembly. This event ended on 24 September and, the very next day, Worthington, Huxley, Monod and Gille took off for Addis Ababa.[14] They returned a week later, on 2 October, having shared with Haile Selassie their fears for the 'deteriorating' state of nature and natural resources[15] and their disdain for an administration which suffered from 'the disadvantage'[16] of not having been colonized by the British.

Did the emperor really say that? It seems highly likely. As historian Bahru Zewde has shown, since the League of Nations had allowed Italy to invade Ethiopia in 1935, Haile Selassie was aware that he was locked into a 'semi-colonial relationship' with Europe. But did he really believe his empire was inferior? Probably not. As long as there was nothing to lose, Haile Selassie was happy to appear to comply with westerners, Bahru observed. Conversely, when his power was at stake it was a very different matter.[17] The emperor may have been prepared to accept the arrogance of a handful of ecologists on 2 October, yet two days later, on 4 October, when he addressed the delegates at the United Nations General Assembly in New York, it was to deliver a resounding declaration to the world – one Bob Marley would revisit in his famous song, 'War': 'until the philosophy which holds one race superior and another inferior is finally and permanently discredited and abandoned. ... We Africans will fight, if necessary, and we know that we shall win.'[18]

Haile Selassie was playing a political game. The same was true for Gizaw Gedlegiorgis, Mebratu Fisseha, Nadew Woreta and Teshome Ashine. These leaders would discuss, impose, obey, negotiate... in short, they would find themselves dealing with human plurality. But how exactly did they do it? When their world was plunged into the postcolonial era, what, in practical terms, did they do in order to impose control over nature and over the nation which was enclosing it inside national parks?

The natural extraversion of the African state. History

A great many researchers have focused their attention on this moment of postcolonial transition. They tell us about dependence and instrumentalization, about extraversion and the art of navigating between several different worlds.

Before we embark on the pathways these researchers have opened up to enable closer observation of the relationships between independent African and the world, it is important to point out that, in the context of postcolonial transition, Ethiopia provides an opportunity to reflect calmly on this subject given that it was never colonized. At the beginning of the 1960s, immediately following independence, many colonial administrators remained in Kenya and in Tanzania or in Zambia, formerly Northern Rhodesia. In these countries, they transformed themselves into international experts but continued to promulgate the ideas and practices of the empire, the same dream of African nature without Africans, and the same socially excluding norms. It is tempting therefore to think in terms of 'neocolonialism' given that colonial domination continued, as evidenced by the ongoing presence of Europeans who were still travelling throughout the whole of East Africa, and could be found even as far as Ethiopia, still doing things exactly as they had done in the past. Yet Ethiopia had never been colonized. Rather than deciding to *stay*, these experts had been invited to *come* by Ethiopia. So, rather than referring to neocolonialism, we should instead think in terms of 'postcolonialism' – all over Africa the colonial past weighs on the present, but African societies have learned how to deal with that situation.

Dependency as a strategy

Environmental historians first drew attention to this in Tanzania. When, in Arusha in 1961, Julius Nyerere, the future president, asked for help from foreign conservationists, he was in fact acting upon their request (according to the historian Stephen Macekura, it was the lobbyist Max Nicholson, from The Nature Conservancy, who wrote the Arusha Manifesto, signed by Nyerere). In private, however, Nyerere described himself as 'not very interested in animals'. 'I do not want to spend my holidays watching crocodiles', he added, but since 'Thousands of Americans and Europeans have the strange urge to see these animals', he was determined to make wild animals one of 'the country's most important sources of income'.[19]

This strategy of dependence could be found across the whole of East Africa. In Kenya, for example, in 1963, President Jomo Kenyatta declared himself a 'protector' of nature in order to prove his commitment to the outside world, and to attract as many tourists as possible. To prove it, he even went so far as to provide a presidential guard for Ahmed, the elephant with enormous tusks who wandered freely in his gardens. And, like Nyerere, like Kenyatta, in Zambia and Malawi (ex-Nyasaland), presidents Hastings Banda and Kenneth Kaunda demonstrated they were 'prepared to act on the potential of tourism in a much more systematic fashion than had the colonial state'.[20]

Their determination was not simply confined to the question of tourism. At the beginning of the 1960s and across the continent as a whole, the 'extraversion' of postcolonial societies had a significant impact on the management of nature. This concept put an end to the idea of Africa's dependence on the world and to the notion of a history made up of impositions with no space for creativity. As political scientist Jean-François Bayart explains, the relationships African societies had with the external world were an integral part of their internal functioning: 'Dependence as a mode of action', he writes.[21] Following in his footsteps, historians have shown that this was already the case during colonialization: the Africans may indeed have been subjugated but that did not mean they were inactive. Historians have demonstrated this, for example, by studying the way in which the West African elites contributed to the making of French ethnography at the beginning of the twentieth century. By observing a professional group in the process of educating itself, they were able to decrypt the subaltern relationship which linked West African ethnographers to European scholars, and they subsequently discovered that their subordination did not prevent them from pursuing their own agenda given that they were accumulating an intellectual, economic and, ultimately, political capital.[22] This process was to accelerate across the entire continent after 1945. Historians have highlighted this by studying the capacity of the colonized elites to embrace the 'notion' of development. The more deftly the African officials and employees of colonization learned to manipulate the key words of this new international discourse – words like 'population control', and references to the need to combat 'overgrazing' – the more familiar they became with the workings of the colonial state. Consequently, when colonialization came to an end at the beginning of the 1960s, they were ready to govern, by using the outside world to their advantage.[23]

The politics of nature worked directly in favour of this extraversion of the state. Of course, the colonial nature of African conservation was, to quote anthropologist Elizabeth Garland, the 'elephant in the room'. At the time of independence, when the new worldwide ecological conscience had come face to face with the new mass culture, African lions, antelope and elephants became part of the 'natural symbolic repertoire of the world'. Their existence was taken for granted everywhere and by everyone, wrote Garland, drawing attention to the inequality of this dynamic since the primary responsibility for protecting these animals fell only 'on African shoulders'.[24] Nevertheless, as historian Julie Weiskopf points out in relation to Garland's work, this is still a matter of 'African modes of production'.

The art of the in-between

Weiskopf even refers to a genuine 'wildlife diplomacy', which she demonstrates with reference to Tanzania. Under the impetus of Nyerere, the Mweka College of African Wildlife Management opened its doors in 1963. The establishment was set up in order to train East African elites in the western norms of conservation. Each foreign leader visiting Tanzania was moreover invited to the Serengeti. This included, amongst many others, President Tito of Yugoslavia, who, in January 1970, was presented with the stuffed trophies of two lions and a zebra. Then, two months later, when Japan was organizing the 1970 Universal Exhibition, the Tanzanian delegation included in their luggage two leopards named Uhuru and Maendeleo, Swahili for 'Freedom' and 'Development' – two key words of the new national doctrine.[25]

This extraversion of nature and of the Tanzanian state satisfied economic goals – since the parks department had become part of the Ministry of Tourism in 1968, its official mission was 'bringing in foreign exchange'. But being able to offer nature to an international audience was also a good way of managing public policies. The expulsion of the inhabitants from the parks of the Serengeti and Ngorongoro is evidence of this. At the end of the 1960s, and then in the mid-1970s, their eviction served both the nature-orientated objectives of the IUCN and the political intentions of the TANU, the government party which was at that time organizing the villagization programme through all the rural areas of the country, a policy which necessitated, de facto, the forced displacement of local people.[26]

Finally, this wildlife diplomacy reveals the historic depth of the extra-version of the Tanzanian state. Named *ujamaa* in Swahili, or 'fraternity', Tanzanian socialism is in fact a 'Fabian socialism' according to historian Andreas Eckert, with reference to the Fabian Colonial Bureau, the agency created by the British in 1940 to promote development in the empire. Until he was named secretary of state for the colonies, immediately after the war, Arthur Creech Jones was one of its directors. Throughout the 1950s, under his direction, considerable numbers of agronomists were sent by the Crown to work on the 'development' of Tanganyika. And twenty years later, it was these same individuals who were employed by the Tanzanian administration in order to implement the *ujamaa*. The leaders wanted to build the new nation, the experts wanted to remain in the former colony, and all of them were united in the conviction that, in addition to being ecologically irresponsible, 'the peasants did not know what was good for them'. For, just like the former colonial administrators who were advising them, the Tanzanian officials felt that 'if the peasants could not be persuaded to act in their own interest, they might have to be coerced'.[27]

The same story was unfolding simultaneously across all of East Africa. In Kenya, at the end of the 1950s, in an attempt to rally the rural populations to their cause, the independentists of the Kenya African National Union (KANU) had come up with a particularly unifying promise which amounted to the lifting of conservationist restrictions. And, as a result, in December 1963, when they were celebrating independence in the Lambwe valley, pastoralists and farmers in the south-west of the country organized a hunting expedition to celebrate the occasion. Then came the Kenyatta state. From that point on, the national parks were run by national managers in association with European conservationists, but contrary to what had been promised, nature still entailed exclusion[28] – in spite of the fact that during that period, nature was protected by, and for, the Kenyans. That at least was the claim of the leaders of East Africa, both in Kenya and in Tanzania. And also in Zambia, formerly Northern Rhodesia, where for Kenneth Kaunda's new state, the protected areas served at the same time to satisfy the international institutions, to boost the economy and to maintain control over both farmers and pastoralists, all thanks to the efforts of provincial administrators to whom the central government paid a share of the income resulting from hunting and tourism. And all of that was happening in partnership with former colonialists subsequently transformed into international experts.[29]

In this way the postcolonial 'household' gradually took shape. As Bayart writes, the state established by the leading African elites was a 'two-tiered' edifice in which they acted with the outside whilst at the same time working on the inside.[30] They 'navigated' between the local and the global, between the old and the new, and as historian Frederick Cooper makes clear, there is nothing contradictory in any of this: '*in between* is as much a place to be at home as any other'. This '*in between*' is difficult to grasp, Cooper adds, but we must endeavour to do so.[31] And Ethiopia enables us to do this all the more easily since the absence of any colonial past facilitates the simultaneous observation of the two most powerful dynamics of the postcolonial era – consensual servitude and indiscipline.

Ethiopia – submissive and assertive

Although few environmental historians have chosen to focus on Ethiopia, there are nevertheless some whose work enables us to gain a deeper understanding of the Ethiopian postcolonial moment.

First of all, we are indebted to historian James McCann for shedding new light on the myth of Ethiopia's lost forests. In 2023, experts, both Ethiopian and foreign, once again agreed that in 1900, 40 per cent of the country had been covered in forests, in contrast with 3 per cent 'today'. Yet, for sixty years, these figures had remained unchanged – since 1961 to be exact, when these percentages were set out for the first time by H.P. Huffnagel. This employee of the FAO spent one month in the country and produced two figures. The first of these came from Friedrich von Breitenbach, a German forester he encountered while in the country. According to Breitenbach, in southern Ethiopia where there was currently only sparse vegetation, in 1900 37 per cent of the land had been covered in woodland. Then Huffnagel came upon another figure, this time in a report written in 1946 by a Canadian forester, William Logan. Logan estimated the forest cover of the town of Addis Ababa to be 5 per cent. These two estimates resulted purely from visual observations. They are moreover incomparable since one was obtained in a rural area and the other in the national capital. But Huffnagel looked no further. Before sending his report to the FAO, the expert increased the first figure from 37 per cent to 40 per cent and lowered the second one to 3 per cent. Already convinced by the human timebomb theory and the imminence of a demographic catastrophe originating in the third world, the United Nations accepted the analysis, broadcasting it widely and repeating its message so that, as McCann explains, it ended up being taken for the truth.[32]

At the very end of the conservation chain, historian Girma Tayachew shows that local populations could benefit from these declinist myths. This was the case, for example, in the Simien where, in February 1965, on the recommendations of UNESCO, the Ethiopian government announced a ban on hunting. In order to impose the ban, the emperor delegated the task to the governor of the region, the highly respected Lieutenant-Colonel Tamrat Yigezu, famous throughout the country for his military exploits against the Italian invader which had led to him being made a captain in the Imperial Army at the age of nineteen. Determined to succeed in the mission consigned to him by the emperor, governor Tamrat entrusted the management of the Simien Mountains to one of his protégés, Nadew Woreta, a former imperial dignitary who was a native of the area. Clive Nicol would later describe Nadew as someone who 'had extorted money and taken bribes' and who consistently 'lied, cheated, got off work',[33] but at that time, he was acting perfectly legitimately. Appointed as park warden by the empire, he recruited guards from amongst the local population and, acting together, they banned the inhabitants of the Simien Park from hunting, whilst at the same time themselves continuing to kill wild animals and to sell the skins to local traders.[34]

The manoeuvre brings us back to the Ethiopian strategy of 'japanization', which consisted in appropriating concepts from outside and using them to meet the objectives pursued within the country.[35] This strategy is the subject of research I carried out in relation to Ethiopia. First UNESCO and then the IUCN sent their experts to the country in 1963 and 1964. On their advice, in 1965, the Ethiopian government set up a Conservation Department, which employed first John Blower and then three wardens to run the country's first three national parks – Peter Hay, George Brown and Laurence Guth (later succeeded by Clive Nicol). The Ethiopian administrators subsequently adopted the declinist discourse of these experts – overexploitation–deforestation–erosion. This brought them recognition and funding from the international institutions thanks to which they were finally able to plant the Ethiopian state flag in areas which had evaded the control of the empire: in 1966, the Ethiopian government sent employees from the Conservation Department, the Ministry of Lands and the National Tourist Agency into the Simien maquis, the semi-nomadic plains of the Awash and the Omo valley on the border with Kenya.[36]

Today we are familiar with this story: the western myths of deterioration, the construction of a two-tier Ethiopian state and the power struggles between the various actors involved in this worldwide African history. But we need to look further still. The archives produced by the foreign experts show the way John Blower reacted *to* Gizaw Gedlegiorgis, or the way Clive Nicol reacted *to* Nadew Woreta. Rereading these archives from the other point of view, and adding to them those produced in Amharic, the Ethiopian national language, we must now attempt to see how Gizaw coped *with* Blower, or Nadew *with* Nicol. What was their personal experience of the in-between?

Current status: Applicant for aid

If we observe the lives of the western experts in the immediate aftermath of the independence process, we are struck first of all by their determination to remain in a colonial environment. Their thirst for Africa was so desperate that we cannot help but find it striking. In contrast, when we turn our attention to the history of the African state, such as the Ethiopian one, for example, we are immediately overwhelmed by the sheer dryness of the paperwork involved. Correspondence, balance sheets, progress reports, new laws or standardized rules, these archives are so mired in protocol that it is all too easy to be discouraged. They are however extremely eloquent. Even the way they are presented is significant – tens of thousands of documents, almost two-thirds of which are written in English, a language which, day after day, was used to request aid.

Calling on the international institutions

For Ethiopia, this appeal for help from the external world began one year after the launch of the African Special Project. In 1962, minister Akelework Habtewold asked UNESCO to help his country create national parks. In 1963 and 1964, Ethiopia was host to three international missions.[37] Then, at the beginning of summer 1965, the empire set up its new Conservation Department with Berhanu Tessema as its first director. A senior official and regular representative of the Ethiopian government in Europe and North America, Berhanu spoke Amharic, Tigrinya and Oromo, three of the main languages of the empire. But he also spoke French, English, Italian and German, languages which he had learned to use to advantage in international discourse. It was therefore with complete confidence that, in the first days of his nomination to the head of the Conservation Department, he turned to the WWF.

In June 1965, Berhanu asked the Fund to finance the training of his staff. The response arrived in July. Such help was 'feasible', replied Sheldon Vance. Vance nevertheless pointed out that 'the Fund is primarily interested in the preservation of rare species … such as the Mountain Nyala and the Ethiopian Ibex'.[38] Berhanu took note. At the beginning of August, he wrote to Fritz Vollmar, the secretary-general of the WWF. He informed him that Leslie Brown, an expert based in Kenya, wanted to come to study the Ethiopian nyala and walia ibex; but '[his] department being already heavily committed financially in connection with the proper management of protected areas, … the WWF might be willing to provide financial assistance to Mr Brown to enable him to complete his research with the adequate required material'.[39] Vollmar accepted. In September he also sent electric generators to Ethiopia, for use in the three new parks of the Awash, the Omo and the Simien.[40] Additional aid then followed. In 1966, the WWF offered a Volkswagen truck to assist the scouts in the Awash Park with their patrols. In 1967, the Fund sent a biologist to survey ungulates in the Omo, and in 1968, it financed the expedition of Bernhard Nievergelt, a Swiss zoologist, who wanted to observe the walia in the Simien Park.[41] In this way, the WWF set out the conditions of any aid it might offer, Ethiopia requested the corresponding aid, and obtained it.

Success was forthcoming but sometimes, or indeed on the majority of occasions, a certain amount of negotiation was required. Gizaw Gedlegiorgis was only too familiar with this. A trained pilot and on the front line in the battles for Ethiopian liberation during the Second World War, Gizaw had risen rapidly up through the ranks of the army, becoming a major in the 1950s. Since then, invariably dressed in a uniform bristling with medals, Major Gizaw had occupied various positions of responsibility in the imperial administration. The most recent of these was as director of the Conservation Department.

Gizaw took over from Berhanu at the beginning of the winter in 1965, and in January 1966 he sent a long letter to the FAO, in Rome. He began by referring to the natural riches of Ethiopia, with its 'fantastic wild fauna … and mountain scenery, unequalled in Africa'. He went on to raise the spectre of deterioration. 'Ethiopia's wildlife has been seriously reduced through indiscriminate hunting, [and] destruction of habitat', Gizaw wrote. The Simien walia, the Somalian wild donkey, the nyala and the gelada baboon were 'still living' but 'in some danger of extinction', he went on, before drawing attention to the 'insufficiency of funds available to protect them'. Which was why his department hoped that the FAO would give 'sympathetic consideration to the assistance requested', namely the financing of three park warden posts over a period of three years. The Ethiopian state would pay them a salary equal to that of its own employees, the FAO would cover the supplement corresponding to the status of expatriate, and in return, 'as discussed earlier', Gizaw promised to call on other financial backers to assure the development of the national parks in question.[42]

The FAO responded favourably to the request and, in February 1966, the Ethiopian administration embarked on the quest for new partners. Yohannes Habtu, director of technical and foreign assistance within the Ministry of Agriculture, contacted David Anstey, former head warden of the Arusha National Park in Tanzania and, at that time, representing the United Nations Development Programme. He asked him whether the UNDP would agree to finance the construction of roads necessary for the efficient functioning of the Ethiopian national parks.[43] Anstey agreed to this request. Then, on his advice, from within the Ethiopian finance ministry and in another department dedicated to foreign aid, Mitiku Gembere made an appeal to Russian engineers asking them to take part in the construction of this road network.[44] They replied in the affirmative and, on the recommendation of the FAO, John Blower took charge of this project in November 1966.

Working with the outside world

British-born Blower had arrived in Ethiopia a year earlier. He occupied the post of 'adviser' to the Conservation Department, but had his own very distinctive way of giving advice. 'Would you please check that our request for Russian aid has actually been sent off to the F.A.O. in Rome?', he asked Gizaw, in what was unmistakeably a warning: 'This should have been done a month ago ... . If there is any further delay we shall give the FAO the impression that we are highly inefficient. Is that what we really want, major?'[45]

Evidently this was not what the major wanted. In February 1967, Gizaw organized the delivery of Russian materials to the Awash.[46] And two years after the work began, he still made it a point of honour to chair each of the follow-up meetings which took place in Addis Ababa, alongside Blower and the two expatriates who were working in the Awash – Peter Hay, the park warden trained in Somaliland and in Uganda, and V. Kostikov, an engineer from the UNDP. In 1969, the major was therefore officially still in charge of this international project. He had however handed over a considerable share of Ethiopian sovereignty to these foreign experts. Warden of the Awash Park, and paid by the FAO, Hay was responsible for the Ethiopian scouts sent to work on the site. In this capacity he was authorized to dismiss 'any trainee who refuses to obey an order or who proves to be incompetent at his work'.[47] As for Kostikov, a Soviet engineer seconded to the United Nations in Ethiopia, as 'chief technician', he was responsible for both the equipment and those using it. Consequently, when the Conservation Department sent some of the material and workmen to the Simien Park without his permission, the Soviet demanded their 'immediate return' to the Awash – a task Gizaw hurried to organize, not forgetting to reassure Kostikov: 'Be certain that it has never been our intention to divert any of the road building machines to other projects.'[48]

Yet that was exactly what Gizaw had attempted to do. The strategy had not worked, but there was nothing particularly serious in that. For, in the eyes of the Ethiopian administration, the Soviet Union was simply one interlocuter among many, including, for example, the United States, who were contacted by the Conservation Department with increasing regularity.

Gizaw, first of all, had since 1967 kept up a regular correspondence with Robert Yost, *chargé d'affaires* at the American embassy in Addis Ababa and in charge of the volunteers at the Peace Corps, an American non-governmental organization set up to foster peace in the world in general and in the developing countries in particular. With Yost's help, in 1968 Major Gizaw was able to send two Peace Corps engineers to the Simien. They carried out ecological surveys in the park, and at the same time, helped with the construction of the park's infrastructures.[49] Then, at the end of summer 1969, Gizaw left the Conservation Department and was replaced by Mebratu Fisseha.

A police officer for more than twenty years, a general in the navy and then ambassador to Nigeria, Mebratu had been made director of the Ethiopian Wildlife Conservation Organization (EWCO), the new name recently adopted by the Conservation Department. Following in Gizaw's footsteps, Mebratu contacted Yost in January 1970. Six of his employees had recently returned from the Mweka College and, Mebratu wrote, in order to transform them into 'true experts', he wanted to send them to American universities to continue their training.[50] Yost put him in contact with James Hyde, an employee at the Rockefeller Foundation in New York. Mebratu sought his help in February 1970, but Hyde did not reply until July.[51] Hyde informed him that 'the Foundation would be pleased to assist Ethiopia'. It would however like, first of all, 'to know more about how the [Omo] park stands' under George Brown: did the former police officer of British Kenya have 'staff' available to him? And what means did he have 'to enforce legislation and regulation'?[52] Clearly, Brown's complaints had got as far as New York, probably through John Blower, who had taken on the role of spokesperson for the expatriate voice in Addis Ababa.

General-ambassador Mebratu showed his credentials. He replied to Hyde a week later, reassuring him that the Omo Park 'is now provided with the adequate staff'. The law would be finalized within 'no more than in one month, or two', the director of the EWCO stated. Then Mebratu mentioned the emperor's visit to the Awash Park. Road networks had already been established, guest infrastructures had been built and the Karayu agro-pastoralists would soon be 'resettled' by the government. Haile Selassie had himself stated that 'priority should now be given to the needs of wild animals rather than that of human beings'. Nevertheless, Mebratu concluded, 'the Ethiopian government may struggle as hard as he [it] can, external assistance remains the major problem for his [its] success'.[53] Explicit as the appeal was, it failed to elicit any response. The former ambassador let the summer go by and, in September, he set aside the pride associated with his role to 'humbly ask one more time the Rockefeller Foundation'. His request had not changed: he was asking for the provision of six study grants for his employees who had recently graduated from the Mweka College.[54] The Foundation's silence implied a refusal and this was officially confirmed by a letter from James Hyde on 20 January 1971. But Mebratu did not give up.[55] On 28 January, he thanked Hyde 'for all the efforts' adding, 'again, the EWCO respectfully call on the Foundation for its assistance'. On that occasion, the director even attached the legal documents which proved that the parks of Awash, Omo and the Simien had now been officially established.[56]

Negotiating and agreeing

The effort did not pay off, but Ethiopia obtained satisfaction elsewhere. Indeed, in 1972, Mebratu thanked the dean of Madison University for accepting a number of Ethiopian students to study agronomy and biology.[57] Teshome Ashine was one of these expatriates. The young graduate returned to Ethiopia in 1973 and became head of the EWCO, immediately reinforcing his links with the United States.

With his meticulously shaven head, a singlet under his starched shirt and an orthodox Christian cross around his neck, Teshome had lost nothing of his Ethiopian appearance over the course of his stay in America. He had however added a western touch in the form of a University of Madison lapel pin displayed on his jacket, an elegant leather satchel worn across the shoulder and the habit of signing off each letter he wrote in English with a *Sincerely yours*. Thanks to this American training and to the contacts he had made during his time there through the Friends of Africa in America association, in 1973 Teshome successfully secured the financing for a number of educational programmes in the Awash Park.[58] That same year, with the Texan company Game Conservation International, he set up a programme of grants to be used for training Ethiopian personnel.[59] Finally, like his predecessors, the director of the EWCO knocked on every door in a systematic, almost mechanical manner.

In 1974, for example, he obtained a number of subventions from the British Foreign and Commonwealth Office. And to ensure these were appropriately used, the latter sent him an 'adviser' called John Stephenson.[60] Former warden in the colonial Tanganyika National Park, the expert shared his contacts with Teshome, who lost no time in approaching the Frankfurt Zoological Society and its president, Bernhard Grzimek, the filmmaker with a passion for zebras. Grzimek agreed to donate a Cessna aircraft to Ethiopia, on condition, he made clear, that the 'foreign adviser' should go in person to Nairobi to collect the plane.[61] A request happily accepted by John Stephenson who, that same year, became the legal holder of the account opened by the EWCO in the Addis Ababa Bank to receive payments from the Frankfurt Zoological Society.[62] As for Bernhard Grzimek, he became a regular guest of Teshome Ashine. 'My country is indeed indebted to you', Ashine wrote in 1977, with reference to the Cessna, thanks to which the EWCO was now able to carry out ecological surveys in its national parks – except when Grzimek went to Ethiopia himself, in which case, he was informed, 'naturally, the plane will be at your personal service'.[63]

Since the Ethiopian government was asking the outside world for help to finance its conservation policy, it also had to accept the omnipresence of the representatives from that world. This was the first consequence of this status of applicant for aid or, at least, the most visible one.

Accepting dependence

John Blower was one of the representatives of the conservation world. Following the recommendation of Julian Huxley, Ian Grimwood and Leslie Brown, the Ethiopian government had recruited him in December 1965. His role was to 'advise' an independent African state, but, in practice, over a period of five years, the Ethiopian conservation managers applied in their own country the policies which the British expert had put in place in the colonies.

Conservation for foreigners, with foreigners

Two months after his arrival in Ethiopia, the imperious John Blower made his theories known to his employer, the equally authoritarian Major Gizaw – 'poaching' was threatening to wipe out wildlife, the 'poachers' must be stopped and therefore 'our staff [within the national parks] should be equipped with good quality firearms'.[64] To this end, he put Gizaw in touch with the director of a New York armament company, a certain A.K. Lang. Blower had met him ten years earlier, when the American had come to hunt in Uganda, and it was from him that, from 1966 onwards, the major had purchased the Winchester rifles he then distributed to the expatriate game wardens and Ethiopian scouts in the Awash, Omo and Simien parks.[65] But Gizaw quickly understood that this measure did not go far enough in the eyes of his 'adviser'.

At the end of summer 1967, he received a long report from Blower. In Dire Dawa, in eastern Ethiopia, Blower wrote, the French consul had informed him that soldiers from the army were hunting big game. And, in the Awash, Ted Shatto, the safari guide, had told him that some inhabitants of Addis Ababa had killed an oryx. 'There are only isolated reports but it is obvious that there are very many other similar incidents', Blower informed the major, before going on to propose the establishment of an 'anti-poaching unit'.[66] Gizaw was quick to reassure him: 'The government is working on this matter ... it will be enforced once all the parks are gazetted.'[67] Then, as the months went by, still unsatisfied, the British expert asked to be put in contact with Gizaw's hierarchical superiors.

The major finally consented in spring 1968. Reluctantly, he introduced Blower to Germatchew Tekle Hawariat, former minister of information and currently president of the council set up by the emperor to monitor the work of the Conservation Department. Germatchew had held one of the highest positions in the empire but Blower wrote to him without the slightest deference. On the contrary, he requested him 'to be kind enough to send [him] a report' on the poaching activity perpetrated in the country, and urged him 'to deploy appropriate actions to stop this'.[68] The archives do not reveal whether Germatchew responded to this request. They do however report that in 1969 the Conservation Department did indeed set up an anti-poaching unit, intended, as the expatriate adviser had requested, 'to stop the continuing slaughter of wildlife by ignorant and greedy people and farmers'.[69] Slaughter for which the blame quite clearly lay entirely with the (greedy) Ethiopian hunters and the (ignorant) inhabitants of the protected areas. For foreign hunters must, for their part, be treated ever more favourably.

In 1964, hoping to encourage foreigners to come and spend their money and their energy in Ethiopia, the minister of agriculture, Akelework Habtewold, had suggested providing two types of hunting licence: one for 'big game' to be sold at a higher price, and another for 'small game' available at a lower price.[70] But this suggestion was deemed 'not attractive enough for visitors', in the words of Russell Berman, adviser to the Ethiopian Justice Ministry. This American lawyer suggested instead that it was time 'to take a fresh start based on the game laws of neighbouring countries', laws inherited from the British who were 'experimented in such matter'.[71] Drawing inspiration from Uganda and Southern Rhodesia, Berman drew up a draft regulation which he had sent to Wolde Mikael, the senior legal officer in the Ministry of Agriculture. The latter had taken careful note of his proposal: an expensive 'professional' licence for safari organizations operating in Ethiopia; a cheap 'visitors' licence for foreigners; and an 'ordinary' licence at a moderate price for nationals.[72] By increasing the cost of permits for the (Ethiopian) majority and reducing the price of licences for the (foreign) minority, this regulation would satisfy both the state and visiting hunters and on the basis of this rationale it came into force in 1965.[73]

This law did not put a stop to John Blower's efforts to encourage tourists to hunt. It was to this end that he became involved in the translocation of wild animals. Blower first of all secured the financial support of the African Wildlife Leadership Foundation (AWLF), the American association of the conservative judge Russell Train. He then obtained the technical assistance of the FAO, who agreed to provide the material needed for capturing the animals, and the veterinary officers responsible for organizing the operation.[74] These began in November 1967. Based in Asmara, in the Eritrean province in northern Ethiopia, Doctor Call captured ibex and transferred them to the Awash, where he collected oryx which were then taken into Gash-Setit, on the Sudanese border.[75] The initiative continued throughout the following year, this time led by Doctor Schultz, a German who had previously worked in Tanzania. In addition to the support of the FAO, Blower had obtained that of the IUCN and the WWF, thanks to which Schultz was able to organize the capture of twelve elephants and two antelopes in the Harar region in eastern Ethiopia. He had the animals transferred to the Awash where, 'in return', the game warden Peter Hay authorized him to proceed with 'capturing' fourteen wild donkeys. Gizaw would only find out about this arrangement between foreigners some weeks later, in the first memo Blower consented to send him, in which he stated: 'this is the way that the Game Departments in East Africa usually arrange for the capture of animals'.[76]

Nature for the former colonists, not for the Ethiopians

Such was the price for being dependent on the outside world: foreign experts were ubiquitous and most of them felt very much at home. That was true for Blower, as it was for Melvin Bolton, the biologist he recruited at the end of 1968. Trained in the national parks of East Africa, Bolton was seconded to Ethiopia by the British Ministry of Foreign Affairs. Thanks to the Land Rover donated by his employers, Bolton was able to conduct ecological surveys in the west and south of the country over the course of a year. He then decided to take a trip to Uganda where the director of the Nuffield Unit of Tropical Animal Ecology had invited him to take part in its game cropping programme. The biologist asked Mebratu to provide him with 'two letters from yourself', one for the immigration services, so that he could return to Ethiopia with his wife, and the other for the attention of the customs authorities authorizing him to leave the country with the department's Land Rover. After all, he wrote to Mebratu, 'In fact ... this Land-Rover has been assigned to me with the British government, not the [Ethiopian] Department of Conservation.'[77]

Although the general-ambassador and now head conservationist bowed to these demands, when Bolton finally returned to Ethiopia, Blower refused to reimburse his petrol costs. But Bolton was adamant. He referred to the 'scientific value' of his trip to Uganda and then added, without troubling himself with any subtleties, that he had 'heard from the British Embassy that a representative of the British Ministry of Overseas Development will be visiting Addis soon to review the question of British aid to Ethiopia'. 'An opportunity to discuss our work, and the way it is carried on here',[78] he told Mebratu, who, eight days later, reimbursed his travel expenses.[79]

Through incidents like these, the Ethiopian administration learned how to deal with the arrogance of these colonial leaders now converted into experts. When Blower left for Nepal in 1970, Ethiopia followed the advice of the IUCN and replaced him with Patrick Stracey, a conservation expert from British India. It was on his advice that the EWCO allocated a third of its budget to the displacement of inhabitants from protected areas.[80] This was in response to Stracey reminding the Organization that it had 'accepted the ideal of National Parks of "international status" with no[t] human presence' and that 'any failure in this area will trouble us like "running sores"!'[81] The expert remained in Ethiopia for four years before being replaced by John Stephenson.[82] The new 'adviser' to the EWCO had been personally recommended by Bernhard Grzimek[83] and John Owen, director of the prestigious Tanzania National Parks, the TANAPA.[84] So, in 1976, when Teshome Ashine heard Stephenson pleading for 'an at last effective wildlife management, through external aid' he made no effort to contradict him.[85] On the contrary, this most American of Ethiopian leaders followed his guidance to the letter. Stephenson ordered him to 'face the problem of wildlife conservation', notably 'the effective removal of the park's inhabitants' and for three years, Teshome did exactly that. Until, in July 1979, he was in a position to announce: 'it is a matter of deep satisfaction that their encroachment has been totally eliminated in the Awash', adding that the same would very soon be the case in the Simien.[86]

In the history which concerns us here, this chronology is a crucial one. In July 1979, several months had elapsed since Stephenson had left Ethiopia to go and live in India. And, most importantly, it was almost a year since UNESCO and the IUCN had included the Simien Park in their brand-new World Heritage List.[87] Ethiopia had obtained this prestigious classification in September 1978 and, a few weeks later, it was able to dismiss the foreign game wardens who were in charge of its national parks.[88] The EWCO did not however dispense completely with the expatriate 'advisers' sent to it by the international institutions. But from that point on, Teshome Ashine would only accept American experts.[89] Although he wrote to Stephenson in July 1979, it was therefore by choice and not by constraint. For the last twenty years, the leaders of the Ethiopian state had chosen this dependence on a daily basis. As a result, they often found themselves having to accept the arrogance of many experts. Nevertheless, for them, as their new slogan officially proclaimed, it would always be a case of *Ityopiya Teqdem*: 'Ethiopia first'.

Ethiopia first

The slogan was that of the *Derg*, the Marxist–Leninist 'committee' which had overthrown Haile Selassie's empire in 1974. Under the regime of Mengistu Haile Mariam, the privileges of government dignitaries were abolished, means of production collectivized, the petty urban bourgeoisie suppressed and the peasant masses taught to read and write – in short, the *Derg* imposed revolution.[90] But it also represented a sense of continuity with the empire. Moreover, like Teshome Ashine, many senior officials remained in their jobs after 1974. For, whether monarchist or Marxist, the government was still the prime promoter of Ethiopian nationalism. In order to 'Ethiopianize' these remote and peripheral regions of the kingdom conquered at the end of the nineteenth century, the leaders of the empire, followed by those of the *Derg*, continued to resort to force. To govern the country, they relied on the same centralized administration, and to construct the nation-state, they turned to the same policy of extraversion. This applied to all areas of public intervention whether economy, health, education or conservation – take whatever was available from the outside, then put it to use in the interests of what needed to be done internally.[91]

The world in the service of the nation

In Ethiopia, as elsewhere on the African continent, since the postcolonial moment had begun in the early 1960s, western norms had shaped national nature policies. Evidence of this can be seen, amongst many other examples, in the 'report' presented by the director of the EWCO to the WWF in 1970. Referring to 'a joint international action' which had been in place 'for nearly a decade', General Mebratu mentioned, in quick succession, the protection of walia and of nyala (species identified as 'endangered' by Leslie Brown, the ornithologist in the woollen sweater), the distribution of educational brochures (designed by UNESCO and Théodore Monod, the naturalist from Dakar), the upcoming eviction of local people from the Awash Park (under the command of Peter Hay, the hunting enthusiast) and the reward offered at that time to anyone in the Omo Park who denounced a poacher (to George Brown, former district commissioner).[92]

Such was Ethiopian policy on wildlife. Since their world had become postcolonial and since, all over East Africa, the colonial administrators had reconverted into international experts, not only did the leaders of the different countries turn to them for help, but they also did what the experts asked. A study of the Ethiopian archives reveals however that they did so in their own way. Since the early 1960s, like any other 'third world' country, Ethiopia needed international recognition in order to build its state and establish itself as a nation. As a result, these decision makers were working towards a phantom Africa: a green, untamed Africa, devoid of human presence. The Ethiopian state had not chosen this fanciful vision of Africa. Its representatives were nevertheless obliged to accept it. Yet there were ways of minimizing the scale of this constraint, and even more importantly, of turning it to their advantage as soon as possible.

In the first instance, this took the form of symbolic gestures. Like that of inviting the president of the WWF, Bernhard de Lippe-Biesterfeld, Prince of the Netherlands, to the Simien Park. Ambassador General Mebratu sent him an official invitation in August 1969, through the intermediary of Fritz Vollmar, the secretary-general of the WWF, with the assurance that 'the resettlement of the people at present living in the park has started'.[93] Mebratu then sent a personal note to the emperor through his closest associate, Abebe Retta, the minister for agriculture. Such a visit 'would contribute to national pride', he wrote to Haile Selassie, the very pride that 'His majesty has commanded us to develop'. Moreover, Mebratu continued, on his advice the Conservation Department had already bought land in the south of the country where those living in the Simien 'would be re-settled'. Twenty of them had already been sent to the site of their future occupancy and had accepted the move. 'The emperor', Mebratu concluded, 'will surely be pleased to announce this to the president of the WWF.'[94] Haile Selassie was indeed pleased. He welcomed Prince Bernhard at the end of the summer of 1969, and the prince publicly congratulated him 'in the name of the world-wide struggle for conservation'.[95] Then, a few months later, having discussed amongst themselves the land proposed by the empire, situated more than 800 kilometres south of where they were currently living, the inhabitants of the Simien Park finally refused to leave their mountains.[96] But that in no way diminished the success of the operation. Thanks to the WWF, the whole world was aware that Ethiopia had stepped onto the stage of the international school of conservation.

Gaining recognition from the outside and then establishing yourself at home

For the Ethiopian state, being recognized as a good student in the school of world governance was a means of accessing the virtuous circle of recognition. Scarcely was the visit of Prince Bernhard over when UNESCO had invited Mebratu to take part in its upcoming 'Man and Biosphere' programme.[97] The EWCO quickly got on board. In 1971, in order to prepare the launch of the MAB programme, it took part in a conference organized by UNESCO in Kenya.[98] As a result, three of the EWCO's employees were allowed to work alongside Perez Olindo, the director of Kenyan National Parks. Throughout 1972, the renowned ecologist introduced them to the various international institutions present in the country. So, when the three men returned to Addis Ababa, they knew how to help Teshome Ashine, their new director, freshly returned from the United States. They applied for around a dozen assistance programmes offered by UNESCO and the UNDP and, in 1973, obtained $218,000 to train staff in the EWCO and to finance the construction of infrastructures within the country's first three national parks.[99]

The EWCO then turned to the IUCN. In 1970, General Mebratu had been keen to introduce this institution to the members of the Organization. 'It is not a branch of the United Nations, but it has the same advisory rights and right of reply as UNESCO or the FAO', he explained to his colleagues, hence 'the necessity of working with the IUCN'.[100] A necessity they quickly embraced by participating in the Conservation Coin Collection in 1973, under the supervision, once again, of the very international Teshome Ashine.

UNESCO had just created its list of 'World Heritage Sites', and it had instructed the IUCN to examine applications for so-called 'natural' sites with a final nomination planned for 1978. So, when the Union set up this much vaunted commemorative Conservation Coin Collection, those aspiring for World Heritage classification rushed to be included. Tanzania was the first country to understand the situation – this was the moment to make a good impression. Ethiopia soon followed suit.[101] Teshome asked the IUCN and the WWF to finance the production of 6,000 gold coins, 15,000 silver ones and 30,000 bronze ones. In order to popularize the conservation cause throughout the whole country, the silver and copper coins would be struck by the National Bank, and then issued on the Ethiopian market with, on one face, an iconic animal representing the country's wildlife, and on the reverse, the logos of the IUCN and the WWF. The gold coins would be sold to collectors for a profit which would be equally shared between Ethiopia on the one hand and the IUCN and WWF on the other.[102] The two institutions suggested four symbols for the coins: the walia, the nyala, the bearded vulture and the Simien fox. Teshome retained only the first three and was adamant that each coin should also feature the heads of famous heroes of the empire. The IUCN and the WWF accepted, on one condition, laid down by Fritz Vollmar – the heads should be designed by Doris Tischler, a German friend and artist living in Addis Ababa.[103] The agreement was sealed and in February 1974, the Ethiopian National Bank began to mint the coins.[104] The revolution however brought the operation to a halt and Teshome had to wait until the *Derg* had stabilized before it could re-start, which finally happened in 1977.[105] These curious coins circulated throughout the country and in western conservationist circles and, a year later, became the symbol of Ethiopia's success. Alongside the Nahanni Park in Canada, Yellowstone in the United States and the Galapagos in Ecuador, the Simien was one of the first sites to feature on the World Heritage List.[106]

The victory was announced in Washington in September 1978 and Melaku Tefera, the governor of Gondar province, officially implemented it on the ground the following year. Melaku suppressed any opponents of the *Derg* with unprecedented ferocity. All the inhabitants of the province were affected by the violence, but in the Simien, which had become a hotbed of resistance to the regime, the government used international injunctions on 'displacement' to strike a decisive blow. The seven villages of Tirwata, Tiya, Dirni, Muchila, Antola, Agedemya and Amba Ber were burnt to the ground and their 1,200 inhabitants expelled. While UNESCO was praising 'the fantastic … vegetation come-back',[107] the Ethiopian government could also congratulate itself on a return to order.

The episode marks both a beginning and an end. On the national scale, the *Derg* was encountering more and more opposition and on the international scale the exclusions associated with African conservation were the target of increasing condemnation. In this double context, the inhabitants of the Simien would return to live in their mountains in 1981. This would be the beginning of a new history – that of community conservation with its new heritage experts, economists, lawyers or specialists in 'international consultancy'. And it would therefore be the end of the history we are concerned with here – that of a postcolonial moment during which the African decision makers and managers worked unfailingly for the benefit of *their* nature and *their* nation.

A little nature, a lot of power

Needless to say, the process unfolded at the highest government levels. In 1969, for example, when the secretary for commerce, Maurice Stans, arrived from the United States to sign an agreement on economic cooperation with Haile Selassie, General Mebratu was at pains to provide him with a 'special licence'. This meant no limits on the number of animals hunted and no species-related restriction for this big game hunter the empire was anxious to win over. Whether it was for oryx, zebra, nyala and even the walia ibex, in Ethiopia, Stans could hunt what he wanted, where he wanted.[108] The same applied to representatives of the East African governments. Since the headquarters of the Organisation of African Unity (OAU) were in Addis Ababa, senior Ethiopian officials regularly met their colleagues from Kenya, Tanzania, Uganda and Zambia there. Consequently, although John Blower was focusing his attention on his new anti-poaching unit, Mebratu had no hesitation in ordering the customs office at Addis Ababa airport to allow OAU delegates to leave the country with the skins of the leopards they had hunted. 'They are not trophies to be sold', he wrote to the customs officers, 'just souvenirs'.[109]

The Ethiopian government transformed nature into a diplomatic tool and at other, lower levels, its agents were able to use it as a means of social promotion. This was the case, for example, with the EWCO staff who were accepted for training at the Tanzanian College in Mweka. Following in the footsteps of Lealem Berhanu, some of them took advantage of their stay in Tanzania to apply for other grants which would enable them to continue their studies in North America, a situation which guaranteed them high-ranking government jobs on their return – Lealem would become the right-hand man of Teshome Ashine in the 1980s and then his successor.[110] For others, on the other hand, much to the displeasure of its director Anthony Mence, the Mweka College offered two opportunities in particular – firstly, access to services then inexistent in Ethiopia, such as the opportunity to consult a cardiologist in one case, and to go bowling in another; and secondly, the assurance of receiving over a three-year period a salary considerably higher than an Ethiopian one, even if their training period ended in failure.[111]

Working for nature was therefore a means of acquiring a small amount of power. This could be seen at all government levels. This power could have a predominantly material dimension, as implied in the reprimands addressed by Peter Hay, head warden in the Awash Park, to two of 'his' scouts at the end of the 1960s. Worka Yohannes and Alemo Bente regularly killed the wild pigs which were devastating the fields of local people, he informed Blower in a letter. 'That is part of their work', but they would then go and sell the animals in Addis Ababa 'and this is unacceptable'. Acceptable or not, for Worka and Alemo, the possibility of topping up their earnings seemed to far outweigh any conservationist deontology.[112]

There were other scenarios too, situations where this time, control of nature seemed to be the source of a symbolic power. So, for example, in the Omo, again at the end of the 1960s, George Brown complained of seeing the 'poachers' he had handed over to the commissariat emerge a few hours later with their leopard skins under their arms. 'The police receive bribes, doubtless', he wrote to Blower, who then passed the information on to Gizaw. But the major informed them that 'things are not that simple in Ethiopia'. As he explained to the two British men, a 'realistic' head of police knew that he would never stop the wildlife trade in a region so far from the seat of power. It would be preferable therefore if he knew how to control it and was able to make the local people understand that 'in this country, everything must go through the state alone', even illegal trading.[113] The major's doctrine in fact echoed that of the *Derg*. For Gizaw, as for most of his colleagues, even when confronted with the external world on which the country depended, Ethiopia came first.

Cursed farenji

Everyone had to be able to deal with other people, that was the rule in any extraverted African state or, indeed, in any of the continent's world-nations. If the former colonialists were still convinced that they were the only ones who could save nature, they now found themselves having to work alongside African leaders. As for these, even if they found themselves acting as subalterns, they were still determined to assert their sovereignty over the foreigners or, as the Ethiopians called them, *farenji* or *farenj*. Tension often arose as a result of this 'in-between' situation. Sometimes this could be explosive but, most of the time, it took the form of a petty comment, a banal demonstration of authority, a short-lived passive-aggressive exchange of remarks. Such small gestures would be anecdotal if the archives did not reveal them in their hundreds, to the point of implying that such gestures constituted the background music in the daily lives of Ethiopian officials.

Disputed sovereignty, imposed sovereignty

Berhanu Tessema, senior director of the Conservation Department and fluent in seven languages, might well have had his suspicions the day he recruited John Blower. Even before he left Uganda, Blower was already stirring things up in Ethiopia. The department had agreed to reimburse his plane tickets, but Blower had reserved six tickets in first class from Kampala to Addis Ababa – for himself, his wife and their four children.[114] The former colonial administrator ended up agreeing to travel second class and Berhanu, for his part, had to hold his tongue in response to a sly commentary on the 'understandable lack of resources ... coming from such an under-developed country as Ethiopia'.[115]

The director of the department welcomed Blower in December 1965, but it was Berhanu's successor, Gizaw Gedlegiorgis, who would work with the British expert. We can imagine the scene. Their offices were in the same building, the 'Chaï na Buna Building', or 'Tea and Coffee building', in the Mexico district of Addis Ababa. Dressed in beige trousers and a colonial jacket and driven by an authoritarian paternalism tinged with racism, Blower worked from an office on the tenth floor while Gizaw occupied an office on the eleventh floor. Proudly wearing his suit and his military medals, the former major was used to being listened to by his staff. But for almost four years, Gizaw found himself on the receiving end of furious memos from his 'adviser'. I had already found and examined about 200 of these, randomly scattered through John Blower's files. But the archives kept in storage at the EWCO contain ten times as many.

These duplicated memos first of all reveal an Ethiopian official with a taste for his own authority. Gizaw demonstrated this in April 1966 when he discovered on his desk the file of a certain G.E. Taylor. Blower was recommending this man as a replacement for Laurence Guth, the former warden of the Simien Park, but the major refused the suggestion outright. He would appreciate it, he informed his British adviser, if Blower would stop trying to get jobs for his 'friends' like 'this Taylor' who had spent twelve years in the national parks of Northern Rhodesia before ending up in the department Blower had headed in Uganda during the colonial era;[116] or like George Brown, another of his acquaintances, to whom he gave the job of head warden in the Omo Park. Two years after his arrival, the former police officer from British Kenya was clearly irritating Gizaw. The major did not, for example, appreciate Brown bursting into his office on discovering that 'his' driver had already left the capital when he was counting on him to go down to the Omo. Gizaw pronounced himself 'disappointed at being interrupted unnecessarily'. Particularly as 'ato [*sir* in Amharic] Balcha and I were discussing an important subject', he wrote to Brown before giving him a stern warning: 'You could have been patient enough to wait … without a flare-up of emotions … . As this kind of behaviour is not acceptable I would advise you to control your temper in future.'[117]

The director of the department was also anxious to protect his employees. He explained this to Blower when the latter complained that an Ethiopian scout was systematically assigned to accompany groups of 'visiting hunters'. Throughout their stay in the country's parks the latter felt as though they were being watched by a 'governmental spy', the British adviser told him. And he also objected to the fact that the tourists were obliged to pay the expenses of this escort, including transport, lodging and meals. It was indeed 'their duty', Gizaw replied, for the scouts were not there to spy on them but 'to help when at times clients encounter trivial problems with local people, police or any government official'. As for the visitors who failed to appreciate the presence of these scouts, the major emphasized that 'except this memo of yours, we have so far received no complaints' either in relation to the expenses pertaining to the scouts or, as Blower had insinuated, to their propensity to 'be open to bribery'. On the other hand, Gizaw concluded, transferring suspicion in the opposite direction, 'as to whether Professional Hunters are trustworthy or not is something that can only be proven through time'. The department would therefore continue 'for the moment' to provide them with 'not "Governmental Spies", but "informative helpers"'.[118]

As someone very much *for* the respect of his position and *for* the sovereignty of his administration, Major Gizaw ultimately revealed himself to be also *against* the former colonizers. He had no hesitation in saying so to his superiors. In May 1968, when his three years in the role were coming to an end, Blower informed the highly regarded Germatchew Tekle Hawariat, former minister of information for Haile Selassie, that he did not wish to see his contract renewed. Unless he were to be 'free' from the authority of the department head, in other words Gizaw, and placed instead under the sole responsibility of the council who oversaw the department, in other words Germatchew.[119] The latter then asked Gizaw for a 'detailed opinion' on the possible extension of his adviser's contract. To which the major replied: 'This employee is not essential to our administration since (1) he is not a biologist; (2) he does not respect the terms of his contract; (3) he is squandering the budget of the government and of the department.' Gizaw then ended his assessment with a final comment: 'This employee has spent seventeen years of his life in colonized nations, which explains his profoundly rigid and dictatorial behaviour.'[120]

Colonial arrogance versus national pride

Gizaw had to put up with Blower for a further year. He would even find himself obliged to grin and bear it when the British adviser succeeded in getting a job with UNESCO. Blower would retain his role as 'adviser' but, from January 1969, he would officially represent that prestigious institution.[121] Blower informed Gizaw about his new role and the major was quick to 'send his congratulations for this well-deserved appointment'. He even went so far as to hope 'that it will facilitate better relations between [them]'.[122] Probably a somewhat hypocritical wish and in any event quickly overtaken by the reality of everyday life. On 20 February 1969, Blower accused Gizaw of being 'unbelievably inefficient', and the latter urged the former to 'stop wasting time on this sort of correspondence'.[123] On 24 February, Blower demanded that his salary be paid 'early next week', and Gizaw asked him 'to write to inform not to impress'.[124] On 13 March, Gizaw sold the Land Rover that the Ford Foundation had donated to the department to enable Blower to get out in the field. Blower was furious – 'a truly remarkable achievement major!' – to which the Ethiopian replied: 'I do not manage to understand what you have in mind.'[125] On the 25 March, Blower once again demanded his salary and, this time, he accused Gizaw of being 'anti British'. But the major preferred to describe himself as 'anti-flagrant liar or anti-dishonest'.[126] Such skirmishes continued until Gizaw's departure in the autumn of 1969.

It was then the turn of Mebratu Fisseha to find himself confronted with Blower. On 24 November, he participated in the 10th General Assembly of the IUCN in New Delhi. Referring to the trading of leopard skins, Mebratu announced, in front of an audience of western conservationists, that, if the threat of extinction was indeed undeniable in his country, it resulted from 'steadily growing, generous incentives given by highly rich leopard-skin traders of the world to poachers in Ethiopia'. It was therefore necessary to take every possible measure 'to stop this illegal trade', urged the general, and to take a stand against 'Overseas buyers' who 'must bear ultimate responsibility for the continued wholesale slaughter of leopard … in Ethiopia.'[127] Mebratu then returned to Addis Ababa and, a few days later, he found a note from John Blower on his desk. The expert sought 'to remind [him] of the extent of the leopard skin trade', and the need 'to fight the Omo poachers'. 'Ethiopia must respond', Blower insisted.[128]

More than a simple clash of personalities, the conflict arose from a radical divergence in viewpoint. Whether addressing Gizaw or Mebratu, Blower was convinced that he alone knew how to protect nature and that it was 'they', the Ethiopians, who were responsible for its decline. But, in his dealings with foreigners like Blower, Gizaw denounced their 'dictatorial' attitude, and Mebratu felt that it was 'difficult to rely on them to oversee conservation … since they are often moulded into a reactionary and imperial attitude' – 'they' being the former colonial administrators now acting as international experts. It was with these words that the director of the Conservation Department addressed his minister, Abebe Retta, who, in December 1969, asked him to look at the application files of candidates applying for Blower's post. His choice was Patrick Stracey, a man born in India during the colonial era. Stracey was currently still working there, but Mebratu trusted him. He had met him during his last trip to India, the two men had got on well and, three months later, Stracey arrived in Ethiopia.[129] Although he remained in post there for four years, the archives have little to say about him. Probably because he took them with him when he returned to India, as suggested by the note sent to him in June 1974 by the Ethiopian minister for the environment: 'I recall', Fikre Mariam Demeke wrote, 'that you are requested to hand over all the registered files in your possession to the Organisation.'[130] Clearly, Stracey did not comply.

Being the winner ... and the loser

Apart from this eloquent letter, a few documents nevertheless give us more insight into the tensions between the Ethiopian managers and the expatriate experts who succeeded Blower. So, for example, in 1971, Mebratu Fisseha ordered a report from a certain Yewand Wassen Fassil, one of three men he had sent to Nairobi to accompany the renowned Kenyan ecologist Perez Olindo. The general wanted to know how the Kenyan wildlife department was run. He hoped to find out about its relationship with the 'advisers' sent by international conservation institutions, and his employee's reply confirmed what he already suspected. Yewand reported to Mebratu that 'the Kenyan National Parks administration has learnt that foreign experts should be handled carefully'. 'Quite a lot have been dismissed', he explained to his superior, 'because they tend to forget their assignment and want to involve themselves in the administration and end up with wishful expectations to run the organization.' 'Failing in this', the EWCO envoy added, 'they try to undermine the organization by trying to convince donating agencies not to help any more.'[131] This was the crux of the problem – without experts, there was no interference but without interference, there was no recognition.

This also explains the attitude of someone like Teshome Ashine towards a man like Patrick Stracey. In a letter he sent him in March 1973 and with his natural diplomacy, the director of the EWCO admitted to the British expert that his 'knowledge' was 'valuable' and that, as a result, 'you could contribute much to our wildlife conservation programmes'. 'But I don't have to tell you, that such contribution cannot be achieved by knowledge and experience alone', Teshome continued. 'One must be able to inspire others, to co-operate with others. It is with this view in my mind [that] I called you on so many occasions to my office. ... But I am afraid that my talks with you have not proved fruitful', the director added before concluding on an emphatic note: 'Complaints are constantly being raised against you that almost every one finds it impossible to work with you.'[132] In the absence of any archives to help us, Stracey's reply remains unknown.

Nevertheless, the two letters he sent to Teshome in May 1973 give some indication of what happened next. 'You spoke of the anticipated aid from UNESCO in next year's budget, including a post of Conservation Specialist', Stracey wrote on 13 May. Clearly his Ethiopian contract was coming to an end and, like Blower before him, the expatriate was now in quest of a job at UNESCO. Consequently, he went straight to the point: 'I will be delighted to discuss the progress of this Department with them, but may I request you suggest my name for the post in question?'[133] The attempted bribery was barely concealed: if he were to find himself unemployed, the expert could indeed tarnish Ethiopia's image with conservation leaders. Yet the threat failed to produce the intended effect. 'Since I have not received an acknowledgement or reply', Stracey wrote to Teshome ten days later, 'I have come to the conclusion that under the circumstances ... I have no desire to see my [Ethiopian] contract extended.'[134]

The expert left the country a month later, leaving Teshome Ashine both winner and loser. The director of conservation had come out on top: he was working first of all for Ethiopia and for the nation and not for the external world and its former colonialists. But a few weeks later, the director found himself welcoming another 'adviser', John Stephenson, also trained in the colonies of the former British Empire. A *farenji* who would help him and annoy him in equal measure.

Revenge

If the expert's first priority was to save nature, the local managers also intended to use ecology in the service of the nation. In the capital, for example, faced with the presence of the expatriates, the Ethiopian administration mastered the art of international discourse – a management-oriented and apolitical discourse the first purpose of which was to conceal the tensions which existed between them and the foreign experts. But on the ground, the Ethiopian government left these expatriates to deal with the political realities of the country – with the provincial administration, the assistant wardens, the scouts and the local inhabitants. It was here that 'the revenge of contexts' was played out, a term used by anthropologist Jean-Pierre Olivier de Sardan to describe a revenge rooted in everyday life, one based in the village, at the precise point where international norms, a national governance and local situations collide.[135]

Murders in a natural environment

This was first apparent in the Omo National Park. In May 1969, the staff seemed to be at the end of their tether. Supervised by their warden, George Brown, the scouts were carrying out daily patrols around Mui, where the park headquarters were situated. They also physically marked out its borders, and inside these, they maintained a road network of 51 kilometres. But once again, Addis Ababa was late in sending their salaries and it was three months since they had been paid. Worse still – for several months now, the Surma had been shooting at them on a regular basis.[136] The Surma people from south-west Ethiopia had been forced to abandon ivory trading in the 1920s, when the demands of European traders in the region had led to the disappearance of wildlife. Since that time, their main activity had been pastoral farming.[137] They also practised a seasonal agriculture based around burning, and they engaged in some occasional hunting, such as for buffalo. It was this animal that they were in the process of hunting when Brown and his scouts came upon them on 16 November 1969.

Shots were fired on both sides, and a Surma fell to the ground, killed outright. Fearing reprisals, the guards informed the Conservation

Department in the capital. General Mebratu in turn contacted the provincial authorities of Jimma, situated 200 kilometres north of the park. Two days later, the police turned up in the Omo. For Brown, the former colonial commissioner, their task was an obvious one: 'Go into the villages and confiscate rifles.' But instead of setting off in search of firearms, the Jimma police arrested Hailu Ayele, 'his' scout, who had killed one of the Surma hunters.[138] Hailu was released on 18 November. And on the morning of 26 November his colleagues discovered his corpse. They did not need to go looking for it since the Surma themselves led them to the grave where they had buried him the previous evening, after killing him with a blow from a spear. Then calm was once again restored.

In November, Germatchew Tekle Hawariat left the capital in order to check on the situation for himself. The local people 'no longer showed any sign of aggressivity', he wrote to the members of the committee which, under his direction, oversaw the Conservation Department. Nevertheless, he told them, 'It is time to bring an end to the conflict between the guards and the local people since failure to do so will mean one side will always want to seek revenge on the other.' Germatchew therefore decided to authorize the Surma to hunt 'if they lacked food'. The former minister of the empire also asked the Jimma police to remain on the spot for a further period. And he ordered George Brown 'not to attempt to expel local people for the time being', informing his colleagues in passing that 'the warden is far more interested in the rights of animals than in those of the local inhabitants'.[139]

The British warden left the Omo a few months later and after his departure, life inside the park seemed to verge on the absurd. In 1971, as a replacement for Brown, General Mebratu chose a man called Fred Duckworth, a game warden from Malawi, the former British Nyasaland. In 1972, Mebratu heard him complaining that 'these nomadic people are relatively harmless ... but they should be moved out of the park, for in the future they will undoubtedly do irreparable damage to the vegetation'. Duckworth added however that 'his' scouts lacked the means of doing so. They had neither uniforms nor medicines, and so rarely received any supplies that they were forced to go and hunt antelope *outside* the borders of the national park – or in other words, in the territory of the Surma and the Mursi, the very people they banned from coming to hunt *inside* the park.[140]

The same contradiction was repeated over the following years. In 1973, assistant warden Mariam Demeke mentioned to his superiors the fines imposed on the Mursi and Surma people who had entered the Omo with their cattle. But he also informed them that, with the help of his scouts, and 'in order to feed themselves', they had managed to clear, burn and then cultivate park land around Mui, where they had set up their 'headquarters'.[141] This land was still being cultivated in 1976 by the new assistant warden Teshome Demena. Although that did not prevent him from informing his superiors that inside the park, scouts had destroyed the 'huts' belonging to the Mursi, while on the outside, they had made a track thanks to which 'visitors can now see the Surma tribes along the road leading to the park'.[142] Nature in one place, farming in another: that was the objective sought within the Omo. But, in 1978, the displaced pastoralists returned. Much to the regret of the EWCO adviser John Stephenson, who observed to Teshome Ashine: 'Scouts do nothing but sit about and talk, as if they were not concerned by the park at all.'[143]

It is difficult to know if Stephenson was distorting the reality. But what is important in this story is to see that the Ethiopian government was indeed giving foreigners power with one hand and taking it back with the other.

Not everyone gets to lay down the law

The Awash Park was a particularly good example of this. In May 1967, Major Gizaw was called to order by John Blower. The 'guidelines' of UNESCO and the IUCN were 'clear', Blower told him. They recommended '[S]etting areas aside to protect wild fauna'. Gizaw therefore gave orders to Peter Hay urging him to put 'a definitive end to the interference of both populations and their stock with fauna'.[144] Surrounded by his scouts, the Awash game warden promptly informed the Karayu, the Ittu and the Afar who were occupying the park that they needed to 'evacuate'. But the latter refused to do so. 'The police did not tell us to leave', they retorted, their guns at the ready. The scouts proceeded to arrest them, or at least those they could catch. They took them to the district police headquarters in Metehara, and after a few hours, the agro-pastoralists were released by a sergeant, who admonished Peter Hay, telling him that even though he was indeed the 'park warden', he 'had no official authority whatsoever to arrest someone'.[145]

On 11 September 1967, 5 December 1967, 12 January 1968, 4 February 1968 and 12 April 1968, identical incidents recurred. The game warden and scouts from the Awash went in pursuit of herdsmen who were grazing their animals, or of farmers who were burning an area of land, and the police always gave them the same response – they alone could act yet nobody had requested them to do so.[146] Then a ministerial delegation arrived from Addis Ababa in May 1968. Peter Hay began to feel hopeful. He thought he would finally be given the authority he had been asking for, but very quickly, as he noted in his monthly report, disappointment set in. Although the 'officials' had told him that he would soon be able to 'expel' the local people, they had also explained to the 'local authorities' that the warden and his scouts were only entitled to 'chase them out, and if they refuse to go [they] have to leave them'.[147] For the former colonial game warden, it was all too much. In June he was to be found in the dock of the district courtroom, accused of molesting children, killing camels and cattle belonging to their parents, burning their crops and then their houses.[148] Although Blower encouraged him to deny the charges, Peter Hay admitted responsibility. 'While you, being in Addis Ababa, and not actually here, might get away with this, I definitely could not as everyone knows we did burn the houses', he told his compatriot. 'The Police, the local governor, all know this.'[149] The warden nevertheless considered himself to be perfectly within his rights: 'We have just performed our job', he wrote to Gizaw.[150]

The Ethiopian administration was perfectly aware of all this. Which is why, thanks to a concerted agreement, Gizaw and the Metehara judge dropped the charges hanging over Hay. The major then asked the warden to resume his duties.[151] At that point he told him, just as he would tell his successor, a certain John Bromley, and what Mebratu would also repeat to the next warden, a man by the name of Mr Vanci, that imposing the 'park order' in these territories was no 'easy task'[152] – particularly for the managers who found themselves having to navigate the 'in-between', they could have added. For their work consisted, on the one hand, in welcoming the foreigners whose enthusiasm was a little too colonial for their tastes and, on the other, in controlling the local people who seemed in the habit of resisting any central authority, whether their own or that of the state. The result was that those in charge needed to be constantly on their guard so as not to overstep the threshold of tolerance above which those people were likely to rebel.

This 'in-between' might seem disconcerting, but, returning to Frederick Cooper and his description of the African elites who were steering a course between the outside and the inside world, the '*in between* is as much a place to be at home as any other'.[153] What the Awash situation adds to our understanding of this way of governing is that it results in a political life which is profoundly global, and deeply conflictual.

The price of prestige

The history of the Simien confirms this. Ever since they found themselves caught up in the conservation world, the Simien Mountains have evolved against the backdrop of global conflict. The mountain range is part of the northern province of Begemder, governed by the famous Tamrat Yigezu, the man who became a captain at the age of nineteen. The emperor asked him to prepare the people of the Simien for the creation of a national park in their mountains, and with this in mind, in the spring of 1965, Tamrat placed the area under the command of Nadew Woreta, a former imperial official originally from Ambaras, in the heart of the Simien. Then, at the beginning of 1966, on the recommendations of UNESCO, the IUCN and John Blower, Nadew was replaced by an expatriate.[154] A new warden, Laurence Guth, was seconded from the American National Parks Service and paid by the association of the highly conservative Russell Train, the judge who had co-founded the African Wildlife Leadership Foundation. Guth spent a year in the Simien Mountains, and over the months, Nadew gradually succeeded in turning the scouts and the inhabitants of the park against him. 'Unable to do his job' and 'driven to the edge', the American warden resigned in the spring of 1967.[155]

Guth's replacement in the park was the British-born Clive Nicol. The young engineer and karateka initially declared he was 'delighted' to move to the Simien, a remote mountain range on the high plains of northern Ethiopia, and to live in a house perched above the village of Gich and at an altitude of 3,800 metres – the 'roof of Africa' as Nicol called it in the book he wrote about his time there. He spent his days with the Ethiopian scouts and, in the evening, together with his wife Sonako, he enjoyed the company of Bernhard Nievergelt, a Swiss zoologist financed by the WWF and also living in Gich.[156] From time to time, the warden received visits from his superiors, John Blower and Gizaw Gedlegiorgis, to whom, from 1968 onwards, he complained with increasing frequency about the difficulty of 'ensuring respect for the park'.[157] Then, in July 1969, Nicol also resigned, under 'pressure', as he put it, from Nadew and his political supporters from the province of Begemder whom he had mobilized on the strength of a single idea: if the *national* park were to be abandoned, restriction on the *local* use of the land would be lifted, and the *international* project for the displacement of local inhabitants would remain a dead letter.[158]

In this way, within the national park, life had become *global*. And it had also become extremely confrontational. The postcolonial moment accelerated connections between individuals, and the more interaction there was between them, the more tensions accumulated.

How did the inhabitants of the Simien react to Bernhard Nievergelt, the zoologist who had travelled from Switzerland in order to observe the walia? Some of them broke into the hut where he kept his provisions and stole them.[159] And what was their attitude to Clive Nicol? Some of them abandoned their fields and their cattle and got jobs as scouts. The warden reproached them for cutting wood in order to cook and keep their families warm but, as long as they received their salary at the end of the month, they accepted his reprimands.[160] On the other hand, when Nicol accused them of being 'illiterate' and described them as 'the worst imaginable quality', or when he refused to pay their salary or sacked them,[161] the scouts would disappear on poaching expeditions for Nadew.[162] After all, what had the Ethiopian warden done before Guth arrived and stole his job? Like the colonial game wardens in East Africa, he had monopolized control of the big game – both in terms of its protection (through the imposition of laws) and of its exploitation (through hunting).[163] Nicol may indeed have referred to Nadew as 'shit', but in reality for him too, nature simply meant power. When he was given the job as warden Nadew imposed himself over his neighbours and then over the entire community. And when he was removed from the post, he took up poaching and then went off to campaign against the park in order to get into the national parliament.[164]

Nicol related all this to Blower and Gizaw,[165] before asking them, in November 1968, if he could be transferred to the Awash Park.[166] However, both the expert and the manager also had their goals. Unbeknown to Nicol, Blower opposed the transfer: 'Mr Nicol is a personal friend of mine', he wrote to Germatchew, 'but he does not have previous African experience, and for this reason I do not think that he is the right man for the post in the Awash'.[167] As for Gizaw, as he confided to Nicol, 'I do feel bound to be assisted with an expatriate warden in the Simien … the WWF demands it.' The major then appealed to his sense of duty: 'Conservation is something new for the local people, who are naturally suspicious of all novelties', he explained to the British warden, 'but I think you will agree with me, it is our moral responsibility to educate them.'[168] Gizaw then visited the Simien Park and, after he had left, there were reports that an 'inflammatory rumour … circulates in the Simien'. Nicol openly accused the major of being responsible: 'You are the one who gave the people permission to cut "small trees", … they all say it.'[169] Whether true or false, the archives do not reveal. They do however tell us how the story ended. On 8 July 1969, the British warden sent his resignation to the minister Abebe Retta. 'I am not going to be away from my family to be an ineffective pawn in Ethiopian prestige politics', Nicol declared, taking care to send a copy of his letter to Morges in Switzerland for the attention of Noel Simon and Fritz Vollmar, the secretary-generals of the IUCN and the WWF, respectively.[170]

It was left to Mebratu therefore to counter this final desperate gesture. 'Even Nicol has failed to develop the Park', he wrote a month later to Simon and Vollmar. 'We have now appointed an experienced Police officer to deal with offenders and introduced new measures to control the cutting and burning of forest and the illegal hunting', the general went on, 'but we still need you: … Would WWF agree to help us again?'[171] The WWF agreed to do so, as did UNESCO and the IUCN, until the Simien National Park was inscribed on the World Heritage List in 1978. The *in-between* is a difficult art, but the leaders knew how to deal with it. Perhaps it was a way of getting their revenge on the outside world. In any case, it was their way of ruling the world-nation and maintaining control over its nature – a nature now far more global than elsewhere, and consequently a more powerful source of conflict.

4

Living in a national park
The global village of the anonymous

The problem of conservation lies with Others. During the Arusha conference in September 1961, the delegates did not discuss the Waata who live in the Tsavo Park in Kenya, nor the Bakiga of the Elizabeth Park in Uganda, nor the Nkoya from Kafue, in Northern Rhodesia. Rather than citing peoples and territories, the speakers at the conference referred to a single world, the fourth world – a world none of them could identify with since this was the distant universe of the 'tribe', of 'nomads', of 'indigenous peoples' and 'traditional societies'. It was the world of Others, that of the small peasantry, of farmers and pastoralists who are governed by the laws of survival, by the needs of the present and the immediate, to the extent that, without even being aware of it, they have become a threat to the very nature on which they rely for survival.

The expert gentlemen gathered together at Arusha were alarmed by the demography of the 'Africans' as population figures continued to exceed the 'carrying capacity' of nature. The field experts were worried about the destructive practices of 'local people' – overgrazing, overexploitation and, above all, poaching. The African heads of state and senior government officials deplored the irresponsible behaviour of this mass of anonymous 'peasants', even though they designated them as the beneficiaries of the new conservation – the one which had replaced preservation in order to support their development.[1] Named, but never specifically identified, these men and women were ultimately the principal focus of a conference to which they had not been invited. But what exactly were these people doing while others discussed them?

Arusha 1961. Nature for some, a way of life for Others

What, for example, were all these anonymous individuals doing in the three future national parks of Ethiopia? In the minds of those attending the Arusha conference they were destroying the nature on which their lives depended. But what were those lives really like?

In 1961, in the sub-desert south-west region of the country, the Omo valley was inhabited by around 5,000 Mursi and Surma people who occupied a territory of approximately 9,000 km² (a surface area equivalent to the French *départements* of the Lozère and Cantal combined, inhabited, at that same, by a population of 250,000). The Mursi had lived on the eastern bank of the Omo since the end of the nineteenth century. Originally part of the Surma group, they had broken away from them and created their own community. They had crossed the river and given themselves a new ethnonym, that of the Mursi. The Surma, for their part, remained on the western bank of the Omo. Genuine differences existed therefore between the two communities but their way of life brought them together.[2]

The Mursi and the Surma lived in a remote area, out of reach of the Ethiopian state. They formed an egalitarian society organized around a collegiate power which was divided into ranks, on the basis of a criterion of descending age. They were transhumant agro-pastoralists who cultivated sorghum and raised cattle, moving from pasture to pasture, according to the seasons. They hunted for their own consumption – mostly for buffalo before the game cropping took place in June, and more rarely, for rhinoceros or leopards, the horns and skins of which could then be traded with the people living on the high plateaux in exchange for guns and cattle. Their weapons were used to defend themselves against neighbouring people, or sometimes to attack them, and cattle played an important role in their social lives.

For in these groups, as anthropologist Jean-Baptiste Eczet points out, people took the name of their cow, chosen according to the colour of its coat. Each individual therefore expressed their relationship with others by borrowing a characteristic from the animal 'with which he or she was in day-to-day proximity: a warlike and migratory proximity for young men (by means of a taurine gesture); a domestic proximity for young women (using gestures borrowed from calves); a managerial one for older women (with gestures intended to represent the herd)'. In this way, in the Omo, the cow lay at the heart of social life. It was a 'source' of milk, or of meat in times of famine, a means of 'mediation' for marriage agreements, a 'payment for the price of blood' and the main focus of ritual sacrifices. The cow was the primary focus of attention and the object of every possible care.[3]

This relationship with an animal is not exclusive to the Omo and can be found in other cattle-rearing societies, for example in the Peul (or Fulani) in West Africa.[4] It is not however a feature of Awash societies.

The Awash valley is a territory made up of low-lying ground with a mixture of wooded savannah, semi-arid savannah and desert, covering a surface area of approximately 850 km² (equivalent to the Île de France district in France). In this valley, in 1961, while the Arusha delegates were discussing the future of African nature, several thousand Karayu and Ittu were cultivating the land and grazing their livestock a hundred kilometres east of Addis Ababa. Like the Surma and the Mursi, they too were transhumant agro-pastoralists.

Originating from the Muslim group of the Oromo, since the beginning of the twentieth century, the Karayu and Ittu had made their living mainly from pastoralism, moving with their cattle and goats from one pasture to another, within the area surrounding the little town of Metehara. But since the 1950s, Afar tribes from the east had spread into their land and taken over their water sources. In addition, central Ethiopian power had arrived from the west to promote the irrigation of the valley and the development of commercial farming and, as a result, existing rights of use were being challenged, leading to expulsions on an increasingly large scale.

All of which explains why in the Awash, in 1961, social relationships with the environment required a continuous process of adaptation. The geographers and anthropologists Girum Getachew, Degefa Tolossa and Getachew Gebru have shown that, since the 1950s, the Karayu, the Ittu and sometimes the Afar had increased the cultivation of barley and sorghum. This enabled them to supplement their subsistence lifestyle with the sale of agricultural products. The agro-pastoralists also collected wood which was then transformed into charcoal either for their own use or for sale. Finally, within their respective clans, structured around a kinship system associated with a particular territory, they urged their chiefs to negotiate with Addis Ababa for access to pastoral lands which were still in communal use.[5]

The same collective management of pasturelands can be found in the Simien Mountains. The Park, with a surface area of 410 km² (i.e. four times the area of Paris *intra-muros*) is perched between altitudes of 2,800 and 4,600 metres, on the edge of the high plateaux of north Ethiopia. In the Simien area, 10,000 mountain people – Amhara Christians or Muslims – combine livestock rearing with working the land. Those with the means to do so occasionally go into town to sell vegetables or milk, which then allows them to buy oil, soap or clothing. Nevertheless, apart from these few inequalities, all of them live in poverty.

Demographic pressure limited both livestock breeding and the size of herds and, as a result, the amounts of dung, essential for enriching the soil, were also reduced. This undermined an agriculture already weakened as a result of the erosion caused by the eucalyptus trees. Introduced into Ethiopia at the end of the nineteenth century, the tree satisfied local firewood needs but caused the soil to dry out. The villagers therefore maximized use of the land by combining terrace farming and slash-and-burn agriculture, and by alternating seasonal and permanent crops. They did not however hunt on any significant scale. They killed any prowling hyenas, threw stones to drive away gelada baboons which threatened their fields, and some of them attempted to kill the walia, the endemic wild goat of the Simien, which lived at altitude on the cliffs and whose skin and horns were highly prized in the capital. Finally, with the exception of this activity, most of the inhabitants maintained a dynamic relationship with the non-human world they referred to as *täfätro*, 'what is created and recreated all around us'.[6]

This was at least the case in 1961, before the *mengest* made them aware of 'nature'. In Amharic, the language of the original Christian kingdom, in the heart of the high Ethiopian plateaux, the term *mengest* means both the state and the holder of power. And the *mengest* was the first common element of the three future parks of the country. The Simien had been part of the Ethiopian kingdom since the seventeenth century, but it was only since the 1940s that the state had decided to impose an absolute central authority there. Yet the more its representatives attempted to achieve this, the more they found themselves confronted with the uprisings of a region which had become a hotbed of resistance.[7]

The same representatives also struggled to control the Awash, a territory conquered at the end of the nineteenth century when Menelik II took advantage of European colonization to extend his kingdom by including the surrounding low lands. Since then, local dignitaries, the *balabat*, were supposed to raise taxes and organize the production of cotton and sugar cane on behalf of the empire. In practice, however, faced with a population still used to living according to their own political organization, they focused their attention on imposing central state power in the Awash – social integration would come later.[8] The same applied in the Omo where, confronted with Mursi and Surma people who sometimes did not even know the word 'Ethiopia', the state leaders were aware that if they tried to impose the nation too brutally, they risked rebellion and even secession. For the time being, the first priority was to get the local populations to recognize the empire.[9]

If the inhabitants of the Simien, Awash and Omo had been part of the Arusha conference, perhaps this is the story they would have told the delegates. The Surma would certainly have spoken about their cows. The Amhara would probably have referred to 'what is created and recreated'. And the Karayu and Ittu would undoubtedly have wanted to discuss the intrusion of commercial agriculture in their grazing lands. What is certain is that none of them would have talked about 'nature' since, in their language, the word does not exist. The question remains as to how all these anonymous agro-pastoralists would respond to the arrival of the postcolonial period in their lives, and to the world of what other people call 'nature'.

In search of subalterns. History

Whether in the context of 'subaltern' or 'postcolonial' studies, over a period of at least forty years, historians have sought to find ways of capturing the everyday lives of those more likely to be subjected to power than to impose it. That challenge still remains, but many new avenues have been opened up in the context of colonial and postcolonial societies.

Listening to the voiceless

First of all, thanks to Edward Said, we know the crucial role of representations and rhetoric in encouraging and justifying colonization. At the end of the nineteenth century, European scholars and administrators had definitively relegated colonized peoples to the world of the Other and the Elsewhere: the 'tribe' or the 'ethnic group', in 'the Orient' or in 'black' Africa'. The colonialists essentialized the 'Africans' or the 'Asians' in this dehumanizing tone, thereby justifying domination. They also anonymized them in their archives, which is why it is so difficult to get any sense of their capacity for action in the face of power.[10] On this subject, by comparing history and literature, some Indian researchers have underlined the ease with which certain intellectuals ended up confining themselves to the discourse of the archives produced by those in power, in both colonial and postcolonial contexts. In order to study the limits of this power, many focused on peasant revolts, and when they could find no trace of rebellion in the archives, they concluded that domination was in fact total. Yet, behind each insurrection, lie a great number of historical strategies, acts of insubordination which though invisible, continued to mark the interaction between the peasants and those in power. At the time of colonization, just as at the time of independence, these relationships, whether in the context of rebellion or not, shaped everyday life.[11] They represented what some have called the 'third space', that of the 'hybridity' which develops from the encounter between dominators and dominated. For, as Homi Bhabba suggests, 'negotiation is what politics is all about. And we do negotiate even when we don't know we are negotiating: we are always negotiating.'[12]

Capacity for action, hybridization, adaptation – these concepts remain a subject of debate even today. Gayatri Chakravorty Spivak, specialist in comparative literature, has even put forward the idea that subalterns do not 'speak'. Though not because they are incapable of doing so, Spivak tells us. The problem lies more with the intellectuals who act as their spokespersons. Quite incapable of understanding the subalterns, their lives or their thinking, researchers end up dispossessing them of a voice which power has already taken from them.[13] As a result, they find themselves falling into the very trap they had set out to expose. Rather like a colonial state which reduced its subjects to 'indigenous people' or 'tribal people', the spokespersons of the dominated also end up locking individuals into abstract categories, divorced from reality – like that of 'subalterns'.[14]

Yet that does not mean we should abandon such ways of studying the past. The Indian historians were the first to remind us of this. What is important is that in both Africa, and Asia, during and since colonization, a history exists in which subalterns produce their own destiny.[15] Their options are more limited than those available to other social categories, but even the disenfranchised still have choices. Historians should therefore attempt to reproduce their choices faithfully, or in other words, without confusing the history they would like to write (that of subalterns capable of achieving everything) with the history as it has unfolded (that of a domination which can be negotiated, but which nevertheless remains a domination). In fact, theorists need to 'listen',[16] not only to those who resist, but also to all the men and women who accept domination and who consent to their own degradation.[17] Nor must the 'big men' be forgotten, those who do not have official status but who know how to exercise control over their neighbours by amassing a small amount of political power, a hint of economic capital and a generous measure of social recognition.[18] Finally, in response to the norms which have come from outside, come those behaviours which political scientists refer to: 'cunning, flight, ... appropriation, or its opposite, rejection'.[19]

Rediscovering modes of action

Once the principles have been established, we can turn our attention to the method which allows us to discover not the 'public transcript' of the subalterns, with reference to the killing of a guard, for example, but their 'hidden transcript', the one which concerns the ordinary and the invisible, such as the squatting of a minuscule patch of land.[20] In order to uncover these traces of everyday life, to reconstitute from the bottom upwards the history of the postcolonial moment, it is important to emphasize the vital importance of beginning our investigation in living and everyday places.[21] It is an approach which means resigning ourselves to observing territories which are sometimes insignificant and then trying to extract from such observations something significant about the anonymous people who live in such places. In this context, the challenge lies in how we handle the archives. First of all, there are the 'low voltage' archives,[22] like the autobiography of a park warden which can refer over and over again to 'local populations', without ever naming a single individual. This kind of source needs to be cross-referenced against administrative archives, although these must be treated with caution since they 'often gives less information on the ordinary lives of individuals than on how the government agents perceive them'. Unless, that is, we read them 'against the grain':[23] that is to say by setting aside the intention of their producers and seeking instead to find out what a particular archive is telling us, about the life of subalterns.[24]

Such methods have enabled environmental specialists to revisit the African history of conservation. But they continue to be divided over one question – are the men and women who live in these natural spaces suffering as a result of conservation? For anthropologists and geographers like Melissa Leach and Robin Mearns, the 'lie' has disastrous effects. Overpopulation, overgrazing, erosion – according to them, these 'preconceived opinions', born out of colonization, explain why in Africa today, just as in the past, conservation involves the denial of local expertise and knowledge and, consequently, the oppression of local people.[25] This argument is challenged by a historian like Helen Tilley, who argues that African ecology is a 'co-constructed' bridge between previously distinct areas of disciplinary expertise and science. The imperial and later international conservationists relied very much on 'indigenous knowledge', Tilley explains. They took into account the knowledge and practical skills of local people and made every effort to ensure these were accepted by the decision makers, who, for their part, were pursuing very different goals. This argument could be a convincing one if the historian substantiated it with evidence other than from accounts produced by the experts themselves.[26] Better to simply conclude with historian Corey Ross that in both the colonial and postcolonial eras 'most conservationists were interested mainly in preserving ecosystems undisturbed by people', a situation which always resulted in 'serious consequences for ordinary people'.[27]

In Africa, these 'consequences' have left particularly visible traces on three separate occasions. First of all, during the creation of the first game reserves at the beginning of the twentieth century, the expulsions of local inhabitants sometimes led to armed rebellions (as in German East Africa, in 1905).[28] Then, in the run up to independence, when the departure of the colonialists was imminent, those who had been under colonial rule were able to give full vent to their resentment (for example, by attacking park wardens and animals in Northern Rhodesia and Kenya).[29] And finally, in the present itself: if the historian knows which elements to look for in the nature archives, it is because he or she has first of all observed them in the field. This is, for example, what Roderick Neumann did in Tanzania. By travelling from one national park to another, he saw crops destroyed by wild animals, but also elephant territory invaded by cattle; people forcibly removed from a park area, but also villages violently disrupted by the arrival of these displaced groups. Neumann observed 'patterns of predation' in the present, and then set about looking for the trace of these in the archives of the past.[30] By proceeding in this manner, we can better understand how postcolonial nature began.

From the present to the past

Since the 2000s, although the life of the Surma in the Omo continues to be organized around a collegial power and a pastoral symbolism, it has also been marked by three major upheavals: the long-term establishment of the Ethiopian state, the expansion of a sugar-producing industry and commercial agriculture, and the arrival of western tourists ready to spend a lot of money in order to see a little 'tribal'[31] folklore. But what were things like in the 1960s? How did the Surma react when George Brown and his guards nailed a sign reading 'Omo National Park' on their new huts in Mui? There was already evidence that the Surma were capable of killing a scout. But in the context of their everyday lives, how did they react when confronted with these British wardens, and these Ethiopian guards, who constantly reminded them that agro-pastoralism and hunting were now forbidden? It is not easy to say with any certainty, since the Surma left no archives behind them.

The same is true for the inhabitants of the Awash. Since the 1990s, the Karayu and the Ittu had been in open conflict with the Afar, since the central state was now fully in control of the park area. The Karayu and the Ittu therefore decided to extend their activity into the pasturelands of the Afar, a move which was rejected by the latter – in their view, the fact that their neighbours had been expelled from their own land did not give them the right to come and occupy Afar land.[32] But what about in 1963, in 1965 and 1966? What did the Karayu and Ittu make of the former colonialists, Ian Grimwood and Leslie Brown, or of Peter Hay and his guards, who turned up on their pasturelands overnight ready to embark on the construction of a 'natural' park? Once again, very little information is available.

As a result, the article written by American journalist Michael Mok during his visit to the Simien in 1970 is even more valuable. Mok interviews a certain John Bromley, referred to as the 'temporary warden' of the park and then a farmer from Gich, the most densely populated village in the Simien. 'You can hear their rifles every day', said Bromley, explaining that the local people 'know we want to relocate them to establish a park to protect the walia, so they figure if they kill off the walia there won't be a park and they won't have to move'. This seems to be confirmed by the Gich resident who describes 'a strange government that cares more about Walia than it does about people'.[33] This information represents the clearest account of all those written on the sudden intrusion of nature in the life of the Ethiopian peasants. As such, it offers a clear demonstration of the importance of starting from the present before calmly turning our attention back to the archives. Only then can we finally attempt to reproduce the content by making that effort of 'imaginative (re)creations' referred to by historian Karl Jacoby in *Shadows at Dawn*, the book from which I tried to draw inspiration in order to write this one.[34]

Since my first stay in the Simien in 2007, many of its inhabitants have allowed me to glimpse the reality of their daily lives. For Samson, the hell of poverty into which he has been plunged since being driven out of Gich in 2016 'has become the fire'. In Debark, the little town which now houses the park management offices, Isayas, the chief warden, insists that, on the contrary, the local people are faring much better than in the past. And nobody contradicts him since the warden's power cannot be challenged. Some people however give a more restrained account. Like Tesfa, a scout who took part in the recent eviction of the inhabitants. But he is merely an employee, he does what he is asked to do and would now like to 'work in confidence' he mutters, angry at the experts from UNESCO who recommended the displacement but who have not been back since. In the village of Ambaras, in the north-west of the park, Philippos continues to work in his field. The authorities have already informed him that he will soon have to leave, but he is determined to stay. 'We're not going', he told me. 'They can kill us if they want, we're not going', he insisted, looking Tesfa straight in the eye. And while we were talking about the 'burden' that the park restrictions represent in the eyes of the inhabitants, we noticed in the distance a young man in the act of cutting down some eucalyptus trees. 'Aren't you going to punish him?' Philippos asked Tesfa, with a sly grin. 'It's the first time this week', the scout replied. 'He knows that tomorrow I'll tell him not to do it, but today he's just getting on with it.'[35]

The resistant, the holder of power, the employee, the poor person and the cunning one. Or in Amharic, *tekelakay, mengest, serateña, dehaw* and *yemiyastekaklew*. They are also to be found in the Omo and the Awash, as I was able to observe in my visits to these two parks. I then searched extensively through the archives hoping to come across them, and eventually I found them, shortly after the Arusha conference in 1961. They appeared only in the form of snippets and fragments, no more than that. Women were absent and elsewhere and when men were described, they were generally lacking any specific identity. But these subalterns do indeed exist. At the risk of incurring some form of strain by endlessly pouring over the archives, we can therefore give them a name thanks to which it will be easier for us to imagine life in the village, the new global, postcolonial life of Tekelakay, Mengest, Serateña, Dehaw and Yemiyastekaklew.

Tekelakay, or how to resist

Of all the people living in the national parks and their surrounding areas, nobody gets mentioned as often as Tekelakay. In progress reports, autobiographical accounts or correspondence, whenever a document touches on the issue of 'local people', he is the first to be cited. Although this rebel leaves more of a mark in the archives than his neighbours, he is not representative of the general attitude. But he embodies a certain mindset, an atmosphere of refusal in the face of the new conservation laws.

Protest on a daily basis

All the Tekelakays of the Awash made it perfectly clear to Peter Hay when he arrived in their valley at the beginning of 1966 that although the old guard of colonial Uganda intended to expel them from the park, they were determined to remain. So much so, that in the middle of the summer certain agro-pastoralists caused him to fear a 'blood bath'. And, as a result, since Hay was unable to get any additional support from Addis Ababa, their eviction was delayed.[36] Then, in November, the

Karayu and the Ittu embarked on their transhumance towards the west. The guards saw this as a glimmer of hope, but the truce was short-lived. A week later, Afar herdsmen arrived in the park accompanied by several hundred cows. A number of Ittu and Karayu groups also returned in the month of December[37] and, in March 1967, most of the agro-pastoralists of the valley returned to the park after the first rains of the year. Some of them grazed their cattle, others also set about constructing *tukul* – small houses made out of wood and mud. They planned to live there for a few months so as to harvest the barley and sorghum they had sowed, after carrying out their annual burning programme.[38]

Most of them were nevertheless forcibly expelled in April 1967 before any of that could happen and, as a result, an increasing number of local people refused to comply with the conservation laws. It mattered little whether these laws were imposed by the state, UNESCO or the IUCN, these people had decided to follow in the footsteps of Tekelakay. Sometimes their resistance was passive, as in Sebober, a village situated in the north of the park where, throughout the month of April, the local people assured the warden that they would leave the next day – and simply failed to do so. At the same time, a little further to the east, in the direction of the Kassem river, on the other side of the park borders, other herdsmen continued to move into the protected areas with their livestock. The guards told them repeatedly that pastoralism was now forbidden, but they claimed not to have seen any boundary markers.[39] Then, confronted with increased insistence on the part of the scouts, their resistance gradually became more and more active.

The first sign of this was evident in June. Around thirty Afar herdsmen led their herd towards Mount Fentale, in the centre of the park. All of them were armed with rifles – the weapons used to protect their livestock from predators and to warn off the *shifta*, or 'bandits' who organized regular raids in the region. But, in June 1967, instead of bandits, the herdsmen encountered a patrol of scouts led by Peter Hay and Clive Nicol, the warden of the Simien Park who had come to visit his counterpart in the Awash. The Afar were ordered to turn back, but instead of complying with the request, they trained their weapons on these men from Addis Ababa. The standoff lasted for several long minutes until the guards finally left, taking with them a young herdsman whom they took to the police post in Metehara. The rest of the troupe continued on their way to Fentale, rifles on their shoulders, wooden staffs in their hands and the herd of cows in front of them.[40] The young man was released a few hours later, but the Afar remained angry. In the following days, they destroyed any boundary markers they encountered on their route. And, on 17 June, when a patrol attempted to arrest them, this time guns were fired. No one was injured, and the three herdsmen arrested were released that same evening. But the following day several men beat up a camp guard from Fiua, before proceeding to make off with all the livestock belonging to the scouts including the sheep they kept as a food source and the mules they used to get around within the park. 'The red line has been crossed', wrote Peter Hay.[41]

Indeed, after that incident, tension flared on a daily basis between Tekelakay and the warden, between the rebels and the scouts. In the middle of the summer of 1967 the Karayu and the Ittu were once again grazing their livestock in the park.[42] At the beginning of the autumn, on the plains of Ilala Sala, in the south of the Awash, the Afar came back from the salt deserts of eastern Ethiopia along with the hundred camels needed to transport their harvest of amoles (the 500 gram bars of salt which serve as currency in the region). Then, once again, the Karayu began burning and cultivating the land, building *tukul* and allowing their herds to use the reservoirs built by the park guards as watering holes for the zebras and antelopes in the Awash Park.[43] Finally, certain agro-pastoralists threatened to carry out retaliation on any scouts seeking to punish them. The scouts demanded the authorization to 'shoot in self-defence'. But the imperial administration refused any such privilege, a situation which would drive the warden into a paroxysm of rage.[44]

In March 1968, prompted by Hay and his scouts, the governor of Metehara ordered all the inhabitants to leave the park. The Karayu and the Ittu made some semblance of complying but in fact they simply brought forward their departure for transhumance. Then, on their return two months later, in May 1968, they pulled down the enormous sign announcing the 'Awash National Park' which the scouts had erected at the entrance to the park, attaching it to a tree at a height of 6 metres above ground level. It was at this point that Peter Hay lost his temper. He launched a violent attack against the herdsmen, their children, their houses and their crops. With the result that in June the local people were successful in bringing him before the tribunal in Metehara.[45] But the warden did not have to account for his actions. Major Gizaw had the charges against him dropped and he would remain in the Awash for a further year, during which a strange status quo was established. On the one hand, the agro-pastoralists regularly threatened the scouts with their rifles and, on many occasions, threw stones at their cars. And on the other hand, the expatriate warden deplored the 'repeating incidents', in particular with reference to the arrest 'of the youngest, some [of whom are] hot-headed who need to be kept in check'. Then, since no one could claim victory, violence became the tacit rule of the cohabitation.[46] That was at least the impression the Karayu and the Ittu gave to the new warden, John Bromley. When this British warden arrived in the Awash at the end of summer 1969, he found 'several thousand people' in the park. And the same global game was repeated once again with a cycle of expulsions, returns and regular outbursts of violence. Encounters with Others increasingly resembled a standoff.[47]

To each their power

For Tekelakay, living in the park seemed therefore to involve living in a state of rebellion, in the Awash and, almost certainly, in the Omo too. George Brown, the warden, devoted almost all his reports to the wildlife of the park. The former commissioner of British Kenya described the park's antelopes (the waterbuck and the lesser and greater kudu), its buffalos, oryx, elephants and a few lions. In contrast, little mention is made of its inhabitants. Except that, at the beginning of 1966, when the park first erupted into their daily lives, the Surma and the Mursi sent a distinctive message of refusal to the representatives from Addis Ababa, all dressed up in their military uniforms, a reminder of the time when their lands had been conquered by the Ethiopian empire at the end of the nineteenth century. Brown and the park scouts arrived in the Omo in February 1966. In March they informed the transhumant agro-pastoralists of the valley that hunting was forbidden from then on. And on 13 April, in the vicinity of Mui, where the park headquarters had just been built, local people shot a dozen antelope. And they did not even pick up the carcasses, instead leaving them to rot in the sun.[48]

The gesture was all the more eloquent given that in normal times the Surma did not hunt with guns. The following year, in March 1967, they explained this to George Brown, with the help of an interpreter sent from the capital 'to explain to them the new regulations'. At the beginning of the transhumance period, they told the warden, when they settled on a plain for several months, every evening they would set wire snares all around their camp. If they were successful in catching an animal, they would have meat which could be dried in order to provide food for several weeks, as well as one or more skins which they would sell on to traders in the region, in exchange for domestic animals or guns.[49] The Surma were still engaged in this kind of hunting in 1968, in spite of the ban which was pointed out to them with increasing frequency. As a result, they were regularly arrested by the park scouts, before being released by the police, who allowed them to leave with the spoils of their hunting.[50]

The guards were determined to conserve the fauna, and the inhabitants of the park were equally determined to continue to exploit it. Consequently, as in the Awash Park, tensions flared. In August 1969, on the western bank of the Omo, some Surma opened fire on a patrol of scouts they had caught dismantling the wire traps set the previous day. The episode was repeated on several further occasions and each time the guards responded more brutally. Until, on 16 November, they shot dead a Surma caught in the act of 'poaching'.[51] Retaliation followed swiftly. Ten days later, the killer was in turn murdered, with a blow from a spear. It was on this note that a brutal status quo was then established.[52] This was evident on several occasions, such as in March 1970 when a Mursi was struck by a bullet shot by a park guard while grazing his herd on the other side of the river. The elders of the group accepted the explanation proffered by George Brown, according to which the scout 'accidentally discharged his gun while cleaning it', But in exchange, the Mursi demanded compensation of 120 Ethiopian dollars – in other words the equivalent of two months of a scout's salary. Half was paid to them in money, the other in sorghum seeds.[53]

No nature without violence

Tekelakay endured and continued to wield the same kind of power in the Simien. However, in northern Ethiopia there seemed to be no possibility of negotiation between those who cultivated the land and those who protected it. The same intensification of tension was evident from 1966 onwards, immediately after the creation of the park. And after 1969, just as in the Awash and the Omo parks, the local people began to demonstrate their resistance openly, and with resort to force.

In May, in the very heart of the park, several men took up position on the Enatye plateau, at an altitude of 3,900 metres, and fired shots at the house belonging to the zoologist Bernhard Nievergelt, built a little further down the mountain, just above the village of Gich. Sent by the WWF to study the walia ibex, the famous wild goat endemic to the Simien Mountains, Nievergelt understood that day why Clive Nicol, the young warden of the park, never went anywhere without the revolver he carried in his belt.[54] And his fears intensified a month later, in June 1969, when the inhabitants of Gich vented their anger on Tag Demment, a Peace Corps volunteer sent to the Simien in order to help Nicol. Demment had hit an adolescent who was cutting eucalyptus, and, at nightfall on the same day, he was beaten up by three men who had been lying in wait, hidden behind his tent.[55] A few farmers also decided to abandon their land for a day, to allow them time to make their way through all the valleys of the park and destroy the boundary posts put in place by the scouts.[56] The operation was largely unsuccessful since the guards systematically followed in their footsteps and a few days later, the same signage was once again back in place along the Simien trails.[57] Which is why, at the beginning of 1970, several mountain dwellers opted for a more radical solution. Rifles at the ready, they climbed to the summit of the cliffs where the walia were generally to be found and shot every single animal dead. For the local people the message was clear: no more walia, no more park.[58]

Perhaps it was the sheer brutality of the gesture which persuaded the Ethiopian state to suspend their expulsion – we do not know. Nevertheless, Tekelakay's dramatic action meant that the several thousand inhabitants of the Simien had gained a moment of respite – they could still occupy their houses and keep their fields. But they were not exempt from the ban on grazing their livestock or from the fines or confiscation of their crops and firewood. Confronted with the park laws, some agro-pastoralists still kept up a strong resistance: by setting fire to the forests they were forbidden to access, as in Ambaras, in 1972;[59] or by attacking foreign tourists who had come to visit their mountains, as in Sankaber, in 1976;[60] or by shooting at patrols of guards, and eventually fatally injuring one of them, as in Arkwaziye, in September 1979.[61] That last event represented the peak of peasant resistance but also, subsequently, the climax of the repression. Two months later, across the entire country, the Marxist regime of the *Derg* was finally able to organize a retaliation against its opponents, which, in the Simien, meant the expulsion of 1,200 inhabitants and the destruction, by fire, of the seven villages they occupied.[62]

Tekelakay was defeated but, wherever he was, he did not lose without putting up a fight. When the Eritrean and Tigray rebels went underground in the Simien in 1981, the people who had been expelled took advantage of the situation to return to their mountains and to destroy as much of the park as they could: signage, scout camps, tourist areas.[63] The same scenario was played out in the country's two other national parks. In 1978, in the Awash, the authorities had this time expelled Afar, Karayu and Ittu pastoralists on a massive scale and in the Omo, the *Derg* had intensified control over hunting and agro-pastoralism – so much so that, at the end of 1979, when Ethiopia found itself engulfed in civil war, agro-pastoralists from the Omo and Awash parks set fire to each of the savannah areas they left behind in the course of their transhumance.[64] Tekelakay did not of course win the battle. But since his world had started to be governed by the new conservation laws – those of the postcolonial era – he had demonstrated to the leaders and to the experts that their power was by its very nature, limited.

Mengest, the local big man

The first people to exercise this power were the scouts who patrolled the national parks. There were about twenty-five of them in the Omo, the same number in the Awash, and thirty or so in the Simien. In the first two parks, where the agro-pastoralists practised transhumance, the personnel tended to come from Addis Ababa, whereas in the Simien Park, most of the guards were recruited from amongst the local inhabitants, and were a settled population. At least, in the absence of any other evidence, that is what the archives tell us. Clive Nicol nevertheless provides us with a useful entry point. Having arrived in the Simien in 1967 as a replacement for the American warden Laurence Guth, the young British warden found himself plunged into a nightmare which lasted for more than two years – a nightmare largely stemming from the 'backward' peasants, and in particular from Nadew Woreta.

Exerting power over nature and over the neighbours

In his 1972 account of his Ethiopian experience, Nicol described Woreta as someone who 'had exhorted money and taken bribes', accusing him of being 'a liar and a thief' and even referring to him as 'a big fart', making it in the end impossible for us to rely on his testimony[65] – at least as far as the facts go since, thanks to this account, written very much from life, we sense that in fact Nadew and Nicol were quite similar in several ways. Like Nicol, for this former imperial dignitary, protecting nature meant exercising power. It was even a way of becoming the legitimate holder of that power.

A former soldier under the empire, then a district administrator in northern Ethiopia, and finally warden of the Simien Park, Nadew found himself quickly ousted by the new postcolonial conservation experts, all of whom were foreigners. First with Guth, in 1966, and then Nicol in 1967, the *farenji* had robbed him of his title of 'warden'. Continuing to work in the park but simply in the role of a scout or 'guard', Nadew then became involved in trafficking skins and hunting trophies, and, in 1969, he embarked on his campaign to enter the national parliament as the representative of the people of the Simien, promising them to do his utmost to ensure that the park would disappear.[66] This about-turn might seem radical but in reality, this man was in quest of stability – his goal was always to remain powerful, to be the 'holder of power', the *mengest*.

Nadew had known Tamrat Yigezu since 1935. They had met on the battlefield, fighting against the Italians. Promoted to the rank of captain at the age of nineteen, Tamrat had since climbed to the highest ranks of the imperial administration, but he had never forgotten his former comrade in arms. When he became governor of the province of Begemder, he made Nadew 'Warden of the Walia' in March 1965. In this job, Nadew made every effort to keep a close eye on the inhabitants of the Simien.[67] Even when he was replaced by Guth, and even after Guth's departure, Nadew still continued to do so – Major Gizaw had ordered him in person 'to continue to protect the region'. With the help of scouts recruited in Ambaras, his native village, he travelled from valley to valley as tax collector, wildlife warden and hunter, selling for high prices a handful of wild animal skins and walia horns to traders from the capital.[68]

Then Nicol came along, and Nadew continued to exert his power over his neighbours. This involved protection – anyone bringing an antelope, a leopard or a walia to Nadew and his scouts would be rewarded with a sheep, and a guarantee of being allowed to graze his herds freely.[69] It also involved extortion – the scout who refused to give part of his salary to Nadew was threatened with a transfer to the low-lying lands of the Awash or, worse, to the Omo in the extreme south of the country.[70] Finally, since this local power came to him from above, Nadew had to appear both threatening and loyal to the state. This was particularly striking at the beginning of 1969. In response to requests from Nicol, the Conservation Department decided to transfer Nadew to the Omo. But Nadew immediately made use of his connections. First, Major Gizaw learned that one of Nadew's brothers was inciting the Simien peasants to rally against the park: 'The government wants to sell the land to a foreigner', he told them.[71] Then it was the turn of General Mebratu to receive a letter from the governor of Begemder. Tamrat Yigezu informed him that, along with other dignitaries of the region, he was one of the people who had co-opted Nadew so as to enable him to enter politics. And now it was a done deal; now that the first 'Warden of the Walia' had a seat in the national parliament in Addis Ababa, he would fight against this park 'managed by foreigners'. And he, Tamrat, would support him in this combat, unless the Conservation Department agreed to guarantee the new deputy that a suitable post would await him in the Simien at the end of his tenure.[72] And so, after three years spent in the capital, Nadew returned to his mountains, his head held high.

As a result of these negotiations, which ranged from the local to the international, Nadew was named 'governor of the Simien district' in 1973.[73] Very quickly, he proved his commitment to conservation by letting the national authorities know that he had burned down new houses built within the park, and that he was going to 'personally sanction' the farmers who had cleared new areas of land.[74] Did Nadew really enforce this new legislation, or did he instead subvert the conservationist laws in order to claim even more power for himself? The archives remain silent on this matter, but it is highly likely that he continued to exert his domination over the inhabitants of the park. In any case, in the east and the south of the country, this was exactly what the employees of the Omo and Awash parks were doing.

Conserve, oversee and punish

In these two parks, there were neither locally recruited staff nor a powerful figure whose authority was already recognized. Nevertheless, wherever they were sent, the guards arriving from the capital were men with power vested in them by the state to control and to sanction. Consequently, as soon as they began working for the national park, they too expected to gain a minimum amount of power.

In the Awash, some of them sought to move up through the hierarchy. This was evident in the case of two brothers, scouts whose names were never known but whose traces can be found in the reports produced by park personnel. These inform us that, in February 1967, the two brothers were brought in front of a 'disciplinary commission' in Addis Ababa, because they had refused to obey the orders of an assistant warden who wanted them to cut down some acacia trees in order to clear the landing strip for the park.[75] Because he wanted to be Mengest, the assistant warden insisted the men be sanctioned. They owed him obedience, he said, because they were 'simple scouts only'. The proof? Just like the British warden, the assistant warden also slept alone in his *tukul*, and not, like them, in bunk beds in a communal hut.[76]

Disputes could therefore develop between the Ethiopian staff of the park. But, confronted with a foreigner, they seemed to adopt a united front. So, for example, as soon as Peter Hay arrived in the Awash and tried to employ 'local' staff, the scouts went on strike. They too were 'local' they informed the warden, and most importantly, they represented the Mengest, in that particular instance, the power of the imperial state.[77] It was in this context, that in March 1967, when the two rebellious brothers came back to the Awash, without any sanction whatsoever being imposed on them, they threatened Peter Hay – if he did not move them to a better camp, they would not carry out any of the tasks that he planned to impose on the 'empire civil servants'.[78] Did the Mengest brothers obtain satisfaction? Once again, we do not know. We do know however that they enforced the same state power over the inhabitants of the Awash Park by forcing the Karayu to pay them for the right to graze their animals,[79] or by selling back to a group of Afar the carcass of an antelope they had killed in the park, but whose skin they could not try to sell in Metehara.[80]

After the Arusha conference, becoming a park guard ultimately meant being able to wield power over others. The limited amount of information available about the Omo Park confirms this. In 1966, a certain Zeleke Asfaw took part in an ecological survey carried out by cadets from Sandhurst, the British Royal Military Academy. The team entered the Omo Park and, once inside, Zeleke tried to stab one of the cadets – in order to stop him killing a wild animal, as he explained in his defence in the report he produced of the incident.[81] The following year it was the turn of a scout called Tessema Tulu to resort to violence, this time against an adolescent from the Omo valley whom he threatened with his rifle, before hitting him with the butt.[82] Then, in 1968, we learn that the Conservation Department had devised a new strategy in their attempt to put an end to the 'poaching' carried out by the Surma. From then on, every scout who succeeded in confiscating a trophy from them would receive a 'reward'. In January, for example, seven guards received 30 Ethiopian dollars each for organizing an ambush of Surma people and seizing merchandise estimated to be worth 3,000 dollars on the black market – twelve leopard skins and a cheetah skin.[83]

For these scouts, who referred to those living in the Omo Park as 'savage tribes' and 'animists' who had remained 'on the edge of civilization',[84] the conservationist mission was therefore both civilizing and lucrative. But it was also exhausting. That was at least the argument advanced in July 1969 by a guard accused of having beaten his wife on returning home after a day on patrol, and then of attacking the scouts who had attempted to restrain him. This life in a 'wasteland' for a 'salary of fifty dollars per month' was pushing him to the limits[85] was the defence pleaded by this Mengest, who though he had only limited power, seemed nevertheless to be exerting it over anyone with even less power than himself – the transhumant agro-pastoralists, his colleagues, his wife.

Serateña, invisible employee

Some people chose to work for the park because the job entailed increased authority. This was the case for Nadew Woreta. Perhaps it was also true for the assistant wardens and even for certain scouts, sometimes called 'guards'. But most of them were simply doing their job and seizing the opportunity represented by this new position of 'park guard'. It was however a risky calculation because at the beginning of the postcolonial era, in an East African country like Ethiopia, the job offered little in the way of material advantages.

The park and precarity

In 1966, for example, when the future scouts for the Omo Park left Addis Ababa, the Conservation Department provided them with only a shirt, a pair of trousers and a pair of shoes, all of which needed to last for a year, in line with the rules. Then, once they arrived in the park, more than 600 kilometres south of the capital, their monthly salary of 50 Ethiopian dollars was only enough to buy food (in comparison, an official like Gizaw earned 700 dollars per month, and an expatriate like Blower, 1,500 dollars).[86] This situation led George Brown, their warden, to remark that the scouts were 'somehow miserable'.[87] But that was characteristic of an insecure job – the person concerned did not live *well*, he or she merely lived *better* than if they did not have a job at all. Which is why the scouts were ready to compile surveys of the wild animals and to supervise the local people, but also to build their own huts, to dig latrines or to asphalt dirt tracks.[88] They had done all that in the 1960s and they continued to do so in the mid-1970s,[89] in the Omo and elsewhere.

In the Simien Mountains, the archives offer a glimpse of similar fragments of lives, like, for example, that of Atekelet Ferede, a scout in the park. His family lived in Asmara, the capital of the Eritrean province, situated 450 kilometres further north, and in March 1968, the park administration agreed to pay his travel costs for a journey he needed to make in order to attend his daughter's funeral. For even if his monthly salary for that year had increased from 50 to 60 dollars, he was still a simple 'employee' a *seratéña*.[90] This applied to the majority of scouts and, in particular, to the mass of invisible inhabitants under their super-vision. One day, they might be taken on to help with the construction of the warden's house.[91] Another day might see them helping the guards install boundary markers along the tracks.[92] Many of those living in the Simien seemed to work for the park on a regular basis, a situation which enabled them to supplement their subsistence economy with some form of income.

The reports written by Guth, Nicol and their successors tell us very little about these activities but, in the Awash, those written by Peter Hay are sufficiently detailed to provide a clearer picture. It is not however a particularly fascinating one, even verging on the tedious at times, but perhaps this is precisely the definition of the everyday lives of Seratéña since 'African nature' first made its appearance.

The first report of the Scottish warden Peter Hay dates from April 1966 and the anonymous workers already seemed omnipresent. Near the Awash Falls, some of these had cleared the land where the first campsite in the park was to be built. They were now building a visitor centre and two residential buildings, the first for Hay, 'a house made of four rooms with concrete floors and a large veranda with mosquito netting', and a second for the scouts, 'one house with five rooms each 3 x 4 metres'. A little further east, others were clearing trees from the site which would serve as the airport for visitors. Hay describes how, in the space of a month, on a strip of land measuring 900 metres long by 40 metres wide, 'every thick Acacia has been cut down'. 'A thankless hot job to which the coolies stuck very well', he wrote, using a term inherited from India and reappropriated by European colonists settled in Asia. And, finally, Seratéña was busy gathering reeds for use in constructing the roofs of the scouts' living quarters.[93] Seratéña's life continued to be organized around these occasional jobs: drilling in order to construct reservoirs, masonry work for the entrance gate of the park, tree cutting along the road which led from Addis Ababa or plumbing to install running water for the campsites. Seratéña would perhaps not have chosen the park but he, or she, was determined to take advantage of whatever it could offer.[94]

The nameless missing

In that year of 1966, many local people found themselves involved in this new enterprise of the 'national park'. This was indeed part of the Scottish warden's strategy, a way 'to sweeten the pill of the soon-to-come eviction'.[95] But, as the months went by, a certain resentment began to spread amongst the Seratéña. When Haile Selassie made a visit to the Awash in December 1966, they spent an entire week cleaning the main camp, from the latrines to the hippopotamus enclosure situated near the park entrance. However, only a few days before the emperor's visit, they learned that they, 'like everyone', were to be expelled. They voiced their anger to the scouts and the warden, and the latter avoided their questions by promising to give them work on a more regular basis,[96] with the result that at the beginning of 1967, the Serateña had once again had their faith in the park restored. In February, Haile Selassie launched the Awash Valley Authority, his grand project involving dam building and irrigation, and again they provided the majority of the labour involved.[97] In March, Peter Hay recruited energetically in order to finish the construction of a new campsite near the Djibouti–Addis Ababa railroad,[98] and then, at the beginning of April, in the Sabober camp, a group of Karayu and Ittu built three *tukul*, some toilets and a kitchen, a shed to house the mules, a hut for the scouts and a reservoir. Yet the guards expelled them two weeks later. This time any sense of equilibrium was shattered.[99]

A few agro-pastoralists still continued to hire out their labour to the administration. In 1968, some of them were involved in painting the façade of the new museum dedicated to the wildlife and flora of the Awash.[100] In 1969, a few people responded to the call from the new warden, John Bromley, who needed workers for various tree-cutting and construction jobs.[101] But, with the exception of these two episodes, since the expulsion of April 1967, the archives seem mostly to indicate the disappearance of Serateña. Could it be that he or she had now joined those actively demonstrating their resistance to the park by attacking its staff and its infrastructures? This was certainly indicated by the scouts who complained that they now had to erect the park boundary markers on their own, a task all the more difficult at this point since they needed to be fixed in concrete because, they reported, more and more local people were uprooting them.[102] Could Serateña have joined forces with Tekelakay? It is highly likely. In any case he, or she, had now joined the ranks of the majority represented by their neighbour – Dehaw.

Dehaw, the poor man

Dehaw makes his first appearance in the archives at the beginning of the 1960s, after the Arusha event. All the speakers at the conference agreed on a single ideal – the need for enclosed natural spaces which would be protected from their inhabitants. For people like Dehaw this meant that life in the village was about to change. When colonization came to an end and a new era of conservation began, those living in the parks were the only ones whose daily lives were genuinely transformed. It was a transformation which would herald the arrival on the scene of a key figure in postcolonial conservation – that of the poor man or woman, the *dehaw* in Amharic. This is the conclusion revealed by the archives if we are prepared to embark on a slow perusal of one archive after another, from one park to another.

Surviving in 'nature'

Still in the Awash, it is clear that, for the majority of the local people, living in a protected area meant submission. From the moment the park came into being, Dehaw was forced first of all to submit to the law. The trouble began in January 1966 when the Conservation Department sent its staff to meet the owner of the Ras Hotel to discuss the construction of 'safari lodges' in the park. The same staff also began to draw up plans for the displacement of the agro-pastoralists and their livestock.[103] The operation finally took place a year later, in April 1967, and Peter Hay was delighted to see that 'for the first time, the Park begins to resemble a park'. But Dehaw's experience was somewhat different – he had seen his village, and that of his neighbours, go up in smoke, burned to the ground by the scouts. The guards had moved them to the western side of the river, and this time, any possibility of return seemed unlikely. Particularly since in Filua, on the eastern bank of the park, near their former grazing lands, the warden had organized the construction of a camp for the scouts which was intended to 'prevent them from crossing back over'.[104] Dehaw tried hard to circumvent this strategy. The following month, a little further south, he was part of a group of around twenty herdsmen who were leading some 400 cows towards Mount Fentale when they were stopped by guards and escorted out of the park with their herds.[105] And since that time, Dehaw encountered the guards constantly. In the month of July alone, he ran into two patrols. On the first occasion he managed to flee with his cattle,[106] but on the second, gunfire from the scouts forced him to run off leaving his animals behind. His herd was 'confiscated', then led out of the park and abandoned.[107]

Dehaw had to submit to the state law, and reading Peter Hay, it is clear that he also had to put up with the contempt of the person enforcing it. Take, for example, one of the reports from the Scottish warden, written in February 1968, 'A lot of talking was needed', wrote Hay referring to the eviction of 'nearly one thousand people and about six thousand head of cows and camels'. 'It is absolutely essential we keep them out for the next two months until the rainy season ends', he added. 'Then they will understand' that the damp grazing areas in the park no longer belong to them, and 'they will end up accepting it for the future'. Did the warden really believe that? Was he genuinely convinced that coercion would persuade a pastoralist to accept the existence of the park? For us, this question is an important one – but Hay did not see it in the same terms. For Dehaw took up barely more than a few lines of his report. The 'two highlights of the month', according to the warden, were the hatching of eleven ostrich eggs in the plains of Ilala Sala, and the sighting of sixteen zebras in the area around Mount Fentale.[108] Dehaw could not compete with this untamed nature. Instead, he was a disruptive element, who had found himself in the equation in spite of himself. And if he had not already understood this, he would no longer be in any doubt in June 1968 when he found himself a victim of the warden's violence – blows raining down on him and his children, bullets killing his sheep and his camels, and then the fire which destroyed his crops and his house.[109]

Finally, as well as the violence of the law and the contempt which accompanied it, there was also a sense of incoherence. This was sometimes short-term, as in February 1968, when the thousand or so evicted agro-pastoralists had to abandon pasturelands providing grazing and water for their flocks, only to find themselves 20 kilometres further away, on land which, at that time of the year, had completely dried out. Then, in the autumn, when Dehaw decided to return to the original pasture, the sense of incoherence became even more obvious. The scouts once again forced him back to the other side of the river – he was obliged to accept defeat. Except that now he could no longer leave his flock on the substitute pastureland, even though this was, after all, where the scouts had moved both him and his livestock. But the governors of Awash and of Metehara both refused to accept the evicted pastoralists, and the latter found themselves blocked outside the park, with no authorization to settle there.[110]

Submitting to injustice

This kind of incoherence veered towards the absurd and, ultimately, became mired in inequalities. This became particularly striking when, at the end of February 1969, the eviction of the inhabitants of the Awash, up until then localized and gradual, suddenly became large scale and rapid. In two or three days at the most, with the help of scouts who had arrived as backup from Addis Ababa, the park guards expelled all the agro-pastoralists. Which meant that, on 4 March, the president of the WWF could be welcomed to a park which was naturally *empty*, where no one noticed that it had in fact been *emptied* of its inhabitants. The operation was a media success and since the visit, a growing number of visitors had flocked to the park gates. Dehaw himself, however, no longer had the right to enter. But, from that time onwards, each month he would see some 500 tourists visiting the park. And, since necessity knows no laws, if the opportunity came up, he would agree to go hunting in order to sell their guides, from the company Safaris International, the meat from the animals that he had previously hunted to provide food for himself.[111] His living environment had become a space for visitors and was becoming less and less accessible to him as the days went by.

In the Simian too, Dehaw found himself forced to submit in much the same way. Since the park had first been established, he had become a victim of the law which forbade him from constructing a *tukul* for his son, now an adult.[112] He was also an object of contempt to Nicol, the young British warden, who accused him of 'the destruction of the habitat' and criticized 'the inability of the peasants to see what they were doing'.[113] He also suffered from the absurdity of this 'conservation' which forbade him from throwing stones at gelada baboons – simply because the tourists enjoyed seeing them. Instead, he was obliged to let them root about on his land in quest of the tiniest blade of grass, the staple food of the baboons.[114] In short, the same moral code brought with it the same injustice, in the truest sense of the term. It meant being deprived of the rights which other people benefited from (those who lived outside the park), in the name of an ethic defined by others (the western experts and the Ethiopian managers).[115]

In the Simien, for Dehaw, injustice began with the arrival of the postcolonial experts in 1963. And ten years later, it permeated his daily existence. First, he was deprived of the right to hunt the gelada and the walia, and even the foxes and hyenas which might attack him. Only those in possession of a permit could kill them, which in practice meant that only a few foreigners were authorized to hunt. Generally, in the Simien, these were accompanied by Ted Shatto, the director of Safaris International, with whose help certain tourists even managed to return home with a walia.[116] This was the case of the British hunter James Mellon, in the early 1970s. Accompanied by Shatto and by Yeinatter, a local guide who had hunted with Nadew a few years earlier, Mellon managed to kill a walia, the 'supremely covetable prize' in his view. Yeinatter expressed his annoyance. 'Besides, why are you foreigners allowed to shoot the walia, when we are not?' he snapped at Mellon, who replied angrily: 'Listen, if you keep shooting walia … you may even be resettled in another part of the country.'[117] But we understand why Mellon chose not to reply that here, as in the other national parks of Africa, only African elites or well-to-do and wealthy whites could join the ranks of *hunters*. If anyone else killed an animal, all the Dehaws like him would be considered to be *poachers*. For according to the rules of postcolonial conservation, they could no longer claim the right to hunt.

Then, Dehaw had to face another of his rights being challenged – that of exploiting the land. Here too, the deprivation began in the very first days of the park's existence. But it intensified in 1970. By then, the national administration was sufficiently organized to achieve its objectives, and from that time onwards, in each valley of the Simien, markers clearly indicated the 'inside' and the 'outside' of the park, or in other words the free area and the protected area.[118] For Dehaw, in real terms, that meant that when he drove his flock along a mule track which coincided with the park boundary, his sheep and goats could graze to the right of the track (therefore outside the park), but when his animals wandered onto the lefthand side of the track (therefore inside the park), he would have to pay a fine were he to encounter the warden. The demarcation also applied to the forest. When he had installed his flock on a relatively large pastureland (on the edge of the park), Dehaw had time to go and cut eucalyptus (in the park). Ideally, he would bring two bundles of wood back on his mule, one to heat his house and to use for cooking, the other to sell in town at the end of the week. The problem was that the eucalyptus forests were to be found either in the park itself or roughly 10 kilometres away. If Dehaw wanted to respect the law, or simply avoid a fine, he needed to do a great deal of walking. Yet if he left his flock for too long, he would run the risk of losing an animal, and if he abandoned the idea of the second bundle it meant losing a supplementary income essential to his survival. Dehaw therefore opted for illegality and continued to cut wood within the park. At least until he received the first warning from a scout who caught him red-handed. He knew he would not get a second chance that week. So, instead of paying a fine, or being arrested, he simply tightened his belt.[119]

Being deprived

Poverty lay in wait for all those living in the park. The managers and the expatriates were well aware of this, yet they still continued to reinforce the conservation laws. In 1972, in all the national parks of the country, the empire officially banned hunting, deforestation, pastoralism, agriculture and habitation.[120] Then, a few months after the revolution in 1975, when the leaders of the *Derg* once again took up the baton in the race for world heritage status, they decided to apply the law even more strictly. As a result, fines became systematic and were fixed at a higher rate.[121] Finally, in 1976, the rationale behind African conservation was extended to its limits. The ideal was one of unspoilt nature with no human presence, and so, on the advice of Colonel John Stephenson, the former guard from colonial Tanganyika, the Ethiopian state decreed the 'exclusion of all human interference' in every one of the country's parks.[122]

The operation began in July 1979 in the Awash, and then, in November, in the Simien, where 1,200 inhabitants saw their homes burnt to the ground in Tirwata, Tiya, Dirni, Muchila, Antola, Agedemya and Amba Ber.[123] Of course, in reality, many agro-pastoralists went on living in their homes, on their land, which they continued to exploit. But from that point onwards, they did so illegally because, in both the Simien and the Awash, they had been deprived of the right to live on the land, and trapped in poverty in a way which was now perfectly legal. For this was indeed the reality of their situation. 'Being poor does not simply mean possessing nothing, or little, or less than another. Being poor means being deprived.'[124] This definition, proposed by Heidegger, justifies the attribution of the nickname Dehaw to the inhabitants of the parks of the Awash and the Simien, as well as to those of the Omo.

While the archives have almost nothing to say about the most ordinary inhabitants of this last park, they nevertheless prompt us to see them as other poor people, other Dehaws. For example, in 1967, the Mursi could see John Blower and his men sharing out the meat from an antelope they had just hunted – a hartebeest – something they themselves were forbidden to do, even though they lived there from day to day.[125] The Mursi still continued to hunt, but now, they regularly had to run away in order to avoid being sanctioned. The same was true of the Surma. When the latter spotted scouts, as a warden recounted in 1969, they were 'routinely crossing the river to escape'. Which meant that, for at least a few days, they had to leave their homes, their children, their relatives and their livestock.[126] Then, at the beginning of 1970, the presence of guards forced them to put a definitive stop to their migration towards Kenya, and therefore to abandon part of their annual transhumance route.[127]

The more time went by, the more the hardships accumulated. One day in 1972, unable to avoid the scouts, a group of Mursi had their wire snares confiscated – snares they had set in place the previous day in the area surrounding their camp, inside the park boundary. And the following day, a kilometre away from the same spot but outside the park, they saw the same scouts hunting the elands they had hoped to hunt themselves.[128] The following year, some Surma were punished with fines for cultivating land, yet they could see the assistant warden burning and working the land around his hut in Mui.[129] Finally, in 1976, a dozen Surma failed to prevent the scouts burning down their huts.[130] They subsequently rebuilt them, once again. But nevertheless, for them, just as for all the Dehaws of the Awash and the Simien, ever since their world became bound up with the universe of conservation, living in the park involved living in poverty since it meant suffering deprivation on a constant basis. They had never been rich, of course, but now 'nature' had ended up reinforcing their poverty and their precarity.

Yemiyastekaklew, the resourceful one

This intensification of power relations applied to everyone. Already unwilling to be subject to a central state, Tekelakay became a rebel. A powerful force in his village, Mengest now wanted to dominate the entire valley. An employee, Serateña now had two jobs. Already poor, Dehaw had become destitute. This was the impact of the postcolonial moment on the village, where daily life had to accommodate to an ever-growing number of ideas and practices – coming from the director of UNESCO, from the new minister, from the expatriate warden, from the scout or the peasant. The village had now become global, and whether they liked it or not, those who lived there would have to learn to accept it. Or, as Tesfa said about the young eucalyptus cutter, they could become 'resourceful'. Yemiyastekaklew is the final character glimpsed in the archives. Even more silent than usual on his account, they nevertheless reveal a few clues.

A thousand and one ways of adapting

The first of these clues come from the administrative file of a certain Amare Gebretsadik, a former Ethiopian soldier. For sixteen years, Amare worked in what he described as the 'deserts of the empire': Ogaden on the Somalian border, Omo to the north of Kenya, and Gambela on the Sudanese border. This military career explains why, in May 1965, the new Conservation Department employed him to train the scouts for the Omo Park. For over a year, Amare Gebretsadik taught them the 'military salute', the 'handling of weapons' and the techniques of 'arrest' and 'interrogation'. Then he was given leave to 'go off and cultivate his field'. The archives do not say where his land was. They do however reveal that Amare returned home taking with him money that belonged to the scouts he had been training. The man had promised that, as soon as he arrived in the capital, he would send them whatever it was they had asked for – knives, shoes, medicines. But the scouts never received anything. They complained to George Brown, who passed the information on to Addis Ababa and, by way of a sanction, Amare was demoted to the rank of a simple scout. It is in this capacity that we encounter him again in 1967, this time in the Simien. Here too, a guard had accused him of having stolen the pay of five other scouts, and made sure that Amare was deprived of a salary for five months – a manoeuvre remarkably similar to those invented by Nadew Woreta as a way of dominating his colleagues. The file on Amare Gebretsadik ends with a period of time spent in the

Awash, where he remained until 1971. Apparently, he was responsible for 'extorting money' from local people. But this was not the reason for his dismissal. He owed that to the expatriate warden, who was exasperated by his refusal to obey orders.[131]

The rebel (*tekelakay*), the holder of power (*mengest*), the employee (*serateña*), the poor one (*dehaw*), were all known to Amare. Not only because he came across them in each park where the new conservation took him. He knew them because he was himself one of them. Amare resisted the authority of the expatriates, he asserted himself over his colleagues, he worked for the park, cultivated the land to feed his family and, very often, found himself deprived of his salary, or of his status. As a result, depending on the context, or the moment, he would change role – he was Tekelakay and he was also Mengest, Serateña, Dehaw, because, in the end, he was Yemiyastekaklew the resourceful one, the one capable of adapting to this new postcolonial world. And there were many others who knew how to do the same thing. If we turn for a final time to the political scientist Jean-François Bayart and his theory of African extraversion, it is clear that when confronted with this externally imposed power, individuals resort to a whole range of strategies, ranging from 'cunning' to 'flight' and even to 'appropriation or its opposite, rejection'.[132]

Rejection sometimes erupted in a violent manner, in the form of shootings and even of murders, as we have seen in both the Simien and the Omo. But it was also a part of everyday life. So much so, that in the Awash, in 1973, the director of the Ethiopian Wildlife Conservation Organization resigned himself to simply accepting it. Since the Karayu, the Ittu and the Afar 'still refuse to acknowledge the park' Teshome Ashine wrote to his superiors, it was pointless to pursue them day after day. Waiting for the means to expel them all, the very international and diplomatic Teshome decided to allocate two grazing areas, one for the Karayu and the Ittu, in the western part of the park, and the other for the Afar, in the eastern part. By separating them in such a clear way, the administration would at least avoid the risk of seeing them join forces against it.[133]

The inhabitants could therefore reject the park space but, at the same time, they could also appropriate it for their own uses. In the Awash, for example, this was the case for the agro-pastoralists expelled from Filua in February 1968. When the Karayu and the Ittu realized that since their departure a moist, grassy savannah now covered the area they had used purely for agriculture, they decided to return there periodically to raise animals and, in order to do so, they integrated this former agricultural land into their new transhumance routes. So, at the end of that year, and much to the regret of Peter Hay, although the park space was no longer inhabited by Karayu and Ittu, it had become part of their 'grazing rotational cycle'.[134] Other means of appropriation were also found and sometimes these were even viewed in a positive light by the expatriate warden. This was the case, for example, in the Omo, in January 1968. When the Mursi and the Suri living some tens of kilometres from the park agreed to work for him, George Brown did not attempt to conceal his enthusiasm. With their help, he said, the expulsion of the Surma would be 'finally feasible'. In reality, the Suri and the Mursi had no intention of working for the cause of nature since they were only inter- ested in dominating the Surma. But if the park could serve their interests at that particular moment in time, they were happy to accept the offer.[135] This was a choice also made by other individuals for more personal reasons – like the man living in the Kefa province, near the Omo, who had become a volunteer in the park. In June 1970, he entered the park on his own. He surprised a group of 'poachers' whom he personally escorted to the police and then wrote to the Conservation Department asking to be taken on as a scout in the park.[136] The plan did not pay off but it is an indication of the range of strategies deployed by Yemiyastekaklew. Sly or smart, depending on the point of view – conservation had certainly forced him to become resourceful.

To each their story

Yemiyastekaklew rejected conservation or used it to his own advantage and then, very often, he tried to circumvent it. In the Simien, he attempted to do this on a daily basis, for example, by continuing to cut firewood. Clive Nicol forbade him from doing so and the scouts confiscated his bundles of wood on a regular basis. But when Gizaw Gedlegiorgis came to visit the park in June 1969, Yemiyastekaklew took advantage of the opportunity. Together with his neighbours he managed to speak to the major, in Amharic, in the presence of Nicol who was incapable of following the conversation. Gizaw would later claim that he had never given them permission 'to cut small trees', but for the moment, the inhabitants won the day – 'The major said so ... and we simply obey.'[137] With this argument they could continue to supply themselves with eucalyptus from the park.

Their respite did not last long. Six months later, the state reinforced the rules and Yemiyastekaklew was forced to play his final card and resort to trickery. In the Simien, he tried to discredit the expatriate warden. In December 1969, in an attempt to prevent Nicol from causing them any further harm, the inhabitants demanded and obtained an audience with the governor of Begemder. The *farenji* was not paying workers, they told him. He punished those who sold eggs in order to survive, and fired his rifle 'close to their ears' 'to frighten them'.[138] Did Nicol really resort to such violence? Here too, the answer does not really matter. Confronted with the power this foreigner had acquired, Yemiyastekaklew was clearly deploying all his powers of ingenuity. Sometimes he invented a rumour, or he tried to bypass the hierarchy. On other occasions he pretended he was unable to control his herd. This manoeuvre was particularly well-honed in the Awash. Since they no longer had the right to graze their animals in the park, early each morning the agro-pastoralists drove them to the entrance of the protected area, just outside the boundary markers. Some cracked their whips, others shot their rifles in the air, and the animals would then run away, heading into the park. They grazed there all day, until the evening, when the scouts finally managed to locate their owners who were then invited to go and recover their herds. Which they did, thanking the guards and apologizing profusely for the 'erratic behaviour of domestic animals'.[139] This was life in the new global village.

We could of course end this last story with a more general discussion, by highlighting, for example, the ever more closely interwoven strands of conservationist action, ranging from the local to the international and including the regional and national. But the nameless ones do not have the same history as the people who were determined to control their lives in the aftermath of the Arusha conference in 1961. It is true that they were increasingly taken into consideration. That was clear in 1975 in Kinshasa during the 12th General Assembly of the IUCN, when the American ecologist Raymond Dasmann called on his colleagues to recognize 'indigenous people' and to acknowledge 'the value and importance of traditional ways of life and the skills ... which enable them to live in harmony with their environment'.[140] It was clear once again in Washington in 1978, when the launch of the World Heritage List brought to a close the era of postcolonial conservation and introduced a new era of community conservation, the era of *Parks for People*.[141] History was played out in much the same way in the Congo or in the United States, but in the village, it was a very different story.

What, for example, at almost the same moment, were the occupants of the Awash Park doing? They were, quite simply, stealing fridges. The first was a park driver, the second his book-keeper, and in October 1977, with the help of a few local people these two nameless individuals stole the refrigerator which had been installed in the little museum destined for tourists at the entrance of the park. They proceeded to sell it to traders in Metehara, before being arrested by the police. With the result that, in September 1978, when UNESCO announced the launch of its 'World Heritage Sites', the two men were still in prison.[142] The event represents an insignificant page in the history of postcolonial conservation but this was the page they had written. From Europe and from North America, the expert gentlemen were busy theorizing about African overpopulation before it was too late. Throughout East Africa, former colonialists continued to save nature, come what may. In Ethiopia, for example, leaders used nature as a tool with which to govern a world-nation. And right at the bottom of the scale, in a park like the Awash, nameless people were stealing fridges.

Epilogue
A little nature, (far) too much humanity

Nature is missing. It should have been the subject of a fifth story, the last voice, that of the Virunga okapi, the Serengeti wildebeests, the Ugandan gorillas, or the Ethiopian ibex. How did these animals get through the postcolonial moment? What was it like for them in the midst of this maelstrom of frenzied human activity? While the question is an important one, it nevertheless results in considerable uncertainty. In order to understand how different ecologies evolved once confined within a park, we would need research focusing at one and the same time on the long term, on the vast territories involved and on all the fauna and flora to be found within them. The experts and the managers with responsibility for nature certainly carried out their own research, the results of which are consigned to the archives. They include inventories of a particular species (in one case, perhaps gorillas, in another wilde-beests), reports of a large mammal killed (on one occasion an elephant, on another a rhinoceros), within a particular park and on a particular date (an ecological survey in Serengeti in 1947 for example, or research carried out in the Murchison Park in 1978). Such investigations were real enough, but there were not enough of them, and, most importantly, they were not sufficiently exhaustive to provide us with any real conclusions.

So, what exactly do we know? In the decades following the post-war period, African levels of production and consumption were increasing and the non-human world was unmistakably under pressure from humans. But what about all the areas populated by agro-pastoralists surviving on a subsistence regime? In all those areas which were inhabited but where 'nature' was still very much present, what valid conclusions do the archives allow us to reach? In fact, we can salvage only one conclusion – notably that during the postcolonial moment which is our focus here (from the 1950s to the 1970s) nature policies corresponded not to the use individuals put them to but to the idea those individuals had of them. In other words, what mattered was not nature as it really was, but nature as people would have liked it to be – an untouched paradise for the expert gentlemen, a stronghold for animals for the ex-colonialists now converted into experts, a place of prestige or of profit for the leaders of the African states and, for each of these, a space empty of any inhabitants.

This was the ideal which had shaped the world of African conservation until the emergence of the notion of 'ecosystem people'. The expression was popularized by the American ecologist Raymond Dasmann. Dasmann first introduced it at Kinshasa in 1975, during the 12th General Assembly of the IUCN, and on his recommendation, the delegates at the conference approved a resolution 'recognising ... indigenous people' with their 'traditional' ways of living.[1] Dasmann further developed his thinking the following year. 'What we really need', he wrote for the Fauna Preservation Society, is '"conservation as if people mattered" and "development as if nature mattered".'[2] The conservationists quickly adopted this discourse and the IUCN put it into action, in its own way, in 1978. Alongside, amongst others, 'parks', natural 'monuments' and wildlife 'sanctuaries', the Union created a new category of protected areas which took the form of the 'anthropological reserve'. Given over to 'natural areas in which man is a component', the first of these reserves would be opened in Africa in the 1980s, with the official objective: 'to allow the way of life of societies living in harmony with the environment to continue undisturbed by modern technology'.[3]

The change of direction seems radical but in reality, with these 'ecosystem people', Dasmann was not inventing anything new. In 1953, when he was vice-president of the FPS, Charles Pitman had already included 'primitive man' as an element of African nature. 'With his primitive weapons and implements, [he] had little lasting effect on the zoological and biological world around him', wrote Pitman from British Kenya.[4] A little further west, in the Congo, the same reasoning led the Belgians to exclude the Hutu and the Tutsi from the Albert Park, while authorizing the 'Pygmies' to go on living there. For, unlike other peoples, these had remained in an almost wild state. This is the crucial factor, according to historian Raf de Bont in his research on this 'naturalization of "primitive people"'. At the end of the 1970s, the idea that the expert gentlemen had formulated of Africa ended up being extended to include the Africans themselves. Where humanized territories had been defined as 'untouched' and 'primeval', some of those living there were now seen as 'primitive' and 'original'. Naturalized in their turn, they would therefore obtain a place in the African national parks – if, and only if, their way of living did not interfere with the natural character of the areas in question.[5]

The change is only a small one but it is precisely developments of this kind which justify reference to a postcolonial moment, that is to say, to an event in its own right. If colonization was indeed synonymous with a whole range of encounters, the fact remained that, between governors and governed, 'there has never been a marriage', as the famous Algerian writer Mouloud Feraoun observed. 'There was still a choice to be made', he wrote, 'and they made it.' For the colonizers and the colonized it mattered little whether there was exploitation, struggle or submission, since between them there existed what was essentially a 'mutual indifference'.[6] Then around ten years before and after independence, those encounters turned into relationships. The history of conservation makes that clear. Between the American ecologist and the Kenyan manager, between the British director of UNESCO and the Tanzanian president, between the big man in an Ethiopian village and the colonial warden turned into an expatriate warden, the process of independence was a game-changer: their relationships intensified, and everybody had to start taking account of the other. It was this rapprochement between different worlds which shaped the postcolonial moment, from the 1950s until the end of the 1970s. Then came the era of the postcolony, a period which lasted until the beginning of the 1980s. But by then the past was already weighing heavily on the present.

When the postcolonial moment ended

Let us first observe the expert gentlemen. In 1979, the United Nations asked them to draw up a 'strategy' which reconciled the imperatives of economic globalization and the need to protect the planet's resources. The IUCN was in charge of the undertaking, and in order to ensure a successful outcome, like the one achieved in Arusha in 1961, the Union turned to experts from two still closely interwoven worlds represented respectively by the conservationists from UNESCO and the WWF, and by the developmentalists from the FAO and other agencies of the United

Nations for the environment. In 1961 they had devised the African Special Project. This time, in 1980, they were devising the World Conservation Strategy. On a planetary scale, the major experts called for a 'sustainable development through the conservation of living resources'. But they also planned to 'take into account' developing countries in general and Africa in particular. They intended to respond to 'the growing demand for people centred development', and in order to achieve that aim, they envisaged 'conservation-based rural development'. The protected areas would still be dedicated to the protection of nature, but theoretically, inside the parks and in the areas immediately surrounding them, local people could now benefit from tourist revenues, from wooded areas which could be cleared and from well-maintained pasturelands and fertilized soil.[7]

The expert gentlemen therefore set about the task of redistributing the cargo of the conservationist ship, though without however changing course. They still dreamed of parks empty of local people in an Africa which was struggling against its runaway demography. This was the case, amongst a great many others, of Jacques Verschuren, the Belgian zoologist. This passionate fan of elephants had already been present at Arusha. And twenty years later, alongside the IUCN and his government, he was still working for nature, for example in Burundi. 'Is it possible for the most densely populated country in Africa, with no wildlife legislation, still to possess a valuable stock of wildlife?' he speculated in 1978. The conservationist set about studying the question in the field and he found his answer: 'The answer, fortunately is yes.' There were, he explained, three reasons for that. First of all, because Burundi was populated with pastoralists. And there, as 'all over Africa', Verschuren wrote, 'this way of life generally engenders respect for wildlife'. Secondly, because the authorities of this former Belgian colony had recently converted to conservation. Turning their attention to the 'bushmen' who, according to Verschuren, had 'condemned' what was once a 'naturalists paradise' with their 'cultivation and cattle', they had given the order that 'not a single tree may be cut down'. Finally, Burundi's wild animals still existed in large numbers because, in addition to the new laws, local people now benefited from an education founded on 'an argument' which Verschuren praises as being 'very simple and persuasive'. 'If you use a thousand litres of water per year, do you prefer 999 litres in January and a single litre for the rest of the year, or three litres each day of the year? So – protect your forest sponge …' Clearly the expert gentleman was still convinced that nature in Africa, although deteriorated, was still intact, just as he continued to think of the Africans as destructive but nevertheless open to being educated. In other words, in 1978, the dream of an African Eden was still being pursued. For, as Verschuren concluded: 'Nature is not completely condemned in Burundi. … If these projects [the parks] can be carried out soon, they will show that some nature conservation can be achieved even in so crowded a country.'[8]

Was it simply that practices were changing but the mindset remained the same? This was also the impression given by the world of the field experts. These now included Africans like Eric Edroma. The Ugandan was barely twenty years old when the Arusha conference was held. At the time, he was a studying at the University of London in Great Britain, returning a few years later to set up the Wildlife Clubs of Uganda, an association aimed to promote conservation education across the entire country. At the end of the 1970s, Edroma became head of the Ugandan Institute of Ecology. It was in this capacity that, in 1980, with the backing of the Fauna Preservation Society, he sounded the alarm. They were witnessing, he said, the 'extermination' of large mammals, such as elephants, rhinos, buffalo, lions and giraffes. He was therefore asking for help from all foreign governments and from all the international conservation agencies – their duty was to 'assist Uganda' by eliminating the world trade in African fauna.[9] His colleague Kes Hillman took a similar view. The British woman was the first female expert to appear in the archives. Having studied zoology in her native country, she had settled in Kenya in 1973, and, like her predecessors, had travelled from Nairobi across all of East Africa. As president of the African Rhino Specialist Group, within the IUCN, she condemned the drastic drop in elephant populations in the 'region'. And, in 1979, following in the footsteps of Edroma with whom she worked regularly, she emphasized the need for international action against traffickers trading elephant tusks, the majority of whom came from the Yemen, Hong Kong and China.[10]

Reading these two conservationists it becomes clear that the experts in the field had cast off their colonial ethos. Instead of attributing predation to 'indigenous' hunters who were hostile to the animal world, they finally saw the destruction of the planet for what it truly was – that is to say, the result of a commercialization of the world from which, since the end of the nineteenth century, there had been no escape, either for individuals or for animals, and from which even the wildlife of East Africa was not immune. The claim was not completely false. Eric Edroma and Kes Hillman were adamant about the global reasons behind the extinction of East African fauna. But that did not prevent them from continuing to blame the men and women who lived in the midst of nature. The British woman deplored the lack of 'involvement of rural people in protecting the rhinos they live close to'. As for the Ugandan expert, he regretted the 'spread of human settlements' and the 'get-rich-quick drive'. According to him, these were the major causes of animal extinction. Where Hillman proposed creating more 'sanctuaries' thanks to financial 'incentive', on the basis that these would encourage local people to protect fauna rather than kill it, Edroma recommended that park guards be provided with 'guns' and 'ammunition' which would enable them to enforce the law.[11] If the two field experts genuinely saw local people as the prime beneficiaries of conservation, at the end of the 1970s, they still continued to think that in East Africa, protecting nature meant, first of all, protecting it from its inhabitants.

In this respect, the African leaders were not always in agreement, and from that time on, they sometimes made that abundantly clear. That was the case, for example, of Maaza Bekele, professor of demography, director of the Ethiopian Planning Office and Ethiopian representative for UNESCO. Since 1974, she had been referring to the United Nations experts as the 'False prophets of doom'. These were engaged in a curious 'numbers game' wrote Maaza in the *UNESCO Courier*. For 'The same year', she insisted, some people had claimed that Africa had 363 million inhabitants, and others calculated its population as 329 million. But western scholars had chosen not to draw attention to this error since they were all pursuing the same goals, according to Maaza, namely 'to prove that the world is threatened with disaster, attributable largely to the "population explosion" occurring in developing regions such as Africa'. The professor insisted that she was not casting doubts on the 'catastrophe' but on the racially prejudiced nature of the argument. For, according to her, by demanding a reduction in *African* birth rates in order to save *world* resources 'the prophets of doom ... are sometimes guilty' of 'hinting in some cases at the threat to white children which a growing coloured population represents', or in other words the threat for those children who will 'consume a much larger proportion of the planet's resources than any child born in Addis Ababa, Accra, Lagos or Algiers'. This is why Maaza Bekele exhorted the international institutions to stop financing programmes of demographic control intended for African governments but instead to help them improve daily life for their populations. This is the new message Ethiopia was sending to the outside world: less money 'to control life' and more to 'promote it'.[12]

At the end of the 1970s, and following in the footsteps of other African states like that of Nyerere who accelerated the Africanization of the Tanzanian administration, the Ethiopian government was addressing both its own citizens and foreigners. The country's new doctrine was *Ityopiya Teqdem*, 'Ethiopia first', and just like Maaza Bekele, the state fully intended to respect that motto. But once again, radical as it was in appearance, the change of direction took place in a context of continuity. This can be seen, for example, in the Omo Park. At a time when the country was descending into civil war, the inhabitants of the Omo tried to take advantage of the situation to free themselves from the central power. But, as during the time of the empire, the Marxist regime of the *Derg* continued to rely on foreign experts, and these continued to advise them to create zones of controlled hunting in the areas around the national parks – these would generate income for 'local people' who would then more readily accept being moved out of the park.[13] And, in the meantime, the warden, Awegeghew Teshome, was working to maintain a 'proper carrying capacity'. He claimed to be conscious of the 'basic needs of local people', but insisted that the Omo must remain 'untouched'. With his scouts and foreign experts, the warden hunted down all those 'poaching to feed themselves', lighting 'small bush fires' in order to cultivate the land or installing hives to produce honey in the park.[14] That was the Ethiopian world-nation. Its leaders were adamant that the demands of the population now came before those of the outside world. But they still made every effort to satisfy the foreign experts, whilst at the same time using them to exert greater control over their citizens. At the beginning of the 1980s, governing a postcolonial state still entailed navigating between one world and the other.

As for the men and women who lived in the national parks, their lives were also affected as a result of these increasingly frequent encounters between worlds which were becoming ever closer to each other. Suddenly, they were no longer ignored. The expert gentlemen had adopted a 'people centred' approach, the field experts no longer attributed to them all the ecological evils of the planet, and their governments even recognized their right to the land. But that did not change the fact that conservation was imposed from outside – for those living in the parks, it was still a case of adapting to a policy which had come from elsewhere. Faced with the experts who had come to study their living environment, they now had a voice. And they used it in the Omo in 1980, when they told American ecologists that they refused 'the park laws'.[15] That said, these foreigners were still advocating their removal. In order to continue living on their lands, the Surma and the Mursi decided therefore to play the card of tribal tourism. The transhumant agro-pastoralists agreed to greet busloads of western visitors, they were willing to smear their bodies in paint in order to be photographed, at a price of course, but in doing so, they were insisting on their legitimate right to live in these 'natural' spaces.[16]

That insistence could also take the form of resistance which had now become official. This can be seen at exactly the same moment in the Simien Park. In 1981, in their fight against the regime of the *Derg*, Eritrean and Tigrayan rebels took control of the mountains, and the agro-pastoralists who had been expelled from their land took advantage of the situation to reclaim it. The result was such that a visitor would soon describe a 'feeling of peace and pastoral prosperity' in the park.[17] But this peace came at a price. The local inhabitants were able to support the opponents of the *Derg* all the more readily in that with them agriculture, pastoralism and wood cutting were once more authorized. However, in the eyes of the soldiers of the regime in the throes of civil war, nothing justified sedition, not even anti-conservationism. In Chenek, in the heart of the park, the peasant caught by the army faced the same destiny as the rebels he might have helped – he was taken to the 'cliff of the dead' and thrown over the edge.[18] At the beginning of the 1980s, life in the global village of conservation meant learning to coexist with power. A power that came simultaneously from international, national and provincial sources and was ultimately ever more global.

When a lasting postcolonial era began

It was on this note that, in Ethiopia, and throughout Africa, the post-colonial *moment* came to an end. And in its place came the postcolonial *era* which would endure for decades to come, swept along by that same blend of abrupt changes of direction and of continuity. For an idea never really dies, nor do the practices associated with it, which are instead simply added to those which went before. And, still today, in the context of 'African' nature, the ideas and practices which have the most impact have been handed down to us from the postcolonial moment. Four examples will demonstrate this, four final stories.

First of all, in 2003, UNESCO acknowledged that, since its creation in 1972, the World Heritage List had been based on a nature–culture dualism which was inherently western. In response, the prestigious insti-tution added the category of 'intangible cultural heritage' to its 'World Cultural and Natural Heritage List', seeking to correct its ethnocentric focus.[19] All of which explains why in 2011 a southern Ethiopian territory like the Konso country could be added to the World Heritage List as a 'cultural landscape' on the basis that it features anthropomorphic wooden statues, in an agro-pastoral area, which, according to the UNESCO experts, represents 'a spectacular example' of 'a living cultural tradition stretching back 21 generations'.[20] The institute has therefore unmistakably reformed its image and its practice. The problem is that reform does not mean revolution. Like all the other national parks in the continent included on the UNESCO list before 2003, the Awash, the Omo and the Simien are still effectively 'natural' sites. They are however areas which are very much 'alive', they too are peopled by agro-pastoralists, their landscapes also have a 'cultural' dimension. But innovation does not erase the past, it simply adds to it. Africa may well have become 'cultural', it still retains all its natural identity.

Botswana's leaders are well placed to know this, given that their country is home to the largest elephant population on the continent, with around 130,000 specimens. In 2019, in the light of such a population density, the national authorities, encouraged by the Botswana Wildlife Producers Association, reinstated elephant hunting, issuing affluent visitors with almost 300 permits. International institutions and experts were quick to criticize this decision. Botswana, they said, was threatening the survival of an endangered species. But the leaders of the former British Bechuanaland stood their ground – with 130,000 elephants, they said, the species was not 'endangered'. They claimed that, on the contrary, it was the pachyderms which were threatening the local people by devastating their crops and even sometimes killing individuals in their path. After the enforced halt to hunting during Covid-19, in 2021, and in conjunction with conservationist-hunting associations, the Botswanan administration issued 287 new licences to kill. It argued that with the licences sold at 50,000 dollars per trophy, local people benefited from the economic impact of tourism, a situation which has rallied local support for the creation of wildlife parks.[21] Postcolonial conservation of nature may indeed have been Africanized, and it was still closely associated with the same predation which had seen it first emerge during the colonial era.

And this conservation is still synonymous with violence, as the Maasai of Loliondo can testify. At the beginning of 2022, in this territory close to the Serengeti Park, the Tanzanian state announced the imminent establishment of a reserve dedicated to hunting, safaris and conservation. The reserve would be managed by the Tanzania National Parks (TANAPA), with the financial and scientific support of the Frankfurt Zoological Society, and in partnership with a company based in the United Arab Emirates, the Otterlo Business Corporation, specialists in the organization of 'hunting trips'. But the creation of the park took a dramatic turn in June 2022. The Maasai, who were destined to be expelled, refused to abandon their houses and the police opened fire. The TANAPA agents and the forces of order killed one person and injured around twenty men and women. Thousands more ran for their lives and many were beaten up because they had filmed the event.[22] African conservation is now as international as it is neoliberal. It has clearly lost none of its violence.

The Maasai understood this, and so did the inhabitants of Gich. It was around this Ethiopian village that I carried out my last research project. In January 2019, in the small town of Debark, 35 kilometres west of the Simien, Samson agreed to answer my questions. This man, who had spent his entire life in Gich, told me about his expulsion in 2016 by park guards who had beaten him with sticks, and described his bitterness on learning that UNESCO had 'congratulated' the Ethiopian government for having, on its advice,[23] at last agreed to displace the some 2,500 inhabitants of Gich. The park was no longer 'in danger' the experts had declared in 2017.[24] But Samson, for his part, is so much poorer since his expulsion that he feels he is living in hell – hence his curious expression: 'it has become the fire'. My research ended at that point and, three months after our interview, the Simien was in flames. In April 2019, 'wild fires' probably deliberately caused by arson had broken out in the heart of the park, in Gich, the very place which, three years before it was destroyed, was the site of Samson's village.[25] If I had got wind of this coincidence, it would probably have formed the conclusion to the story I was trying to write at that time, that of *The Invention of Green Colonialism*.[26] But I would not have interpreted it in the same way as I do today, after continuing my research in the archives. For these archives reveal the decisive importance of the postcolonial moment and of the previously unprecedented rapprochement which took place at that time – shortly before and shortly after independence – between the great thinkers of conservation, the field experts, the African leaders and those living in the parks.

When Ernesto Ottone Ramirez, the assistant director-general of UNESCO, insisted in 2020 that the institution had not demanded the expulsion of the Simien villagers, and when he declared that he had simply 'supported' Ethiopia in its task of naturalizing certain places,[27] what exactly was he doing? He was subscribing to the tradition of the expert gentlemen who had decided to respond to African independence by launching the African Special Project in 1961, when the colonial period was still sufficiently close to be able to declare without embarrassment that UNESCO would be there 'to help [African] Governments to help themselves'.[28]

Similarly, when in 2017, after the destruction of the village of Gich, the IUCN expert Jaeger Tilman emphasized the need to teach other agro-pastoralists in the area to stop interfering with 'urgently needed conservation and restoration needs',[29] what exactly was he saying? He was reproducing the declinist rhetoric and myth mutually adopted by the field experts gathered at Arusha in 1961, following the example of Leslie Brown, the ornithologist who, in East Africa, had proposed 'increasing and restoring the value of wild life resource in areas where it has diminished'. After all, as he pointed out, 'African pastoral usage of such country is almost invariably destructive and usually results in destruction'.[30]

Alongside Brown and still in Arusha in his role of spokesperson for the new independent African states, Julius Nyerere then promised that he would do 'everything in [his] power' to preserve nature within the parks created by the British colonists.[31] And that was exactly what he did during the 1960s, and ultimately, it is also what the current leaders of Botswana, Tanzania and Ethiopia are doing. Their parks were created as a result of the postcolonial event and even today, in order to obtain the international recognition which will strengthen their economy and their nations, the East African heads of state will stop at nothing, and certainly not at the expulsion of farming communities.

As for the latter, they too demonstrate a remarkable stability. When the expert gentlemen launched their African Special Project in 1961, they acknowledged that in terms of protecting nature 'The major issues of Governments lie not directly with animals, vegetation or soil, but with people.'[32] Sixty years later this still applies. In the name of 'African nature' the international conservation institutions are still prepared to sacrifice the men and women who live in its midst. In the parks of East Africa, field experts continue to judge them as being too destructive, and if necessary, today as in the past, their governments take action against them. But they too will stop at nothing. And, in the Simien they did not hesitate, for example, to set fire to the land which was to be taken from them. The conservation that has been imposed on them for sixty years corresponds to a universal principle, according to which humans only have one 'planet' or one 'nature'. But by this incendiary gesture, the inhabitants of the Ethiopian park were seeking to remind the international institutions, the experts and their leaders that, behind this supposed universality of nature, there are first of all societies, that is to say women and men with their own unique past and present. And for them, as for so many other people living in the parks of the continent, ever since the start of the African Special Project, conservation has been synonymous with violence. For this unspoilt African ecology with its untamed nature and teaming wildlife cannot belong to the men and women who live amongst it but only to those who are more powerful than them.

Acknowledgements

After so many months spent thinking 'in fours' in order to tell this story, I cannot quite shake off the idea that the writing of it also belongs to four different worlds. Except that these are 'my' own worlds, and without necessarily realizing it, the women and men who live in them have brought me invaluable help.

First there is the world of the historians who specialize in Africa, the (post)colony and nature. There are far too many of them to be mentioned individually here, but I would at least like to thank Hélène Blais, Raf de Bont, Diana Davis, Richard Drayton, François-Xavier Fauvelle and Isabelle Surun. They were the first ones who agreed to read this text, and all of them helped me in many other ways. Isabelle Surun demonstrated a confidence in my work which was as generous as it was inspiring and an admirable patience in the face of my writing foibles. Thanks to her own research she also encouraged me to see the history of the 'colonial encounter' in a different light. Hélène Blais also offered me her support, first of all in teaching me that a plant or a garden could reveal the true nature of the empire and then in making me realize that I too had the right to 'belong' to the academic community. Raf de Bont, for his part, gave me a concept that I had still not fully defined in ten years of research: without his 'expert gentlemen' I would have struggled to fully complete this book. Diana Davis was one of the first to introduce me to the environmental history of Africa, and she has continued to show me that this history could perhaps contribute to bringing some small change to our present. As for Richard Drayton, even without ever having met me, he was ready to read the three manuscripts, including this one, that French researchers have to write in order to be 'accredited to supervise research'. I had already encountered the wisdom of this global historian; thanks to him I had learned that governing nature first of all meant governing men, but as a result of his generous gesture I was also able to discover his qualities as a friend. A quality for which I would finally like to thank François-Xavier Fauvelle. In the world of historians specializing in Africa, he is one of those who taught me to 'de-africanize' my approach, or in other words, to turn my back on the so-called exceptionality of the continent. He also enabled me to belong to another world – that of the historians specializing in Ethiopia, a country I was able to visit for the first time in 2007, thanks to a 'field study' scholarship he was kind enough to award me.

Here too, I owe a great deal to far too many people. I would therefore like to at least thank the 'experts' on the subject which is the focus of my book. Jean-Baptiste Eczet agreed to share with me his meticulously detailed knowledge of the Mursi and the Surma. Laurent Fourchard encouraged me to observe postcolonial violence in its everyday form rather than in its more spectacular dimension. My capacity for mispronouncing Ethiopian languages knows no limits and I needed the invaluable help of Pierre Guidi to correctly pronounce Dehaw, Tekelakay and Yemiyastekaklew. To penetrate the everyday lives of these anonymous individuals, Antonin Plarier also helped me, in particular by teaching me to cross-reference questions of environmental history with those of social history. And if I succeeded in understanding even a little of these ordinary lives, I owe it first of all to Ophélie Rillon, who showed me just how much politics weighs on the personal. I also owe it to Thibaud Trochu, who allowed me to benefit from a little of his astute insight and enabled me to make the link between the science and the dream. I hope finally to have proved myself worthy of the analyses of Marie Bridonneau and Jean-Nicolas Bach, both capable of interrogating, at the same time, the policies of the Ethiopian state and the international institutions, the practice of their agents and experts, and their very real effects on people's daily lives. Marie and Jean-Nicolas also went out of their way to welcome me in Ethiopia. Without them, I would never have had access to the third world on which this story depends: the world of the archives.

In Addis Ababa, nothing would have been possible without the help of the staff at the *Centre français des etudes éthiopiennes* (CFEE) and the Ethiopian Wildlife Conservation Authority and in particular Hanna Siyum Tadesse and Kumura Wakijira. It was also thanks to the sheer force of work and the incredible sense of diplomacy of Kidanemariam Woldegiorgis that, with the CFEE and the EWCA, we were able to establish the first archive collection on the environmental history of

Ethiopia. Only the determination of Lidya Adane Workie and Kalehiwot Ayele Gebregiorgis enabled us to save and then sort through the Ethiopian archives which were used in the writing of this book. Already filed, indexed and accessible, the archives kept in Great Britain were of course less demanding to access. But if Younis Assadi had not agreed to help me collect and photograph tens of thousands of pages of archives, I would still be shuttling between the Cambridge library and the botanical gardens at Kew. Finally, if Brigitte Marin and Laura Pettinaroli had not invited me to the *École française de Rome*, it would have been far more difficult for me to access the Italian archives of the FAO, the Food and Agriculture Organization. And, I should add, thanks to this stay in Rome, never has the reading of dry documents seemed such a pleasure.

That pleasure brings us to the fourth world, the last one, that of intellectual complicity which turns into friendship, of encounters between one city and another, of unwavering camaraderie, of love, and even, sometimes, of family. This world is the most precious of all, but it is also the one about which words always fail me. I hope that all those who have accompanied me throughout the writing of this book know that I would not have had the courage or the desire to finish it if they had not been there.

Acronyms

AWLF	African Wildlife Leadership Foundation
CAWM	College of African Wildlife Management
CITES	The Convention on International Trade in Endangered Species of Wild Fauna and Flora
CTCA	Commission for Technical Cooperation in Africa South of the Sahara (CCTA Commission de coopération technique en Afrique au sud du Sahara)
EWCA	Ethiopian Wildlife Conservation Authority
EWCO	Ethiopian Wildlife Conservation Organization
FAO	Food and Agriculture Organization
FPS	Fauna Preservation Society (founded 1950)
GEF	Global Environmental Fund
IBP	International Biological Program
IFAN	Institut français en Afrique noire
IOPN	International Office for the Protection of Nature (OIDCPN Office international de la documentation et de corrélation pour la protection de la nature) (since 1928)
IUCN	International Union for the Conservation of Nature (UICN Union internationale pour la conservation de la nature) (since 1956)
IUPN	International Union for the Protection of Nature (UIPN Union internationale pour la protection de la nature) (since 1948)
KANU	Kenya African National Union
MAB	Man and Biosphere
NUTAE	Nuffield Unit of Tropical Animal Ecology
OAU	Organisation of African Unity (OUA Organisation de l'unité africaine)
SCA	The Scientific Council for Africa South of the Sahara (CSA Conseil scientifique pour l'Afrique au sud du Sahara)

SPFE   Society for the Preservation of the Fauna of the Empire (1919)

SPWFE   Society for the Preservation of the Wild Fauna of the Empire (1903)

TANAPA   Tanzania National Parks

TANU   Tanganyika African National Union

UNEP   United Nations Environment Programme

UNESCO   United Nations Educational, Scientific and Cultural Organization

UNIP   United National Independence Party (Zambia)

UNDP   United Nations Development Programme

UPC   Uganda People's Congress

WWF   World Wildlife Fund

Notes

Preliminary text

1 IUCN, 'Warsaw and Cracow meeting', *Oryx*, vol. 5, no. 6, 1960, pp. 373–80.
2 Oryx, 'African Special Project, stage 1', *Oryx*, vol. 6, no. 3, 1961, p. 143.
3 Ibid.
4 Julian Huxley, 'The treasure house of wildlife', *The Observer*, 13 November 1960, pp. 23–4.
5 WWF, 'We must save the world's wildlife. An international declaration', Morges, 1961, p. 1 (https://wwfeu.awsassets.panda.org/downloads/morgesmanifesto .pdf).
6 John Hillaby, 'African Special Project. Stage two – The Arusha Conference', *Oryx*, vol. 6, no. 4, 1962, p. 213.

Introduction

1 Karl Jacoby, *Shadows at Dawn. An Apache Massacre and the Violence of History*, London: Penguin, 2008, p. 7.
2 Romain Bertrand, *L'Histoire à parts égales*, Paris: Points Seuil, 2014, pp. 16 and 23.
3 Raf de Bont, *Nature's Diplomats. Science, Internationalism, and Preservation*, Pittsburgh: University of Pittsburgh Press, 2021, p. 170.
4 The Ethiopian language does not follow the rule of name and first name. First comes the name (used by the individual in question), then the name of the father and finally that of the grandfather.
5 W.E.B. Du Bois, *The Souls of Black Folk*, New York: First Vintage Books, 1990, p. 68.
6 For the most recent update on this issue, see: Fiore Longo, *Décolonisons la protection de la nature! Plaidoyer pour les peuples autochtones et l'environnement*, Paris: Double ponctuation, 2023.
7 Guillaume Blanc, *The Invention of Green Colonialism*, Cambridge: Polity, 2022. See also: Guillaume Blanc, 'Préface. La planète brûle, et les incendi-aires courent toujours', *in* Fréderic Bourdier and Patrick Kulezza (eds.), *La Combustion du monde. Peuples autochtones, conservation et marchandisation de la nature en Asie du Sud et du Sud-Est*, Paris: L'Harmattan, 2024, pp. 7–15.

8 See Marie-Christine Cormier-Salem, Dominique Juhé-Beaulaton, Jean Boutrais and Vernard Roussel (eds.), *Patrimonialiser la nature tropicale. Dynamiques locales, enjeux internationaux*, Paris: IRD Éditions, 2005; Marie Christine Cormier-Salem, Dominique Juhé-Beaulaton, Yves Girault and Dominique Guillaud (eds.), *Ambivalences patrimoniales au Sud. Mises en scène et jeux d'acteurs*, Paris: IRD Editions and Karthala, 2016.

9 Achille Mbembe, *De la postcolonie. Essai sur l'imagination politique dans l'Afrique contemporaine*, Paris: Karthala, 2000, p. 26.

10 See in particular: Jean-François Bayart, 'Africa in the world: a history of extraversion', *Africa Affairs*, vol. 99, no. 395, April 2000, pp. 217–67.

11 See in particular: Frederick Cooper, *Africa in the World. Capitalism, Empire, Nation State*, Cambridge, MA: Harvard University Press, 2014.

12 Corey Ross, *Ecology and Power in the Age of Empire. Europe and the Transformation of the Tropical World*, Oxford: Oxford University Press, 2017, p. 395.

13 William Adams, 'Nature and the colonial mind', *in* W. Adams and Martin Mulligan (eds.), *Decolonizing Nature. Strategies for Conservation in a Post-colonial Era*, London: Earthscan, 2003, pp. 42–3.

14 Diana Davis, *The Arid Lands. History, Power, Knowledge*, Cambridge, MA: The MIT Press, 2016.

15 Jacob Dlamini, *Safari Nation. A Social History of the Kruger National Park*, Athens: Ohio University Press, 2020.

16 Thomas Lekan, *Our Gigantic Zoo. A German Quest to Save the Serengeti*, Oxford: Oxford University Press, 2020. Thomas Lekan used the same cover image as the one chosen for this book to illustrate Bernhard Grzimek's attempt to 'save' the Serengeti. While here I have extended the scope of analysis to East Africa, I believe that no other image so strikingly illustrates the western quest for African nature.

17 Anna-Katharine Wöbse, '"The world after all was one": the international environmental network of UNESCO and IUCN 1945–1949', *Contemporary European History*, vol. 20, no. 3, 2011, pp. 331–48.

18 Yannick Mahrane, Frédéric Thomas and Christophe Bonneuil, 'Mettre en valeur, préserver ou conserver? Genèse et déclin du préservationniste dans l'empire colonial français (1870–1960)', *in* Charles-François Mathis and Jean-François Mouhot (eds.), *Une protection de l'environnement à la française? (XIX–XX siècles)*, Seyssel: Champ Vallon, 2013, p. 79.

19 Daniel Brockington and James Igoe, 'Eviction for conservation: a global overview', *Conservation and Society*, vol. 4, no. 3, 2006, pp. 424–70.

20 Charles Geisler and Ragendra de Sousa, 'From refuge to refugee: the African case', *Public Administration and Development*, vol. 21, no. 2, 2001, pp. 159–70.

21 William Adams, *Against Extinction. The Story of Conservation*, London and New York: Earthscan, 2004.

22 Guillaume Blanc, 'L'expert, le dirigeant et l'habitant. La fabrique globale de la nature éthiopienne (1965–1970)', *Genèses*, vol. 115, no. 2, 2019, pp. 53–74.

23 Anthony Kirk-Green, 'Decolonization: the ultimate diaspora', *Journal of Contemporary History*, vol. 36, no. 1, 2001, p. 145.

24 Gilbert Rist, 'Le prix des mots', *in* Gilbert Rist (ed.) *Les Mots du pouvoir. Sens et non-sens de la rhétorique internationale*, Paris and Geneva: Presses universitaires de France et Institut universitaire d'études du développement, 2002, p. 10.

Chapter 1: Protecting Africa from the Africans

1 IUCN, 'Seventh General Assembly, Warsaw, June 1960. Proceedings', Brussels, 1960, p. 27 [UICN-GA-7th-006].

2 Ibid., p. 48. My thanks to Raf de Bont for allowing me to discover this (post) colonial history of the headquarters of the IUCN.

3 Ibid., p. 151.

4 Abdallah Said Fundikira, Julius Nyerere and Tewa Said Tewa, 'The Arusha Manifesto', *in* Gerald Watterson (compiled with the help of other members of the IUCN secretariat), 'Conservation of Nature and Natural Resources in Modern African States. Report of symposium organised by CCTA and IUCN and held under the auspices of FAO and UNESCO at Arusha, Tanganyika, September 1961', Morges, 1963, p. 12 [IUCN-NS-no. 001].

5 Gerald Watterson, 'Conservation of Nature…', op. cit., pp. 9–25.

6 Ibid., p. 19

7 Frank Fraser Darling, 'The habitat', *in* Gerald Watterson, 'Conservation of Nature…', op. cit., pp. 130–2.

8 Bernhard Grzimek, 'Value of the tourist industry', *in* Gerald Watterson, 'Conservation of Nature…', op. cit., pp. 189–92.

9 Jacques Verschuren, 'Developing an appreciation of the need for conservation of nature and natural resources', *in* Gerald Watterson, 'Conservation of Nature…', op. cit., pp. 348–50.

10 Julian Huxley, 'Wild fauna and flora of Africa as a cultural and economic asset, and the world interest therein', *in* Gerald Watterson, 'Conservation of Nature…', op. cit., pp. 203–7.

11 Gerald Watterson, 'Conservation of Nature…', op. cit., pp. 62 and 73.

12 IUCN, 'The Arusha Conservation Conference', *IUCN Bulletin*, no. 2, 1961, pp. 1 and 7 [UNESCO, UIC/8].

13 Oryx, 'African Special Project. Stage two – The Arusha Conference', *Oryx*, vol. 6, no. 3, 1961, p. 143.

14 John Hillaby, 'African Special Project. Stage two', op. cit., pp. 211–14.

15 Joseph Murumbi, in IUCN, 'Eighth General Assembly. Nairobi, Kenya, September 1963. Proceedings', Morges, 1964, p. 39.

16 Tanganyika became independent in 1961, Zanzibar in 1963 and, in 1964, the two states merged to form 'Tanzania'. However, in order to avoid confusion with the colonial period, when discussing the period post 1961, we will refer to Tanzania.

17 IUCN, 'Eighth General Assembly. Nairobi, Kenya, September 1963. Proceedings', Morges, 1964, pp. 39–40 [IUCN-NS-SP-no.001].

18 Théodore Monod, 'Man's dependence on nature and her resources', in Gerald Watterson, 'Conservation of Nature…', op. cit., pp. 242–6.

19 Diana Davis, 'Introduction', in Diana Davis and Edmund Burke (eds.), Environmental Imaginaries of the Middle East and North Africa, Athens: Ohio University Press, 2011, pp. 1–22.

20 Raf de Bont, 'Europe and its environmental other(s): imagining natures for "global" conservation', in Anna-Katharine Wöbse and Patrick Jupper (eds.), Greening Europe. Environmental Protection in the Long Twentieth Century. A Handbook, Berlin and Boston: Oldenbourg, 2022, pp. 47–72.

21 William Beinart and Katie McKeown, 'Wildlife media and representations of Africa, 1950s to the 1970s', Environmental History, vol. 14, no. 3, 2009, pp. 429–52.

22 William Beinart, 'The Adamsons, Born Free and the late colonial era: images that helped to change the animal world', in Guillaume Blanc, Mathieu Guerin and Gregory Quenet (eds.), Tropical Nature. Colonial and Post-Colonial Conservation in Africa and Asia, London and New York: Berghahn Books, 2015, pp. 159–78.

23 William Beinart and Lotte Hughes, 'Empire and the visual representations of nature, 1860–1960', History Compass, vol. 6, no. 5, 2008, pp. 1177–93.

24 Jim Igoe, The Nature of the Spectacle. On Images, Money, and Conserving Capitalism, Tucson: The University of Arizona Press, 2017, pp. 20–6.

25 Peter Fitter and Sir Peter Scott, The Penitent Butchers. The Fauna Preservation Society 1903–1978, London: Collins, 1978.

26 Guillaume Blanc, The Invention of Green Colonialism, op. cit., pp. 27–43

27 Jennifer Gold, 'The reconfiguration of scientific career networks in the late colonial period: the case of the Food and Agriculture Organization and the British Colonial Forestry Service', in Brett Bennett and Joseph Hodge (eds.), Science and Empire. Knowledge and Networks of Science across the British Empire, 1800–1970, Basingstoke and New York: Palgrave Macmillan, 2011, pp. 297–320.

28 Corinna Unger, *International Development. A Postwar History*, London: Bloomsbury Academic, 2022 [2018], pp. 49–56.

29 Thomas Jundt, 'Duelling visions for the postwar world: the UN and UNESCO 1949 conferences on resources and the origins of environmentalism', *Journal of American History*, vol. 101, no. 1, 2014, pp. 44–70.

30 Anna-Katharine Wöbse, 'L'Unesco et l'Union internationale pour la protection de la nature: une impossible transmission de valeurs?', *Relations internationales*, vol. 152, no. 4, 2012, pp. 29–38.

31 Raf de Bont, *Nature's Diplomats*, op. cit., pp. 169–206.

32 Simone Schleper, 'Conservation compromises: the MAB and the legacy of the international biological program, 1964–1974', *Journal of the History of Biology*, vol. 50, no. 1, 2017, pp. 133–67.

33 Simone Schleper, *Planning for the Planet. Environmental Expertise and the International Union for Conservation of Nature and Natural Resources, 1960–1980*, New York and Oxford: Berghahn Books, 2019, pp. 26–60.

34 Anna-Katharina Wöbse, 'Framing the heritage of mankind: national parks on the international agenda', *in* Bernhard Gissibl, Sabine Höller and Patrick Jupper (eds.), *Civilizing Nature. National Parks in Global Historical Perspective*, New York and Oxford: Berghahn Books, 2012, pp. 140–56.

35 William Adams, *Against Extinction. The Story of Conservation*, London and New York: Earthscan, 2004, pp. 50–7 and 97–100.

36 Thomas Robertson, *The Malthusian Moment. Global Population Growth and the Birth of American Environmentalism*, New Brunswick, NJ: Rutgers University Press, 2012, pp. 5–7.

37 Fabien Locher, 'Cold War pastures: Garrett Hardin and the tragedy of the commons', *Revue d'histoire moderne et contemporaine*, vol. 60, no. 1, 2013, pp. 7–36.

38 Marie-Claude Smouts, *Tropical Forests, International Jungle. The Underside of Global Ecopolitics*, New York: Palgrave Macmillan, 2003, pp. 85 and 97.

39 Gregory Maddox, '"Degradation narratives" and "population time bombs": myths and realities about African environments', *in* Stephen Dovers, Ruth Edgecombe and Bill Guest (eds.), *South Africa's Environmental History. Cases and Comparisons*, Athens: Ohio University Press, 2003, pp. 250–8.

40 Claude Lévi-Strauss, *Structural Anthropology*, London: Hachette UK, 2008, p. 45.

41 Roderick Neumann, 'Moral and discursive geographies in the war for biodiversity in Africa', *Political Geography*, vol. 23, no. 7, 2004, pp. 813–37.

42 IUPN, 'International Conference for the Protection of Nature, Brunnen, 1947. Proceedings, resolutions and reports', Basel, 1947, pp. 168–70 [IUCN, Bios-cons-Nat-040].

43 UIPN, 'Conférence pour l'établissement de l'Union internationale pour la protection de la nature. Fontainebleau, France. 30 septembre–7 octobre 1948', Paris, 1948 [UICN, NS/UIPN/5].

44 'UNESCO scientists at Fontainebleau study nature preservation', *UNESCO Courier*, vol. 1, no. 9, 1948, p. 6.

45 UIPN, 'Conférence pour l'établissement de l'Union internationale pour la protection de la nature. Fontainebleau, France. 30 septembre–7 octobre 1948', Paris, 1948, p. 5 [UICN, NS/UIPN/8].

46 Ibid.

47 IUPN, 'UNESCO. International Technical Conference on the Protection of Nature. Lake Success, 22–29 – VIII – 1949. Proceedings and papers', UNESCO, Paris and Brussels, 1950 [UNESCO, IUPN/ CONF.2].

48 IUPN, 'Proceedings and papers of the Fourth General Assembly held at Copenhagen (Denmark), 25 August to 3 September 1954', Brussels, 1955, pp. 34–42 [IUCN-GA-4th-003].

49 IUCN, 'Cinquième Assemblée générale. Fifth General Assembly. Edinburgh, 20–28.6.1956, Proces-verbaux. Proceedings', Brussels, 1957, pp. 32, 75 and 68 [IUCN-GA-5th-004].

50 IUCN, 'Sixième Assemblée générale. Sixth General Assembly, Athens, Sept. 1958. Proces-verbaux. Proceedings', Brussels, 1960, pp. 32–56 [IUCN-GA-6th-005].

51 Daniel Vigier, 'La Commission de coopération technique en Afrique au sud du Sahara', *Politique étrangere*, vol. 19, no. 3, 1954, pp. 335–49.

52 Letter from the Colonial Office to Keith Caldwell, 'Flora & Fauna. Society for the promotion of nature reserves', undated (u.d.) [National Archives (NA), Colonial Office (CO) 847/53/1].

53 NA, CO 936/62/2, 'International Union for the Protection of Nature', u.d., no page number provided (n.p.).

54 Jean-Paul Harroy, 'Comptes rendus de la Troisième Conférence internationale pour la protection de la faune et de la flore en Afrique, Bukavu, 26–31 octobre 1953, Congo belge', UIPN, 1953 [IUCN-1953-002].

55 NA, CO 936/62/2, 'International Union...', op. cit.

56 NA, CO 847/58, 'Resolution by UN Economic and Social Council on listing of national parks and reserves in Africa 1958–1959', u.d., n.p.

57 John McCormick, *The Global Environmental Movement*, Hoboken, NJ: John Wiley, 1995 [1991], p. 46.

58 WWF, 'We must save the world's wildlife', op. cit., p. 1.

59 Peter Scott (ed.), *The Launching of a New Ark. First Report of the World Wildlife Fund*, London: WWF and Collins, 1965 [UICN, SPE-Inst-002].

60 *IUCN Bulletin*, vol. 1, no. 2, 1961, p. 2 [UNESCO, UIC/8].

61 *IUCN Bulletin*, vol. 2, no. 18, 1971, p. 156 [ibid.].

62 *IUCN Bulletin*, vol. 3, no. 12, 1972, p. 55 [ibid.].

63 C. 403, u.d., n.p. [Cambridge University Library (CUL), GBR/0012/MS Scott, C. 400-403 'The Council for Nature, 1962'].

64 C. 434, u.d., n.p. [CUL, GBR/0012/MS Scott, C. 434-438 'The Fauna Preservation Society'].

65 Oryx, 'The FPS/WWF Revolving Fund', *Oryx*, vol. 10, no. 5, 1970, pp. 291–2.

66 *IUCN Bulletin*, vol. 1, no. 17, 1965, p. 1 [UNESCO, UIC/8].

67 *IUCN Bulletin*, vol. 2, no. 11, 1969, p. 92 [ibid.].

68 *IUCN Bulletin*, vol. 5, no. 4, 1974, pp. 13–14 [ibid.].

69 Isebill V. Gruhn, 'The Commission for Technical Cooperation in Africa, 1950–65', *The Journal of Modern African Studies*, vol. 9, no. 3, 1971, pp. 459–69.

70 Gerald Watterson, 'Conservation of Nature...', op. cit., pp. 210 and 355.

71 Alexander B. Adams (ed.), 'First World Conference on National Parks. Proceedings. Seattle, June 30–July 7, 1962', National Park Service, Washington, 1964, pp. 302–36 [UNESCO, UIC/16].

72 *IUCN Bulletin*, vol. 1, no. 8, 1963, p. 1 [UNESCO, UIC/8].

73 *IUCN Bulletin*, vol. 1, no. 9, 1963, p. 2 [ibid.].

74 UNESCO and United Nations Economic Commission for Africa, 'Final report of the Lagos Conference', Paris, 1965, pp. 37 and 59 [UNESCO, NS.64/D.36/A].

75 UNESCO and United Nations Economic Commission for Africa, 'Lagos Conference. Selected documents. International Conference on the organization of research and training in Africa in relation to the study, conservation and utilization of natural resources, Lagos, 1964', Paris, 1965, pp. 9–20 [UNESCO, NS.64/ D.38/A/F].

76 IUCN, *IUCN 1970 Yearbook. Annual Report of the International Union for Conservation of Nature and Natural Resources for 1970*, Morges, 1971 [IUCN-1971-003].

77 IUCN, 'Ninth General Assembly, Lucerne, Suisse, 25 juin–2 juillet 1966: proceedings', Morges, 1969, p. 73 [IUCN-NS-SP-no.008, Fr].

78 IUCN, *IUCN 1970 Yearbook...*, op. cit., pp. 25–6.

79 IUCN, *IUCN 1971 Yearbook. Annual Report of the International Union for Conservation of Nature and Natural Resources for 1971*, Morges, 1972 [IUCN-1972-001].

80 UNESCO, 'Records of the General Conference, 17th session, Paris, 17 October to 21 November 1972, v. 1, Resolutions, recommendations', Paris, 1973, pp. 133–5 [UNESCO, 17/C Resolutions].

81 IUCN, 'Eleventh General Assembly, Banff, Alberta, Canada, 11–16 September 1972: proceedings', Morges, 1973, p. 97 [IUCN-NS-SP-no.040, Fr].

82 UNESCO, 'Intergovernmental Committee for the Protection of the World Cultural and Natural Heritage', Second Session, Washington, D.C. (USA), 5–8 September 1978.

83 IUCN, 'Ninth General Assembly', op. cit., pp. 80 and 161.

84 UNESCO, 'Use and conservation of the biosphere. Proceedings of the international conference of experts on the scientific basis for rational use and conservation of the biosphere. Paris, 4–13 September 1968', Paris, 1970 [UNESCO, SC.69/XII.16/A].

85 UNESCO, 'Report of the director-general on the activities of the organization in 1971, communicated to member states and the executive board in accordance with article VI.3.b of the Constitution', Paris, 1972, pp. 113–29 [UNESCO, 17 C/3].

86 IUCN, 'Twelfth General Assembly, Kinshasa, Zaire, 8–18 September 1975: Proceedings', Morges, 1976, p. 48 [IUCN-NS-SP-no.044, Fr].

87 UNESCO and United Nations Economic Commission for Africa, 'Final report...', op. cit., p. 101.

88 IUCN, 'Tenth General Assembly, Vigyan Bhavan, New Delhi, 24 November–1 December 1969. Volume II. Proceedings and summary of business', Morges, 1970, p. 108 [IUCN-NS-SP-no.027].

89 FAO, 'African Forestry and Wildlife Commission. First session (Ibadan, Nigeria, 31 October–7 November 1960). Final report', 1960 [FAO-AFC-60/9 Rev. 1].

90 FAO, 'Report of the African Forestry Commission Ad hoc working party on wildlife management (Kampala, Uganda, 21–25 September 1965)', 1965, p. 6 [FAO-AFC/WPWM-65/8].

91 FAO, 'Papers presented at the third session of the working party on wildlife management of the African Forestry Commission (Lome, Togo, 15–18 January 1969)', 1969, n.p. [FAO-AFC/WL-69/1].

92 FAO, 'Papers presented at the fourth session of the Ad hoc working party on wildlife management of the African Forestry Commission (Nairobi, Kenya, 1–3 February 1972)', 1972, n.p. [FAO-AFC/WL-72].

93 Ibid.

94 FAO, 'The economic value of wildlife in certain African countries', 1978, p. 1 [FAO-AFC/WL-78/4.1].

95 FAO, 'Report of the fifth session of the working party on wildlife management and national parks of the African Forestry Commission (Bangui, Central African Republic, 17–19 March 1976)', 1976, n.p. [FAO-AFC/WL-76/Rep].

96　See for example: Jean Le Goff, 'Des effets des discours positifs sur les angoisses liées au changement climatique', *Nouvelle revue de psychosociologie*, vol. 24, no. 2, 2017, pp. 145–56.

97　Alain Gille, 'Preservation of nature', *UNESCO Courier*, vol. 2, no. 1, 1952, p. 4.

98　Maurice Goldsmith, 'Deforestation and its abuses', *UNESCO Courier*, vol. 5, no. 1, 1952, p. 14.

99　Roger Heim, 'Are we headed for catastrophe?' and Maurice Burton, 'Man against nature', *UNESCO Courier*, vol. 11, no. 1, 1958, pp. 3 and 16; K.-H. Oedekoven, 'Saving our vanishing forests', *UNESCO Courier*, vol. XIV, no. 11, 1961, p. 5.

100　*UNESCO Courier*, 'Our thirsty hungry world', April 1966.

101　U. Thant, 'Man, the killer of nature', *UNESCO Courier*, 23rd year, August–September 1970, p. 46.

102　Linton K. Caldwell, 'A world policy for the environment', *UNESCO Courier*, 26th year, 1973, p. 46. On the subject of the construction of Earth as a space ship, see Sebastian Vincent Grevsmühl, *La Terre vue d'en haut. L'invention de l'environement global*, Paris: Seuil, 2014.

103　*UNESCO Courier*, 27th year, July–August 1974, pp. 19–20 [Unesdoc, online]; Yoshio Abe et al., 'The roots of a growing world crisis', *UNESCO Courier*, 29th year, March 1976, pp. 4–7.

104　Maurice Burton, 'Man against nature', op. cit., pp. 4–5.

105　UNESCO, 'Last refuge', *UNESCO Courier*, vol. 11, no. 1, pp. 9 and 11.

106　Gerald Watterson, '"Fire and axe" farming on the way out', *UNESCO Courier*, vol. 11, no. 1, p. 17. For some citations see also the French version of the article, Gerald Watterson, 'Jungle et fertilité ne sont plus synonymes', ibid., p. 17.

107　François Bourlière, 'The vanishing herds', *UNESCO Courier* [Unesdoc, online], p. 34.

108　Julian Huxley, 'Poaching: the shocking slaughter of Africa's wildlife', *UNESCO Courier*, vol. 14, no. 9, pp. 8–16.

109　François Bourlière, 'The vanishing herds', op. cit.; Julian Huxley, 'Poaching...', ibid., pp. 10 and 12.

110　U. Thant, 'Man the killer of nature', op. cit., p. 46.

111　*IUCN Bulletin*, vol. 2, no. 1, 1966, p. 1 [UNESCO, UIC/8].

112　*IUCN Bulletin*, vol. 1, no. 1, 1961, p. 1 [ibid.].

113　*IUCN Bulletin*, New Series 17, October–December 1965, p. 4 [ibid.].

114　*IUCN Bulletin*, vol. 2, no. 19, April–June 1971, p. 165 [ibid.].

115　Ibid.

116　*IUCN Bulletin*, vol. 1, no. 4, 1962, p. 2 [UNESCO, UIC/8].

117　*IUCN Bulletin*, vol. 1, no. 14, 1965, January–March, p. 6 [ibid.].

118 *IUCN Bulletin*, New Series, vol. 2, no. 9, October–December 1968, p. 68 [ibid.].

119 *IUCN Bulletin*, New Series, vol. 5, no. 9, September 1974, pp. 33 and 34 [ibid.].

120 David Hulme and Murphree Marshall, 'Communities, wildlife and the "new conservation" in Africa', *Journal of International Development*, vol. 11, no. 2, 1999, pp. 277–85.

121 Gerardo Bukowski, 'The problems of conservation in the third world', *IUCN Bulletin*, New Series, vol. 6, no. 10, October 1975, p. 37 [UNESCO, UIC/8].

122 See in particular: Patricia Van Schuylenbergh, 'De l'appropriation à la conservation de la faune sauvage. Pratiques d'une colonisation: le cas du Congo belge (1885–1960)', PhD thesis, history, Université catholique de Louvain, 2006, p. 616.

123 Jean-Paul Harroy, *Afrique. Terre qui meurt. La dégradation des sols africains sous l'influence de la colonisation*, Brussels: Marcel Ayez, 1949 [1944], pp. 3–7.

124 Edgar Worthington, *Science in the Development of Africa. A Review of the Contribution of Physical and Biological Knowledge South of the Sahara*, London: CCTA-CSA, 1958, p. xiv. See also: Damiano Matasci, 'Internationalising colonial knowledge: Edgar Barton Worthington and the Scientific Council for Africa, 1949–1956', *The Journal of Imperial and Commonwealth History*, vol. 48, no. 5, 2020, pp. 892–913.

125 Edgar Worthington, 'The future of the African fauna', *Oryx*, vol. 1, no. 1, 1950, pp. 44–50.

126 Roderick Neumann, 'The postwar conservation boom in British colonial Africa', *Environmental History*, vol. 7, no. 1, 2002, pp. 22–47.

127 Frederick Cooper, 'Modernizing bureaucrats, backward Africans and the development concept', *in* F. Cooper and Randall Packard (eds.), *International Development and the Social Sciences. Essays on the History and Politics of Knowledge*, Berkeley: University of California Press, 1997, p. 64.

128 IUCN, 'The position of nature protection throughout the world in 1950', Brussels, 1951, pp. 240 and 290 [UNESCO, UIC/10].

129 Letter from Keith Caldwell to the secretary of the IUPN, 'Nature protection in Kenya', January 1950, n.p. [NA, Colonial Office 847/53/1].

130 Keith Caldwell, 'The Bukavu conference', *Oryx*, vol. 2, no. 4, 1954, pp. 234–7.

131 Gerald Watterson, 'Can the harmful effects of shifting cultivation be restricted by cooperative movements?', FAO, 1955 [FAO, 062072].

132 Max Nicholson, 'The new outlook in ecology', *Oryx*, vol. 4, no. 3, 1957, pp. 196–8.

133 Peder Anker, *Imperial Ecology. Environmental Order in British Empire, 1895–1945*, Cambridge, MA: Harvard University Press, 2001, p. 235.

134 Anna-Katharina Wöbse, 'Framing the heritage...', op. cit., p. 148.

135 Edgar Worthington, 'The problem of influencing African native opinion on conservation', 11 April 1960, n.p. [CUL, GBR/0012/MS Scott, C. 853-859 'Correspondence etc., 1960–1961', C.854].

136 Julian Huxley, 'The conservation of wild life and natural habitats in Central and East Africa. Report on a mission accomplished for UNESCO, July–September 1960', UNESCO, 1961, pp. 12–14 and 92 [UNESCO, NS.61/D.31/F].

137 Edgar Worthington, 'Dynamic conservation in Africa', *Oryx*, vol. 5, no. 6, 1960, p. 345.

138 IUCN, 'African Special Project, stage 1', *Oryx*, vol. 6, no. 3, 1961, pp. 143–70.

139 Abdallah Said Fundikira et al., 'The Arusha Manifesto', op. cit., p. 12.

140 André Villiers, 'Our mother nature: the conservation of nature and natural resources in the Sudan-Sahel zone of Africa', IUCN, Morges, 1963, pp. 60–7 [IUCN-NS-SP-no.002].

141 Thane Riney, 'Conservation and management of African wildlife', FAO, 1967, pp. 8–31 [FAO, 456443/719 R47 (E)].

142 IUCN, 'Ninth technical meeting. Nairobi, September 1963. Proceedings and papers. The ecology of man in the tropical environment', Morges, 1964, p. 281 [IUCN-NS-no.004].

143 André Villiers, 'Our mother nature: the conservation of nature and natural resources in the Sudan-Sahel zone of Africa (revised by L.H. Brown, I.R. Grimwood and P. Walshe)', IUCN and UNESCO, Addis Ababa, 1965 [Ethiopian Wildlife Conservation Authority (EWCA), file John Blower (JB) 2].

144 John Morton Boyd, 'Ministry of Overseas Development 1967 July–1974 Aug.', u.d., n.p. [NA, FT 3/180].

145 Kai Curry-Lindahl, 'The new African conservation convention', *Oryx*, vol. 10, no. 2, 1969, pp. 116–19.

146 UNESCO, 'Séminaire régional de l'Unesco sur la méthodologie écologique et la conservation des ressources naturelles en Afrique tropicale', *Nature et ressources*, vol. 8, no. 2, 1972, pp. 18–20 [UNESCO, 339.5].

147 FAO, 'Papers presented at the fourth session of the Ad hoc working party on wildlife management of the African Forestry Commission (Nairobi, Kenya, 1–3 February 1972)', 1972, n.p. [FAO-AFC/WL-72/1].

148 Perez Olindo, 'Park values, changes, and problems in developing countries', *in* Hugh Elliott (ed.), 'Second World Conference on National Parks, Yellowstone and Grand Teton National Parks, USA, September 18–27, 1972. Proceedings', IUCN, Morges, 1974, p. 56 [IUCN-1974-002].

149 IUCN, 'Twelfth General Assembly', op. cit., pp. 153–4.

150 Cited *in* Stephen Macekura, *Of Limits and Growth. The Rise of Global Sustainable Development in the Twentieth Century*, Cambridge: Cambridge University Press, 2015, p. 1.

151 Jean-Paul Harroy, 'A century in the growth of the "national park" concept throughout the world', *in* Hugh Elliott (ed.), 'Second World Conference on National Parks...', op. cit., p. 24.

152 Max Nicholson, *The Environmental Revolution. A Guide for the New Masters of the World*, London: Hodder and Stoughton, 1970, pp. 5 and 283.

153 Max Nicholson, 'What is wrong with the national park movement?', *in* Hugh Elliott, 'Second World Conference on National Parks...', op. cit., p. 32.

154 Patricia Van Schuylenbergh, 'Virunga, star des médias. Les tribulations du plus ancien parc naturel d'Afrique', *Le Temps des médias*, vol. 25, no. 2, 2015, pp. 85–103.

155 *IUCN Bulletin*, vol. 1, no. 1, 1961, p. 4 [UNESCO, UIC/8].

156 Kai Curry-Lindahl, 'The current situation in the Albert and Garamba National Parks, Congo', *IUCN Bulletin*, vol. 1, no. 20, 1966, p. 3 [ibid.].

157 IUCN, 'Prevailing conditions in the Albert National Park, Congo (Kinshasa)', *IUCN Bulletin*, vol. 2, no. 9, 1968, p. 67 [ibid.] and 'The current situation in the Albert National Park', *IUCN Bulletin*, vol. 2, no. 11, April–June 1969, p. 92.

158 IUCN, 'World news. Congo: the Albert National Park', *IUCN Bulletin*, vol. 2, no. 10, 1969, p. 78 [ibid.].

159 IUCN, 'Prevailing conditions in the Albert National Park, Congo (Kinshasa)', *IUCN Bulletin*, vol. 2, no. 11, 1969, p. 92 [ibid.].

160 Oryx, 'African president looks at nature conservation', *Oryx*, vol. 13, no. 3, 1976, pp. 255–6.

161 Richard Fitter, 'IUCN Nairobi, 1963', *Oryx*, vol. 7, no. 4, 1964, p. 155.

162 Jeff Schauer, '"We hold it in trust": global wildlife conservation, Africanization, and the end of empire', *Journal of British Studies*, vol. 57, no. 3, 2018, pp. 516–42.

163 Charles Boyle, 'What of the Serengeti?', *Oryx*, vol. 3, no. 6, 1956, pp. 303–18.

164 Fauna Preservation Society, 'The Serengeti', *Oryx*, vol. 4, no. 6, 1958, pp. 351–2.

165 Pauline Bentley, 'The drama of Serengeti: two men and a "flying zebra"', *UNESCO Courier*, 14th year, September 1961, pp. 19–21 [UNESCO online].

166 Julian Huxley, 'Nature's fight for life at Ngorongoro crater', *UNESCO Courier*, vol. 14, no. 9, p. 23 [ibid.].

167 IUCN, 'Ngorongoro rhino', *IUCN Bulletin*, vol. 1, no. 16, 1965, p. 5 [ibid.].

168 Thomas Lekan, '*Serengeti Shall Not Die*: Bernhard Grzimek, wildlife film, and

the making of a tourist landscape in Africa', *German History*, vol. 20, no. 2, 2011, p. 260.

169 UICN, 'Kenya. Liste des organisations s'occupant de conservation et information', *Bulletin UICN*, supplément no. 7, décembre 1963, n.p. [UNESCO, UIC/8].

170 UICN, 'Ouganda. Liste des organisations s'occupant de conservation et information', *Bulletin UICN*, supplément no. 8, décembre 1963, n.p. [ibid.].

171 IUCN, 'Aircraft for Uganda national parks', *IUCN Bulletin*, vol. 2, no. 1, 1966, p. 5 [ibid.].

172 IUCN, 'Ethiopia', *IUCN Bulletin*, vol. 1, no. 9, 1963, p. 5 [ibid.].

173 UICN, 'Liste des organisations s'occupant de conservation et informations', *Bulletin UICN*, supplément no. 17, mars 1967, n.p. [ibid.].

174 UICN, 'Éthiopie', *Bulletin UICN*, vol. 2, no. 10, 1969, p. 82 [ibid.].

175 Cited *in* Hugh Elliott (ed.), 'Second World Conference on National Parks...', op. cit., p. 86.

Chapter 2: Saving the East African stronghold

1 Cited in Ian Michael Wright, letter to Richard H. Nolte (Institute of Current World Affairs), 'Arusha Wildlife Conference', Nairobi, 22 September 1961 (www.icwa.org/wp-content/uploads/2015/10/IMW-6.pdf). My thanks to Fiore Longo for drawing my attention to this correspondence.

2 Martin Booth, 'Cowie, Mervyn (1909–1996)', *Oxford Dictionary of National Biography*, 2004 (https://doi.org/10.1093/ref:odnb/39752).

3 Wade Greene, 'Keeping "the African experience" African', *The New York Times*, 15 August 1971 (https://legendsandlegacies-ofafrica.org/johnowen.php, accessed 17 May 2023).

4 For an overview of the period before and after independence in Africa, see in particular, Frederick Cooper, *Africa Since 1940. The Past of the Present*, Cambridge: Cambridge University Press, 2002; Guillaume Blanc, *Décolonisations. Histoires situées d'Afrique et d'Asie (19e–21e siècle)*, Paris: Points Seuil, 2022.

5 *UNESCO Courier*, 'Africa's wild life in peril', 14th year, September 1961, p. 7 [Unesdoc, online].

6 See in particular: Catherine Baroin and Jean Boutrais, 'Bétail et société en Afrique', *Journal des africanistes*, vol. 78, no. 1–2, 2008, pp. 9–52.

7 Lee Talbot, 'Comparison of the efficiency of wild animals and domestic livestock in utilization of East African range-lands', *in* Gerald Watterson, 'Conservation of Nature...', op. cit., p. 330.

8 Mike Everett, 'Obituary. Leslie Hilton Brown, OBE, BSc, PhD (1917–1980)', *British Birds*, vol. 74, no. 5, 1981, p. 224.

9 Leslie Brown, 'Wild animals, agriculture, and animal industry', *in* Gerald Watterson, 'Conservation of Nature...', op. cit., pp. 109–12.

10 John Owen, 'Awakening public opinion to the value of the Tanganyika national parks', *in* Gerald Watterson, 'Conservation of Nature...', op. cit., pp. 261–4.

11 Jacques Verschuren, 'Developing an appreciation of the need for conservation of nature and natural resources', *in* Gerald Watterson, 'Conservation of Nature...', op. cit., p. 350.

12 Tewa Said Tewa, 'The value of tourist industry in the conservation of natural resources in Tanganyika', *in* Gerald Watterson, 'Conservation of Nature...', op. cit., pp. 336–9.

13 Anthony Shepherd, *Flight of the Unicorns*, London: Elek Books, 1965, p. 141.

14 Ian Grimwood, 'The fauna and flora of East Africa', *in* Gerald Watterson, 'Conservation of Nature...', op. cit., pp. 179–88.

15 John Blower, 'Development and utilisation of wildlife resources in Uganda', *in* Gerald Watterson, 'Conservation of Nature...', op. cit., pp. 97–8.

16 R.I.G. Attwel and B.L. Mitchell, 'Special problems of controlled areas, national parks, "strict natural reserves", other nature reserves and forest reserves which contain wildlife', *in* Gerald Watterson, 'Conservation of Nature...', op. cit., pp. 82–5.

17 IUCN, 'Eighth General Assembly', op. cit., p. 59.

18 Reiner Grundmann, 'The problem of expertise in knowledge societies', *Minerva*, vol. 55, no. 1, 2017, pp. 25–48.

19 Sabine Clarke, 'A technocratic imperial state? The Colonial Office and scientific research, 1940–1960', *Twentieth Century British History*, vol. 18, no. 4, 2007, pp. 453–80.

20 Joseph Hodge, 'Colonial experts, developmental and environmental doctrines and the legacies of late British colonialism', *in* Karen Oslund, Neil Brimnes, Niklas Thode Jenson and Christina Folke Ax (eds.), *Cultivating the Colony. Colonial States and Their Environmental Legacies*, Athens: Ohio University Press, 2011, pp. 300–26.

21 Roy MacLeod, 'Nature and empire. Science and the colonial enterprise: Introduction', *Osiris*, no. 15, 2000, pp. 1–13. See also: David Gilmartin, 'Scientific empire and imperial science: colonialism and irrigation technology in the Indus basin', *The Journal of Asian Studies*, vol. 53, no. 4, 1994, pp. 1127–49.

22 Anthony Kirk-Green, 'Decolonization: the ultimate diaspora', *Journal of Contemporary History*, vol. 36, no. 1, 2001, pp. 133–51.

23 Joseph Hodge, 'The hybridity of colonial knowledge: British tropical

agricultural science and African farming practices at the End of Empire',
in Brett Bennett and Joseph Hodge (eds.), *Science and Empire*, op. cit.,
pp. 209–31.

24 Sandrine Kott, 'Les organisations internationales, terrains d'étude de la
globalisation. Jalons pour une approche socio-historique', *Critique internationale*, vol. 52, no. 3, 2011, pp. 9–16. Kott borrows the notion of 'nebula' from
Christian Topalov.

25 Wolf Feuerhahn and Pascale Rabault-Feuerhahn, 'La science à l'échelle internationale', *Revue germanique internationale*, no. 12, 2010, p. 6.

26 Jean-Pierre Olivier de Sardan, 'Les paysans africains face au développement',
in BLACT (ed.), *Introduction à la coopération en Afrique noire*, Paris: Karthala,
1983, p. 10.

27 Frederick Cooper, 'Modernizing bureaucrats, backward Africans…', op. cit.,
p. 81.

28 Roderick Neumann, 'The post-war conservation boom…', op. cit., pp. 29–31.

29 Raf de Bont, 'Abattre pour conserver. Protéines, organisations internationales
et faune sauvage africaine', *in* Guillaume Blanc, Mathieu Guérin and Grégory
Quenet (eds.), *Protéger et détruire. Gouverner la nature sous les tropiques
(20e–21e siècle)*, Paris: CNRS Éditions, 2022, pp. 189–211. The author takes the
concept of 'sociotechnical imaginaries' from Sheila Jasanoff.

30 Simone Schleper, 'Pister les gnous. Médiation technologique entre humains
et faune sauvage au Serengeti', *in* Guillaume Blanc, Mathieu Guérin and
Grégory Quenet (eds.), *Protéger et détruire*, op. cit., pp. 269–97.

31 Etienne Benson, 'Territorial claims: experts, antelopes, and the biology of
land use in Uganda, 1955–75', *Comparative Studies of South Asia, Africa and
the Middle East*, vol. 35, no. 1, 2015, p. 137–55; Jeff Schauer, *Wildlife between
Empire and Nation in Twentieth-Century Africa*, Cham: Palgrave Macmillan,
2019, pp. 157–84.

32 Clark Gibson, *Politicians and Poachers. The Political Economy of Wildlife Policy
in Africa*, Cambridge: Cambridge University Press, 1999, pp. 21–33.

33 Roderick Neumann, *Imposing Wilderness. Struggles over Livelihood and Nature
Preservation in Africa*, Berkeley and Los Angeles: University of California
Press, 1998. See also: Jevgeniy Bluwstein, 'From colonial fortress to neoliberal
landscape in Northern Tanzania: a biopolitical ecology of wildlife conservation', *Journal of Political Ecology*, vol. 25, no. 1, 2018, pp. 144–68.

34 Tim Stapleton, 'Gamekeepers and counter-insurgency in Kenya and Rhodesia
(Zimbabwe), 1952–1980', *International Journal of African Historical Studies*,
vol. 49, no. 2, 2016, pp. 213–34.

35 Reuben Matheka, 'The international dimension of the politics of wildlife

conservation in Kenya, 1958–1968', *Journal of Eastern African Studies*, vol. 2, no. 1, 2008, pp. 112–33.

36 See in particular: Simone Schleper, *Planning for the Planet*, op. cit., p. 5.

37 Raf de Bont, Simone Schleper and Hans Schouwenburg, 'Conservation conferences and expert networks in the short twentieth century', *Environment and History*, vol. 23, no. 4, 2017, p. 583.

38 George Petrides and Wendell Swank, 'The status of wildlife and wilderness areas in East Africa', *Oryx*, vol. 5, no. 4–5, 1960, pp. 295–306.

39 Oryx, 'The FPS East African tour', *Oryx*, vol. 8, no. 4, 1966, pp. 219–20.

40 Hugh Elliott, 'The 1966 East African tour', *Oryx*, vol. 9, no. 1, 1967, p. 16.

41 Hugh Elliott (ed.), 'Second World Conference on National Parks...', op. cit., p. 441.

42 IUCN, FAO, UNEP and WWF, 'Proceedings of a regional meeting on the creation of a co-ordinated system of national parks and reserves in Eastern Africa, Seronera Lodge, Serengeti National Park, Tanzania, 14–19 October 1974', Morges, 1976, p. 18 [IUCN-NS-SP-no.045].

43 Edgar Worthington, 'Report on the wild resources of East and Central Africa, by Dr E. B. Worthington 1960–1962', July 1960, p. 18 [National Archives (NA), Colonial Office (CO) 847/78].

44 Oryx, 'African Special Project, stage I', op. cit., pp. 143–70.

45 Leonard Clayton Beadle, 'The education and training of Africans for senior posts concerned with wildlife conservation', *in* Gerald Watterson, 'Conservation of Nature...', op. cit., pp. 86–7.

46 Helmut Buechner, 'Training programmes for personnel concerned with conservation of African wild animals', *in* Gerald Watterson, 'Conservation of Nature...', op. cit., pp. 113–16.

47 NA, FT 3/172 'Overseas conservation organisations, chiefly USA 1964 June–1970 Mar.', u.d., n.p.

48 Jeff Schauer, '"We hold it in trust"', op. cit., p. 522.

49 On the subject of the Mweka College, see also Raf de Bont, *Nature's Diplomats*, op. cit., pp. 239–67.

50 IUCN, 'Tanganyika', *IUCN Bulletin*, vol. 1, no. 5, 1962, p. 5 [UNESCO, UIC/8].

51 Anthony Mence, 'Training in control of dangerous animals by use of a high-powered rifle', FAO, 1968, n.p. [FAO-FO-AFC/WL-69/2]; Patrick Hemingway, 'Tourist hunting in Kenya', FAO, 1968, n.p. [FAO-FO-AFC/WL-69/7]; Leslie Robinette, 'Game animal survey', FAO, 1968, n.p. [FAO-FO-AFC/WL-69/15].

52 Anthony Mence, 'College of African Wildlife Management, Mweka, Tanzania', FAO, 1971, n.p. [FAO-FO-WCFET/71/21].

53 G.R Francis and G.S. Child, 'College of African Wildlife Management, Mweka, United Republic of Tanzania. Report of the UNDP/FAO review and programming mission', FAO, 1975, n.p. [FAO-FO-DP/URT/70/530].

54 G.S. Child, 'Report on follow-up of graduates of the College of African Wildlife Management, Mweka, Tanzania, 1965–1972', FAO, 1976, n.p. [FAO-FO-AFC/WL-76/4.2].

55 NA, CO 847/62, 'Preservation of wild life in colonies in Africa 1959–1960', u.d., n.p.

56 Pierre-Yves Saunier, 'Les régimes circulatoires du domaine social 1800–1940: projets et ingénierie de la convergence et de la différence', Genèses, vol. 71, no. 2, 2008, p. 8.

57 John Morton Boyd, 'Travels in the Middle East and East Africa', 1968 [Zoological Society of London (ZLS), 7AP].

58 Letter from Thane Riney to D. von Hegel, 25 February 1966 [Ethiopian Wildlife Conservation Authority (EWCA), John Blower file (JB) 8].

59 Letter from Alain Gille to John Blower, Addis Ababa, 16 May 1967 [ibid.].

60 Leslie Brown, 'Ethiopia. Progress report on the imperial Ethiopian government's three year wildlife development plan', Nairobi, 7 June 1968 [ibid.].

61 Daniel Hedinger and Nadin Heé, 'Transimperial history – connectivity, cooperation and competition', Journal of Modern European History, vol. 16, no. 4, 2018, p. 439.

62 Pierre-Yves Saunier, 'Les régimes circulatoires...', op. cit., p. 13.

63 Uganda National Parks, 'Notes from Uganda', Oryx, vol. 4, no. 3, 1957, pp. 177–9.

64 Colonial Office, 'National parks & game reserve, Uganda', 1959, n.p. [NA, CO 847/63 'Preservation of national parks and game reserves in colonies' 1957–1959'].

65 John Blower, 'Development and utilisation of wildlife resources in Uganda', in Gerald Watterson, 'Conservation of Nature...', op. cit., pp. 96–101.

66 John Savidge, 'The introduction of white rhinoceros into the Murchison Falls national park, Uganda', Oryx, vol. 6, no. 3, 1961, pp. 184–9.

67 R.J. Wheater, 'The need for co-ordinated land use in areas adjoining national parks', in FAO, 'Papers presented at the third session of the working party on wildlife management of the African Forestry Commission (Lome, Togo, 15–18 Jan 1969)', 1969, n.p. [FAO-FO-AFC/WL/69].

68 Mervyn Cowie, 'Preserve or destroy?', Oryx, vol. 3, no. 1, 1955, pp. 9–11.

69 Mervyn Cowie, 'Royal National Parks of Kenya: plan for game in Masai', 1956, n.p. [NA, CO 847/66 'Report for 1956 by Game Policy Committee of Kenya 1957–1959'].

70 Colony and Protectorate of Kenya, 'Game Department annual report 1961', 1962, pp. 10–11 [NA, CO 822/266 'Kenya Game Department. Annual reports 1961–1962'].

71 Ian Parker, 'The development of wildlife use as a food source', *in* FAO, 'Papers presented at the third session...', op. cit., n.p.

72 R.K. Davis, 'Problems in developing and managing trade in wildlife products', *in* FAO, 'Papers presented at the third session...', op. cit., n.p.

73 Patrick Hemingway, 'Tourist hunting in Kenya', *in* FAO, 'Papers presented at the third session...', op. cit., n.p.

74 C. 437, u.d., n.p. [Cambridge University Library (CUL), GBR/0012/MS Scott, C. 434-438 'The Fauna Preservation Society'].

75 Walter Russell, 'The elephant problem in the Serengeti', *Oryx*, vol. 9, no. 6, 1968, pp. 404–6.

76 Hugh Lamprey, 'Management of flora and fauna in national parks', *in* Hugh Elliott (ed.), 'Second World Conference on National Parks...', op. cit., pp. 237–48.

77 Romain Gary, *The Roots of Heaven*, London: Penguin, 1960, pp. 258–9 and 286.

78 Keith Caldwell, 'Report on a visit to East Africa', *Oryx*, vol. 1, no. 4, 1951, pp. 174–7.

79 George Petrides and Wendell Swank, 'The status of wildlife...', op. cit., pp. 299–304.

80 Antonie Harthoorn, 'Translocation as a means of preserving wild animals', *Oryx*, vol. 6, no. 4, 1962, pp. 215–27.

81 Peter Jewell, 'Wild life research in East and Central Africa', *Oryx*, vol. 7, no. 2–3, 1963, pp. 77–87.

82 Oryx, 'Should the elephants be killed?', *Oryx*, vol. 10, no. 2, 1969, pp. 101–2.

83 D.F. Lovemore, 'The effects of anti-tsetse shooting operations on the game populations as observed in the Sebungwe district, Southern Rhodesia', *in* Gerald Watterson, 'Conservation of Nature...', op. cit., pp. 232–4.

84 Edgar Worthington, 'Report on the wild resources...', op. cit., p. 17.

85 Colony and Protectorate of Kenya, 'Royal national parks and game reserves in Kenya 1960–1961', u.d., n.p. [NA, CO 847/79].

86 C.W. Benson, 'The problem of the cropping of Lechwe on the Kafue flats, Northern Rhodesia', *in* Gerald Watterson, 'Conservation of Nature...', op. cit., pp. 88–9.

87 IUCN, 'Zambia: aid for black lechwe', *IUCN Bulletin*, vol. 2, no. 11, 1969, p. 89 [UNESCO, UIC/8].

88 IUCN, 'Aircraft for Ugandan national parks', *IUCN Bulletin*, vol. 2, no. 1, 1966, p. 5 [ibid.].

89 Fauna Preservation Society, 'World Wildlife Fund. Printed papers with some correspondence', u.d., n.p. [Natural History Museum (NHM), MSS Fisher coll. G77].

90 Correspondence between Charles Boyle and George Dudley Hayes, in 'Colonial game policy in Africa 1960–1961', n.p. [NA, CO 847/75].

91 George Dudley Hayes, 'How independence saved an African reserve', *Oryx*, vol. 9, no. 1, 1967, pp. 25–7.

92 George Dudley Hayes, 'Wildlife conservation in Malawi', *Society Malawi Journal*, vol. 25, no. 2, 1972, pp. 22–31; George Dudley Hayes, 'Conservation in Malawi – old and new', *Oryx*, vol. 12, no. 3, 1974, pp. 334–40; Brian Morris, 'G. D. Hayes and the Nyasaland Fauna Preservation Society', *The Society of Malawi Journal*, vol. 50, no. 1, 1997, pp. 1–12.

93 *UNESCO Courier*, 'Africa's wildlife in peril', op. cit., p. 7.

94 Ian Parker and Stan Bleazard (eds.), *An Impossible Dream. Some of Kenya's Last Colonial Wardens Recall the Game Department in the British Empire's Closing Years*, Moray: Librario, 2001, p. v.

95 Mike Everett, 'Obituary. Leslie Hilton Brown…', op. cit., pp. 223–6.

96 Letter from Leslie Brown to MacDonald, (Karen, Kenya), 19 April 1962 [NHM, Z. MSS PIT-C27 'Correspondence and offprints on ornithology. Grimwood'].

97 Leslie Brown, 'A note on the flamingo situation at Magadi, Kenya', *IUCN Bulletin*, vol. 1, no. 5, 1962, p. 7 [UNESCO, UIC/8].

98 Correspondence between Leslie Brown (Karen, Kenya) and Noel Simon (Morges, Suisse), letters dating 26 December 1963, and 2, 8 and 16 January 1964 [EWCA, JB 8].

99 Leslie Brown, 'Ethiopia. Conservation of nature and natural resources (30 December 1964 to 1 April 1965)', UNESCO, 1965, pp. 8–12 [UNESCO, WS/0865.192-AVS].

100 Hugh Elliott, '*Ethiopian Episode*, by Leslie Brown. Country Life, 42s.', *Oryx*, vol. 8, no. 3, 1965, p. 202.

101 See in particular: Emil Urban and Leslie Brown, 'Wildlife in an Ethiopian valley', *Oryx*, vol. 9, no. 5, 1968, pp. 342–53; Leslie Brown with J. Cocheme, 'Technical report on a study of the agroclimatology of the highlands of eastern Africa', UNESCO and WMO, Paris and Geneva 1969, n.p. [FAO, LIB, M, 551.5 F732].

102 Leslie Brown, 'Wildlife v sheep and cattle in Africa', *Oryx*, vol. 10, no. 2, 1969, p. 92.

103 Correspondence between Leslie Brown, Peter Scott and Ph. S, June 1969 [CUL, GBR/0012/MS Scott, D. 231-242 'East Africa, August–September 1969', D. 238].

104 Leslie Brown, 'Lectures on conservation', Addis Ababa, 1971, p. 4 [EWCA, JB 8].

105 Leslie Brown, *Conservation for Survival. Ethiopia's Choice*, Addis Ababa, Haile Sellassie I University Press, 1973.

106 Letter from Leslie Brown to Peter Scott (Karen, Kenya), 27 June 1973 [CUL, GBR/0012/MS Scott, M. 1785-1789, 'General correspondence, B, 1973', M. 1787].

107 Letter from M.J.C. Brocklehurst to Prince Philip, London, 21 May 1981 [ibid.].

108 Royal National Parks of Kenya, 'Report 1960–1961', Nairobi, 30 June 1961, n.p. [Zoological Society of London (ZSL), G66 'Report – Kenya National Parks'].

109 Ian Grimwood, 'Operation Oryx', *Oryx*, vol. 6, no. 6, 1962, pp. 308–34.

110 Ian Grimwood, 'Airlift for Hunter's antelope: rescue operation in Kenya', *Oryx*, vol. 7, no. 4, 1964, pp. 164–7.

111 Letter from M.J.C. Brocklehurst to Prince Philip, op. cit.

112 Ian Grimwood, '"Operation Oryx". The second stage', *Oryx*, vol. 7, no. 5, 1964, pp. 223–5.

113 Ian Grimwood, 'Ethiopia: conservation of natural resources (November 1964–February 1965)', UNESCO, 1965, p. 4 [UNESCO, WS/0865.66 Rev.-AVS].

114 Letter from Ian Grimwood to Noel Simon, Nairobi, 10 February 1965 [CUL, GBR/0012/MS Scott, M. 1040-1046 'General correspondence', M. 1042].

115 M. 1282, u.d., n.p. [CUL, GBR/0012/MS Scott, M. 1278-1284 'General correspondence'].

116 Ian Grimwood, 'The economic value of indigenous wildlife. Schedule showing', *in* FAO, 'Papers presented at the fourth session of the Ad hoc working party on wildlife management of the African Forestry Commission, Nairobi, Kenya, 1–3 Feb 1972', 1972 [FAO-FO-AFC/WL/72].

117 Letter from Ian Grimwood to Charles Pitman, Nairobi, 4 March 1974 [NHM, Z. MSS PIT-C27 – 'Correspondence and offprints on ornithology. Grimwood'].

118 Letter from M.J.C. Brocklehurst to Prince Philip, op. cit.

119 John Blower, *Banagi Hill. A Game Warden's Africa*, Moray: Librario, 2004, p. 17.

120 Ibid., p. 117.

121 John Blower, 'Development and utilisation of wildlife...', op. cit., p. 96.

122 John Blower, 'The wildlife of Ethiopia', *Oryx*, vol. 9, no. 4, 1968, p. 277.

123 Correspondence between John Blower and David Maddox, letters of 9 June to 3 August 1966 [EWCA, JB 5].

124 Letter from John Blower to Hugh Elliott, Addis Ababa, January 1966 [EWCA, JB 4].

125 Richard Fitter, 'Notice of a meeting of the council', London, 20 October 1966 [NHM, MSS Fisher coll. G16 'Fauna Preservation Society. Printed papers'].

126 Letter from Bernhard Grzimek to John Blower, Frankfurt, 14 June 1968 [EWCA, JB 5].

127 John Blower, *In Ethiopia. A Game Warden's Adventures in Haile Selassie's Medieval Empire*, Moray: Librario, 2005.

128 John Blower, 'Ethiopia. Wildlife conservation and national parks. September 1965–September 1969', UNESCO, 1971, p. 8 [UNESCO, 2351/RMS.RS/SCE, FR/TA/ETHIOPES 5].

129 Letter from John Blower to Abebe Retta, Addis Ababa, 4 April 1969 [EWCA, JB 6].

130 John Blower, *Banagi Hill*, op. cit., p. 17.

131 Ibid., p. 133.

132 John Blower, *In Ethiopia*, op. cit., p. 13.

133 John Blower, 'The wildlife of Ethiopia', op. cit., p. 277.

134 John Blower, 'Rhinos – and other problems – in Nepal', *Oryx*, vol. 12, no. 2, 1973, pp. 270–80.

135 John Blower, 'New look in Indonesia', *Oryx*, vol. 15, no. 1, 1979, pp. 50–4.

136 John Blower, *The Plundered Forests*, Moray: Librario, 2007, p. 263.

137 Letter from John Blower to John Morton Boyd, Addis Ababa, 11 August 1969 [EWCA, JB 4].

138 John Blower, 'Provision of tourist facilities. Awash National Park', Addis Ababa, 7 August 1967, n.p. [EWCA, JB 6].

139 Letter from John Blower to Yohannes Kidane Mariam, 19 December 1967 [ibid.].

140 Peter Hay, *One Long Safari*, Agoura: Trophy Room Books, 1998.

141 Peter Hay, 'Awash National Park. Annual Report 1968', Metehara, December 1968, n.p.

142 Ibid.

143 Letter from George Brown to John Blower, Omo Reserve, 6 May 1969 [EWCA, JB 5].

144 Imperial Ethiopian government, 'Regulations issued pursuant to the game proclamation of 1944 and the wildlife conservation order of 1970', *Negarit Gazeta*, vol. 31, no. 7, 19 January 1972, p. 37 [EWCA].

145 Letter from Clive Nicol to John Blower, Gondar, 30 May 1969 [EWCA, JB 11]; letter from Clive Nicol to Abebe Retta, Gondar, 8 July 1969 [EWCA, JB 1].

146 Clive Nicol, *From the Roof of Africa*, London: Hodder and Stoughton, 1972, p. 8.

147 Ibid., p. 31.

148 Ibid., pp. 71 and 265–6.

Chapter 3: Governing Ethiopia

1 Hannah Arendt, *The Human Condition*, Chicago and London: University of Chicago Press, 1998, p. 7.

2 Thomas Odhiambo, 'Human and sociological factors', *in* Gerald Watterson 'Conservation of Nature...', op. cit., pp. 256–60.

3 H.S. Mahinda, 'An experiment in spreading propaganda among indigenous people as to the value of wild life, and the need for its conservation', *in* Gerald Watterson 'Conservation of Nature...', op. cit., pp. 235–7.

4 M.K. Shawki, 'Integration of the conservation and development of wild resources with programs of economic development in modern states', *in* Gerald Watterson, 'Conservation of Nature...', op. cit., pp. 321–4.

5 Tewa Said Tewa, 'The value of the tourist industry in the conservation of natural resources in Tanganyika', *in* Gerald Watterson 'Conservation of Nature...', op. cit., pp. 336–9.

6 Edgar Worthington, 'The problem of influencing African native opinion on conservation', 11 April 1960 [Cambridge University Library (CUL), GBR/0012/MS Scott, C. 853-859 'Correspondence etc., 1960–1961', C. 854].

7 David Wasawo, 'Wild fauna and flora of Africa as a cultural and economic asset and the world interest therein', *in* Gerald Watterson, 'Conservation of Nature...', op. cit., p. 352.

8 Ibid., p. 354.

9 David Wasawo, 'African culture and African parks', *in* Alexander B. Adams (ed.), 'First World Conference on National Parks', op. cit., pp. 139–44.

10 Julian Huxley, Alain Gille, Théodore Monod, Lloyd Swift and Edgar Worthington, 'The conservation of nature and natural resources in Ethiopia', UNESCO, 1964, pp. 5 and 23 [UNESCO, NS/NR/47].

11 Edgar Worthington, *The Ecological Century. A Personal Appraisal*, Oxford: Oxford University Press, 1983, p. 152.

12 H.P. Huffnagel, 'Agriculture in Ethiopia', FAO, 1961 [FAO, 065241].

13 UNESCO, 'Resolution adopted by the General Conference of Unesco at its 12th Session', Paris, 12 December 1963, p. 6 [UNESCO, 12 C/DR/64].

14 IUCN, 'Eighth General Assembly', op. cit., p. 5.

15 Julian Huxley et al., 'The conservation of nature...', op. cit., p. 5.

16 Edgar Worthington, *The Ecological Century*, op. cit.

17 See in particular: Bahru Zewde, *A History of Modern Ethiopia 1855–1991*, Oxford: James Currey, 2002, p. 85.

18 Haile Selassie I, 'Address to the United Nations. October 4, 1963', *The Proud Reader*, 2022, n.p.

19 Stephen Macekura, *Of Limits and Growth. The Rise of Global Sustainable Development in the Twentieth Century*, Cambridge: Cambridge University Press, 2015, pp. 57–61.

20 Jeff Schauer, '"We hold it in trust"', op. cit., pp. 530–1.

21 Jean-François Bayart, 'Africa in the world', op. cit., p. 218.

22 Jean-Hervé Jézéquel, 'Voices of their own? African participation in the production of colonial knowledge in French West Africa, 1910–1950', *in* Helen Tilley with Robert Gordon (eds.), *Ordering Africa. Anthropology, European Imperialism, and the Politics of Knowledge*, Manchester and New York: Manchester University Press, 2007, pp. 145–72.

23 Frederick Cooper and Randall Packard, 'Introduction', *in* F. Cooper and R. Packard (eds.), *International Development and the Social Sciences*, op. cit., pp. 1–39.

24 Elizabeth Garland, 'The elephant in the room: confronting the colonial character of wildlife conservation in Africa', *African Studies Review*, vol. 51, no. 3, 2008, p. 52.

25 Julie Weiskopf, 'Socialism on safari: wildlife and nation-building in postcolonial Tanzania, 1961–77', *Journal of African History*, vol. 56, no. 3, 2015, pp. 430–7.

26 Roderick Neumann, *Imposing Wilderness*, op. cit., pp. 143–5.

27 Andreas Eckert, 'Julius Nyerere, Tanzanian elites, and the project of African socialism', *in* Jost Dülffer and Marc Frey (eds.), *Elites and Decolonization in the Twentieth Century*, London: Palgrave Macmillan, 2011, p. 231.

28 Reuben Matheka, 'The international dimension…', op. cit., pp. 112–33.

29 Clark Gibson, *Politicians and Poachers*, op. cit., pp. 33–40.

30 Jean-François Bayart, 'La revanche des sociétés africaines', *Politique africaine*, no. 11, 1983, p. 112.

31 Frederick Cooper, 'Conflict and connection: rethinking colonial African history', *The American Historical Review*, vol. 99, no. 5, 1994, p. 1539.

32 James McCann, 'The plow and the forest: narratives of deforestation in Ethiopia, 1840–1992', *Environmental History*, vol. 2, no. 2, 1997, pp. 138–59.

33 Clive Nicol, *From the Roof of Africa*, op. cit., p. 171.

34 Girma Tayachew, 'The Simen wild fauna under the protection of the government of Haile Selassie: from endangered prey to national symbol (1941–1969)', *Annales d'Éthiopie*, no. 31, 2016–17, pp. 73–4.

35 Bahru Zewde, 'The concept of japanization in the intellectual history of

modern Ethiopia', *in* Bahru Zewde (ed.), *Proceedings of the Fifth Seminar of the Department of History*, Addis Ababa: Addis Ababa University, 1990, pp. 1–17.

36 Guillaume Blanc, 'Governing nature and Ethiopia: struggles around world heritage, nation-building and ecologies (1963–2012)', *Northeast African Studies*, vol. 18, no. 1–2, 2018, pp. 137–64.

37 Julian Huxley et al., 'The conservation of nature...', op. cit.; Ian Grimwood, 'Ethiopia: conservation of natural resources', op. cit.; Leslie Brown, 'Ethiopia: conservation of nature and natural resources', op. cit.

38 Letter from Sheldon Vance to Berhanu Tessema, Addis Ababa, 19 July 1965 [Ethiopian Wildlife Conservation Authority (EWCA), 9.B.2 '1957–1961 Ethiopian calendar (Et. c.), The World Wildlife Fund Different Aids'].

39 Letter from Berhanu Tessema to Fritz Vollmar, Addis Ababa, 3 August 1965 [ibid.].

40 Letter from Fritz Vollmar to John Blower, Morges, 15 September 1965 [ibid.].

41 Correspondence between Gizaw Gedlegiorgis and Fritz Vollmar, Addis Ababa and Morges, 1966–1968 [ibid.].

42 Letter from Gizaw Gedlegiorgis to the FAO, Forestry and Forestry products division, Addis Ababa, 3 January 1966 [EWCA, JB 8].

43 Letter from J.L. Craig to Yohannes Habtu, Addis Ababa, 25 February 1966 [ibid.].

44 Letter from Gizaw Gedlegiorgis to Mitiku Gembere, Addis Ababa, 14 November 1966 [ibid.].

45 Letter from John Blower to Gizaw Gedlegiorgis, Addis Ababa, 21 November 1966 [ibid.].

46 Letter from Gizaw Gedlegiorgis to John Blower, Addis Ababa, 17 July 1967 [ibid.].

47 Conservation Department, 'Minutes of the meeting presided by major Gizaw, general manager of the Wildlife Conservation Department held on January 8th 1969 in the Awash National Park', Addis Ababa, 8 January 1969, n.p. [ibid.].

48 Correspondence between Gizaw Gedlegiorgis and V. Kostikov, Addis Ababa and Metehara, April–June 1969 [ibid.].

49 Correspondence between Gizaw Gedlegiorgis and Robert Yost, Addis Ababa, 1968–1969 [EWCA, 9.B.4 '1962–1978, American different aids'].

50 Letter from Mebratu Fisseha to Robert Yost, Addis Ababa, 9 January 1970 [ibid.].

51 Letter from Mebratu Fisseha to Rockefeller Brothers Fund, Addis Ababa, 12 February 1970 [ibid.].

52 Letter from James Hyde to Mebratu Fisseha, New York, 13 July 1970 [ibid.].

53 Letter from Mebratu Fisseha to James Hyde, Addis Ababa, 20 July 1970 [ibid.].

54 Letter from Mebratu Fisseha to William Moody, Addis Ababa, 26 September 1970 [ibid.].

55 Letter from James Hyde to Mebratu Fisseha, New York, 20 January 1971 [ibid.].

56 Letter from Mebratu Fisseha to James Hyde, Addis Ababa, 28 January 1971 [ibid.].

57 Letter from Mebratu Fisseha to Glenn Pound, Addis Ababa, 17 January 1972 [EWCA, 10.A.5 '1964 Et. c., Correspondence'].

58 Letter from Clement Merowit to the secretary of the Ethiopian Ministry of Foreign Affairs, New York, 17 November 1973 [EWCA, 9.B.4 '1962–1978, American different aids'].

59 Letter from Lealem Berhanu to Bob Holleron, Addis Ababa, 4 March 1976 [ibid.].

60 Letter from Fritz Vollmar to John Stephenson, Morges, 4 July 1974 [EWCA, 1.A.S.9 & 1.A.T.1 'John G. Stephenson, 1967–1970 Et. c.'].

61 Letter from Teshome Ashine to Bernhard Grzimek, Addis Ababa, 15 May 1975 [EWCA, 9.B.10 '1969–2004, Frankfurt Zoological Society aids'].

62 Letter from Teshome Ashine to the Addis Ababa Bank, Addis Ababa, 29 May 1975 [ibid.].

63 Letter from Teshome Ashine to Bernhard Grzimek, Addis Ababa, 9 June 1977 [ibid.].

64 Letter from John Blower to Gizaw Gedlegiorgis, Addis Ababa, 26 February 1966 [EWCA, JB 6].

65 Letter from John Blower to Gizaw Gedlegiorgis, Addis Ababa, 28 April 1966 [ibid.].

66 Letter from John Blower to Gizaw Gedlegiorgis, Addis Ababa, 28 August 1967 [EWCA, JB 7].

67 Letter from Gizaw Gedlegiorgis to John Blower, Addis Ababa, 13 September 1967 [ibid.].

68 Letter from John Blower to Germatchew Tekle Hawariat, Addis Ababa, 3 April 1968 [ibid.].

69 Correspondence between John Blower and Mebratu Fisseha, Addis Ababa, April–July 1969 [EWCA, JB 6].

70 Akelework Habtewold, 'Regulations issued pursuant to the game proclamation, 1944', Addis Ababa, 27 July 1964, n.p. [EWCA, JB 1].

71 Letter from Russell Berman to Akelework Habtewold, Addis Ababa, 21 February 1964 [ibid.].

72 Letter from Russell Berman to Wolfe Mikael Kelecha, Addis Ababa, 16 March 1964 [ibid.].

73 EWCO, 'Improvement of services for tourist hunter, professional hunters and export of wildlife products from Ethiopia', Addis Ababa, 30 January 1975, n.p. [ibid.].

74 Letter from John Blower to George Pournelle, Addis Ababa, 7 June 1967 [EWCA, JB 7]; letter from H.H. Roth to John Blower, Mexico, 28 June 1967 [ibid.]; letter from H.H. Roth to John Blower, Mexico, 1 August 1967 [ibid.].

75 Letter from John Blower to Balcha Edesa, Addis Ababa, 22 November 1967 [ibid.].

76 Letter from John Blower to Gizaw Gedlegiorgis, 4 March 1968 [ibid.].

77 Letter from Melvin Bolton to Mebratu Fisseha, Addis Ababa, 20 September 1969 [EWCA, 1.A.B.10 'Melvin Bolton, 1969–1972'].

78 Letter from Melvin Bolton to Mebratu Fisseha, Addis Ababa, 11 February 1970 [ibid.].

79 Letter from Mebratu Fisseha to the Conservation Department, Addis Ababa, 19 February 1970 [ibid.].

80 EWCO, 'Fourth five year plan', Addis Ababa, 1973, p. 19 [EWCA].

81 Patrick Stracey, 'A brief note on a visit to Simien national park', Addis Ababa, 11 February 1972, p. 3 [EWCA, JB 11].

82 Letter from Fritz Vollmar to John Stephenson, Morges, 4 July 1974 [EWCA, 1.A.S.9 & 1.A.T.1 'John G. Stephenson, 1967–1970 Et. c.'].

83 Bernhard Grzimek, 'To whom it may concern', Frankfurt, 25 March 1974, n.p. [ibid.].

84 John Owen, 'Mr. J.G. Stephenson', 1 March 1973, n.p. [ibid.].

85 Letter from John Stephenson to Teshome Ashine, Addis Ababa, 22 June 1976 [ibid.].

86 Letter from Teshome Ashine to John Stephenson, Addis Ababa, 17 July 1979 [ibid.].

87 UNESCO, 'Intergovernmental Committee for the Protection of the World Cultural and Natural Heritage. Second Session. Final report', Washington, 1978, p. 7 [UNESCO, CC 78/ CONF.010/10 Rev].

88 EWCO, 'Annual report', Addis Ababa, 1978, n.p. [EWCA].

89 Jesse Hillman, 'Conservation in Bale Mountains national park, Ethiopia', Oryx, vol. 20, no. 2, 1986, pp. 89–94.

90 See notably: Donald Donham, Marxist Modern. An Ethnographic History of the Ethiopian Revolution, Berkeley and Oxford: University of California Press and James Currey, 1999.

91 Bahru Zewde, 'The concept of japanization…', op. cit.

92 Letter from Mebratu Fisseha to Fritz Vollmar, Addis Ababa, 28 July 1970 [EWCA, 10.A.4 '1964 Et. c., Correspondence'].

93 Letter from Mebratu Fisseha to Fritz Vollmar, Addis Ababa, 5 August 1969 [EWCA, JB 6].

94 Letter from Mebratu Fisseha to Abebe Retta, Addis Ababa, 26 September 1969 [EWCA, 9.B.3 '1962–1964 Et. c., Prince Bernhard of Netherlands visit'].

95 EWCO, 'Comments of the Wildlife Conservation Organization', Addis Ababa, 1972, n.p. [EWCA, JB 9].

96 Patrick Stracey, 'A brief note...', op. cit., p. 3.

97 Letter from Alain Gille to Mebratu Fisseha, Nairobi, 27 September 1969 [EWCA, 9.B.11 '1968–1975, UNESCO'].

98 Letter from Mebratu Fisseha to Perez Olindo, Addis Ababa, 29 October 1971 [ibid.].

99 Letter from Teshome Ashine to the planning office committee, Addis Ababa, 19 November 1973 [ibid.].

100 Letter from Mebratu Fisseha to the committee of the EWCO, Addis Ababa, July 1970 [EWCA, 9.B.14 '1971–1974, IUCN meeting reports'].

101 IUCN, 'Conservation coins', *IUCN Bulletin*, vol. 6, no. 10, 1975, p. 38 [UNESCO, UIC/8].

102 Letter from Fritz Vollmar to Teshome Ashine, Morges, 13 June 1973 [EWCA, 9.B.15 '1972–1974, Building conservation coins'].

103 Correspondence between Kassa Woldemariam and Fritz Vollmar, Addis Ababa and Morges, July–August 1973 [ibid.].

104 EWCO, IUCN and WWF, 'Conservation coinage issue. Minutes', Addis Ababa, 20–25 February 1974, n.p. [ibid.].

105 Ethiopia Tikdem, 'Endangered species of wildlife conservation commemorative coins regulations', *Negarit Gazeta*, vol. 37, no. 13, 21 June 1978, p. 76 [EWCA].

106 UNESCO, 'Intergovernmental Committee for the Protection of the World Cultural and Natural Heritage...', op. cit., p. 7.

107 Ermias Bekele, 'A description of the conservation status and future outlooks of Ethiopia's Semien mountains, Bale mountains, and Abijata-Shall lakes national parks. UNESCO's world heritage mission to Ethiopia. April 24, 1982', Addis Ababa, 1982, p. 12 [EWCA].

108 Letter from Robert Yost to Mebratu Fisseha, Addis Ababa, 1969 [EWCA, 2.A.6.1 '1960–1973 Et. c., Field visits'].

109 Letter from Mebratu Fisseha to the Customs Office at Addis Ababa airport, 19 February 1969 [EWCA, JB 7].

110 Anthony Mence, 'Certificate', Mweka, 29 June 1968, n.p. [EWCA, 1.A.K.9 & 1.A.L.1 'Lealem Berhanu, 1958–1970 Et. c.'].

111 Letter from Anthony Mence to Mebratu Fisseha, Mweka, 6 December 1971 [EWCA, 9.B.3 '1961–1964 Et. c., College of African Wildlife Management'].

112 Letter from Peter Hay to John Blower, Awash, 30 January 1968 [EWCA, JB 7].

113 Letter from Gizaw Gedlegiorgis to John Blower and George Brown, Addis Ababa, 19 January 1968 [ibid.].

114 Letter from Berhanu Tessema to John Blower, Addis Ababa, 30 May 1965 [EWCA, 1.A.B.10 'John Blower, 1965–1970'].

115 Letter from John Blower to Berhanu Tessema, Kampala, 1 July 1965 [ibid.].

116 Letter from John Blower to Gizaw Gedlegiorgis, Addis Ababa, 22 April 1966 [EWCA, JB 4].

117 Letter from Gizaw Gedlegiorgis to George Brown, Addis Ababa, 1 February 1968 [EWCA, 1.A.B.11 'George Brown, 1965–1970'].

118 Letter from Gizaw Gedlegiorgis to John Blower, Addis Ababa, 8 May 1968 [EWCA, 1.A.B.10 'John Blower, 1965–1970'].

119 Letter from John Blower to Germatchew Tekle Hawariat, Addis Ababa, 15 May 1968 [ibid.].

120 Letter from Gizaw Gedlegiorgis to Germatchew Tekle Hawariat, 18 May 1968 [ibid.].

121 Letter from John Blower to Gizaw Gedlegiorgis, Guernsey, 27 November 1968 [ibid.].

122 Letter from Gizaw Gedlegiorgis to John Blower, Addis Ababa, 7 December 1968 [ibid.].

123 Letter from Gizaw Gedlegiorgis to John Blower, Addis Ababa, 20 February 1969 [ibid.].

124 Letter from Gizaw Gedlegiorgis to John Blower, Addis Ababa, 24 February 1969 [ibid.].

125 Letter from Gizaw Gedlegiorgis to John Blower, Addis Ababa, 13 March 1969 [ibid.].

126 Letter from Gizaw Gedlegiorgis to John Blower, Addis Ababa, 25 March 1969 [ibid.].

127 Mebratu Fisseha, 'Statement. Incentives by leopard-skin traders to illegal poachers in Ethiopia', in IUCN, 'Tenth General Assembly, Vigyan Bhavan, New Delhi, 24 November–1 December 1969. Volume II. Proceedings and summary of business', Morges, 1970, p. 167 [IUCN- NS-SP-no.027].

128 Letter from John Blower to Mebratu Fisseha, Addis Ababa, 3 December 1969 [EWCA, JB 8].

129 Letter from Mebratu Fisseha to Abebe Retta, Addis Ababa, 10 December 1969 [ibid.].

130 Letter from Fikre Mariam Demeke to Patrick Stracey, Addis Ababa, 25 June 1974 [ibid.].

131 Yewand Wassen Fassil, 'A "report" on Kenya Game Department', Addis Ababa, 3 November 1971, n.p. [EWCA, 6.A.2 '1962–1973 Et. c., EWCO general reports'].

132 Letter from Teshome Ashine to Patrick Stracey, Addis Ababa, 7 March 1973 [EWCA, 1.A.S.9 & 1.A.T.1 'P.D. Stracey, 1963–1966 Et. c.'].

133 Letter from Patrick Stracey to Teshome Ashine, Addis Ababa, 13 May 1973 [ibid.].

134 Letter from Patrick Stracey to Teshome Ashine, Addis Ababa, 25 May 1973 [ibid.].

135 Jean-Pierre Olivier de Sardan, *Travelling Models and Practical Norms. The Misadventures of Social Engineering in Africa and Beyond*, New York and Oxford: Berghahn Books, 2025, p. 2.

136 Letter from George Brown to John Blower, Omo, 6 May 1969 [EWCA, JB 6].

137 Jon Abbink, 'Authority and leadership in Surma society (Ethiopia)', *Africa: Rivista trimestrale di studi e documentazione dell'Istituto italiano per l'Africa e l'Oriente*, vol. 52, no. 3, 1997, p. 325.

138 Letter from George Brown to John Blower, Omo, 18 November 1969 [EWCA, JB 8].

139 Letter from Germatchew Tekle Hawariat to the EWCO, Maji, 10 February 1970 [EWCA, 2.B.5.3 '1962 Et. c., Omo. Different issues'].

140 Letter from Frederick Duckworth to Mebratu Fisseha, Addis Ababa, 1 March 1972 [EWCA, 2.B.5.1 '1959–1970 Et. c., Reports'].

141 Letter from Mariam Demeke to the EWCO, Omo, 1 December 1973 [ibid.].

142 Letter from Teshome Demena to the EWCO, Omo, 2 February 1976 [ibid.].

143 Letter from Akinori Mizuno and John Stephenson to Teshome Ashine, Addis Ababa, 18 January 1978 [ibid.].

144 Letter from John Blower to Gizaw Gedlegiorgis, Addis Ababa, 31 May 1967 [EWCA, JB 6].

145 Letter from John Blower to Gizaw Gedlegiorgis, Addis Ababa, 21 July 1967 [EWCA, JB 3].

146 Letters from Peter Hay to Gizaw Gedlegiorgis, Awash, 11 September 1967, 5 December 1967, 12 January 1968, 4 February 1968 and 12 April 1968 [ibid.].

147 Peter Hay, 'Awash Park monthly report. May 1968' Awash, 1968, n.p. [ibid.].

148 Letter from John Blower to Gizaw Gedlegiorgis, Addis Ababa, 24 June 1968 [ibid.].

149 Letter from Peter Hay to John Blower, Awash, 28 June 1968 [ibid.].

150 Letter from Peter Hay to Gizaw Gedlegiorgis, Awash, 28 June 1968 [ibid.].

151 Letter from Tadesse Mickael to Gizaw Gedlegiorgis, Awash, 9 January 1969 [EWCA, JB 6].

152 John Bromley, 'People and domesticated stock in the national park', Awash, 6 June 1969, n.p. [ibid.]; letter from the EWCO to Mr. Vanci, 'Indiscipline of operators', Metehara, 29 April 1970 [EWCA, 2.A.6.1 '1960–1973 Et. c., Field visits'].

153 Frederick Cooper, 'Conflict and connection', op. cit., p. 1539.

154 Letter from Gizaw Gedlegiorgis to Laurence Guth, Addis Ababa, 12 October 1966 [EWCA, JB 4].

155 Letter from John Blower to Gizaw Gedlegiorgis, Addis Ababa, 12 April 1967 [ibid.].

156 Letter from John Blower to Gizaw Gedlegiorgis, Addis Ababa, 7 November 1967 [ibid.].

157 Letter from John Blower to Gizaw Gedlegiorgis, Addis Ababa, 14 March 1968 [ibid.].

158 Letter from Clive Nicol to Gizaw Gedlegiorgis, Gondar, 5 February 1969 [ibid.].

159 Letter from Gizaw Gedlegiorgis to Clive Nicol, Addis Ababa, 30 June 1969 [EWCA, 2.B.8.1 '1961–1970 Et. c., Reports'].

160 Letter from Gizaw Gedlegiorgis to Clive Nicol, Addis Ababa, 18 June 1969 [ibid.].

161 Letter from Clive Nicol to John Blower, Gondar, 30 May 1969 [EWCA, JB 11].

162 Letter from Clive Nicol to Abebe Retta, Gondar, 8 July 1969 [EWCA, JB 1].

163 Girma Tayachew, 'The Simen wild fauna...', op. cit., pp. 73–4.

164 Letter from Clive Nicol to John Blower, Gondar, 30 May 1969 [EWCA, JB 11].

165 Letter from Clive Nicol to John Blower, Gondar, 21 August 1968 [EWCA, 2.B.8.1 '1961–1970 Et. c., Reports'].

166 Letter from Clive Nicol to Gizaw Gedlegiorgis, Gondar, 12 November 1968 [EWCA, JB 4].

167 Letter from John Blower to Germatchew Tekle Hawariat, Addis Ababa, 10 February 1969 [ibid.].

168 Letter from Gizaw Gedlegiorgis to Clive Nicol, Addis Ababa, 8 March 1969 [EWCA, 2.B.8.1 '1961–1970 Et. c., Reports'].

169 Letter from Clive Nicol to Gizaw Gedlegiorgis, Addis Ababa, 25 June 1969 [ibid.].

170 Letter from Clive Nicol to Abebe Retta, Gondar, 8 July 1969 [EWCA, JB 1].

171 Letter from Mebratu Fisseha to Noel Simon and Fritz Vollmar, Addis Ababa, 5 August 1969 [EWCA, NOTES 313 2.B.8.1 '1961–1970 Et. c., Reports'].

Chapter 4: Living in a national park

1 See, amongst others, the titles of contributions made during the conference: 'Alphabetical list of authors', *in* Gerald Watterson, 'Conservation of Nature…', op. cit., pp. 359–61.

2 For more detail on the history of the Surma and the Mursi people, the most specialized reference is probably Jean-Baptiste Eczet's book, *Amour vache. Esthétique sociale en pays mursi (Éthiopie)*, Milan: Mimésis, 2019 (*Cattle Poetics: How Aesthetics Shapes Politics in Mursiland*, New York and Oxford: Berghahn Books, 2021).

3 Jean-Baptiste Eczet, 'Des hommes et des vaches: l'attachement entre les personnes et leurs bovins en pays Mursi (Éthiopie)', *Anthropologie et Sociétés*, vol. 39, no. 1–2, 2015, pp. 121–44.

4 Alfâ Ibrâhîm Sow (ed.), *La Femme. La Vache. La Foi. Écrivains et poètes du Fuuta-Jalon*, Paris: Julliard, 1966; Yassine Kervella-Mansaré, 'Le Peul au miroir de sa vache', *in* Sergio Dalla Bernardina (ed.), *De la bête au non-humain: perspectives et controverses autour de la condition animale*, Paris: Éditions du CTHS, 2020, pp. 135–46.

5 Girum Getachew, Degefa Tolossa and Getachew Gebru, 'Risk perception and coping strategies among the Karrayu pastoralists of Upper Awash valley, Central Ethiopia', *Nomadic Peoples*, vol. 12, no. 1, 2008, pp. 93–107. See also: Yihew Biru, Zewdu Tessema and Mengistu Urge, 'Perception and attitude of pastoralists on livestock–wildlife interactions around Awash national park, Ethiopia: implication for biodiversity conservation', *Ecological Processes*, vol. 6, 2017 (https://doi.org/10.1186/s13717-017-0081-9).

6 Guillaume Blanc, 'Violence et incohérence en milieu naturel: une histoire du parc éthiopien du Semēn', *Études rurales*, no. 197, 2016, pp. 147–9.

7 See in particular: Bahru Zewde, *A History of Modern Ethiopia*, op. cit., pp. 201–8 and 216–19.

8 See in particular: Helmut Kloos, 'Development, drought, and famine in the Awash Valley of Ethiopia', *African Studies Review*, vol. 25, no. 4, 1982, pp. 21–48.

9 See in particular: Jon Abbink, 'Authority and leadership in Surma society', op. cit., pp. 317–42.

10 Edward Said, *Orientalism. Western Conceptions of the Orient*, London and New York: Vintage Books, 1979.

11 Ranajit Guha, 'The prose of counter-insurgency', *in* Ranajit Guha (ed.), *Subaltern Studies II. Writings on South Asian History and Society*, Delhi: Oxford University Press, 1983.

12 Jonathan Rutherford, 'The third space: interview with Homi Bhabha', *in*

Jonathan Rutherford (ed.), *Identity: Community, Culture, Difference*, London: Lawrence and Wishart, 1990, pp. 207–21.

13 Gayatri Chakravorty Spivak, *Can the Subaltern Speak?* New York: Columbia University Press, 2010.

14 Christine Chivallon, 'La quête pathétique des *postcolonial studies* ou la révolution manquée', *Mouvements*, no. 51, 2007, pp. 32–9.

15 Dipesh Chakrabarty, 'Subaltern studies and postcolonial historiography', *Nepantla. Views from South*, vol. 1, no. 1, 2000, pp. 15–16.

16 Frederick Cooper, 'Conflict and connection', op. cit., p. 1528.

17 bell hooks, *Feminist Theory. From Margin to Centre*, Abingdon and New York: Routledge, 2015.

18 Jean-François Médard, 'L'État-néopatrimonial', *in* Jean-François Médard (ed.), *États d'Afrique noire. Formations, mécanismes et crise*, Paris: Karthala, 1991, pp. 323–53. The concept and definition of *big man* come from anthropologist Marshall Sahlins ('Poor man, rich man, big man, chief. Political types in Melanesia and Polynesia', *Comparative Studies in Society and History*, vol. 5, no. 3, 1963, pp. 285–303) and Maurice Godelier (*La Production des grands hommes. Pouvoir et domination masculine chez les Maruya de Nouvelle-Guinée*, Paris: Fayard, 1982).

19 Jean-François Bayart, 'Africa in the world', op. cit., pp. 217–67.

20 James Scott, *Domination and the Arts of Resistance. Hidden Transcripts*, New Haven, CT: Yale University Press, 1990; James Scott, 'Infra-politique des groups subalternes', *Vacarme*, vol. 36, no. 3, 2006, pp. 25–9.

21 Lahouari Addi, 'Sociologie du savoir sur autrui. Contributions au débat sur les études postcoloniales', *Mouvements*, vol. 72, no, 4, 2012, p. 55.

22 Philippe Artières, 'Archives de basse tension', *in* Laure Pressac (ed.), *Sur les murs. Histoire(s) de graffitis*, Paris: Éditions du patrimoine et Centre des monuments nationaux, 2018, pp. 54–8.

23 Ann Laura Stoler, *Along the Archival Grain. Epistemic Anxieties and Colonial Common Sense*, Princeton, NJ: Princeton University Press, 2009.

24 Pierre Guidi and Ophélie Rillon, 'Penser les violences politiques au prisme de l'intime', *20 & 21. Revue d'histoire*, no. 151, 2021, p. 16.

25 Melissa Leach and Robin Mearns, 'Challenging received wisdom in Africa', *in* Melissa Leach and Robin Mearns (eds.), *The Lie of the Land. Challenging Received Wisdom on the African Environment*, Oxford and Portsmouth: James Currey and Heinemann, 1996, pp. 1–33.

26 Helen Tilley, *Africa as Living Laboratory. Empire, Development and the Problem of Scientific Knowledge, 1870–1950*, Chicago: University of Chicago Press, 2011, see in particular pp. 122, 314–15 and 320.

27 Corey Ross, 'Tropical nature as global *patrimoine*: imperialism and international nature protection in the early twentieth century', *Past and Present*, vol. 226, no. 10, 2015, pp. 234–7.

28 Bernhard Gissibl, *The Nature of German Imperialism. Conservation and the Politics of Wildlife in Colonial East Africa*, New York and Oxford: Berghahn Books, 2019 [2016], pp. 109–40.

29 Jeff Schauer, *Wildlife between Empire and Nation*, op. cit., pp. 81–7; Reuben Matheka, 'The international dimension…', op. cit., p. 119.

30 Roderick Neumann, *Imposing Wilderness*, op. cit., see in particular pp. 157–73.

31 David Turton, 'Wilderness, wasteland or home? Three ways of imagining the Lower Omo valley', *Journal of Eastern African Studies*, vol. 5, no. 1, 2011, pp. 158–76; Jean-Baptiste Eczet, *Cattle Poetics*, op. cit.

32 Solomon Belay, Aklilu Amsalu and Eyualem Abebe, 'Awash National Park, Ethiopia: use policy, ethnic conflict and sustainable resources conservation in the context of decentralization', *African Journal of Ecology*, vol. 51, no. 1, 2012, pp. 122–9.

33 Michael Mok, 'The losing fight for game parks', *Life*, vol. 69, no. 22, 27 November 1970, p. 57.

34 Karl Jacoby, *Shadows at Dawn*, op. cit., p. 28.

35 Interviews with the author, Simien, January 2019.

36 Peter Hay, 'Awash monthly report – Sept. 1966', Metehara, October 1966, n.p. [EWCA, JB 2].

37 Peter Hay, 'November monthly report, 1966. Awash Falls Park', Metehara, December 1966, n.p. [ibid.].

38 Peter Hay, 'Monthly report Awash Park. February 1967', Metehara, March 1967, n.p. [ibid.].

39 Peter Hay, 'Awash monthly report. April – 1967', Metehara, May 1967, n.p. [ibid.].

40 Peter Hay, 'Awash National Park monthly report. June, 1967', Metehara, July 1967, n.p. [ibid.]; Clive Nicol, *From the Roof of Africa*, op. cit., pp. 9–10.

41 Letter from John Blower to Gizaw Gedlegiorgis, Addis Ababa, 21 June 1967 [EWCA, JB 3].

42 Letter from John Blower to Gizaw Gedlegiorgis, Addis Ababa, 21 July 1967 [EWCA, JB 6].

43 Peter Hay, 'Awash monthly report. September, 1967', Awash, October 1967, n.p. [EWCA, JB 2].

44 Peter Hay, 'Annual report 1967. Awash Falls National Park', Awash, 1968, n.p. [ibid.].

45 Letter from John Blower to Gizaw Gedlegiorgis, Addis Ababa, 24 June 1968 [ibid.].

46 Peter Hay, 'Annual report 1968. Awash Falls National Park', Awash, 1969, n.p. [EWCA, JB 6].

47 John Bromley, 'People and domesticated stock in the national park', Awash, 6 June 1969, n.p. [EWCA].

48 Letter from John Blower to Gizaw Gedlegiorgis, Addis Ababa, 13 April 1966 [EWCA, JB 4].

49 Letter from George Brown to John Blower, Omo, March 1967 [EWCA, JB 6].

50 Letter from George Brown to John Blower, Omo, September 1968 [ibid.].

51 Letter from George Brown to John Blower, Omo, 18 November 1969 [EWCA, JB 8].

52 Letter from Germatchew Tekle Hawariat to the EWCO, Maji, 10 February 1970 [EWCA, 2.B.5.3 '1962 Et. c., Omo. Different issues'].

53 Letter from George Brown to Mebratu Fisseha, Omo, 25 March 1970 [EWCA, 1.A.B.6 'Berhanu Bisetegn, 1960–1984 Et. c.'].

54 Letter from Clive Nicol to John Blower, Gondar, 30 May 1969 [EWCA, JB 11].

55 Letter from Jerry Dandoi to Tag Demment, Addis Ababa, 12 June 1969 [EWCA, JB 8]; Clive Nicol, *From the Roof of Africa*, op. cit., pp. 177–8.

56 John Blower, 'Draft of report prepared for board. Summary of progress', Addis Ababa, May 1969, n.p. [EWCA, JB 5].

57 Peter Stähli and Max Zurbuchen, 'Two topographic maps 1:25 000 of Simen, Ethiopia', *in* Bruno Messerli and Klaus Aerni (eds.), *Geographica Bernensia Simen Mountains – Ethiopia*, Berne: Geographische Institut der Universitat Bern, 1978, p. 21.

58 Michael Mok, 'The losing fight...', op. cit.

59 Letter from Gebrechristos Leggesne to the EWCO, Gondar, 9 June 1972 [EWCA, 10.A.5 '1964 Et. c., Correspondence'].

60 Ethiopian Tourism Commission, 'Simien national park information sheet', Addis Ababa, 1976, n.p. [EWCA].

61 Letter from Teshome Ashine to Wendesen Mesele, Addis Ababa, 21 September 1979 [EWCA, 10.A.6 '1967–1972 Et. c., Notes for ministers from general managers'].

62 Ermias Bekele, 'A description of the conservation status and future outlooks...', op. cit., p. 12.

63 Letter from Berihun Asfaw to the Office of the Simien National Park, Debark, 8 July 1980 [EWCA, 1.A.B.7 'Berihun Asfaw, 1963–1984 Et. c.'].

64 Letter from Teshome Ashine to the Forest and Wildlife Protection and Development Department, Addis Ababa, 3 November 1979 [EWCA, 10.A.6 '1967–1972 Et. c., Notes for ministers from general managers'].

65 Clive Nicol, *From the Roof of Africa*, op. cit., see in particular chapters 10, 11, 13, 17 and 19.

66 See in particular: Girma Tayachew, 'The Simen wild fauna...', op. cit., pp. 65–80.

67 Letter from Gizaw Gedlegiorgis to Nadew Woreta, Addis Ababa, 4 February 1966 [EWCA, 1.A.M.12 & 1.A.N.1 'Nadew Woreta, 1959–1989 Et. c.'].

68 Letter from Balcha Edesa to Hagos Yohannes and Nadew Woreta, Addis Ababa, 5 January 1967 [ibid.].

69 Berihun Asfaw, quoted by Clive Nicol, letter to Gizaw Gedlegiorgis, Gondar, 29 October 1968 [ibid.].

70 Amare Gebrew, quoted by Clive Nicol and his interpreter, letter to Gizaw Gedlegiorgis, Gondar, 30 October 1968 [ibid.].

71 Letter from Gizaw Gedlegiorgis to Nadew Woreta, Addis Ababa, 2 February 1969 [ibid.].

72 Letter from Tamrat Yigezu to Mebratu Fisseha, Debark, 12 May 1970 [ibid.].

73 Letter from Tamrat Yigezu to Kassa Woldemariam, Debark, 10 October 1973 [ibid.].

74 Letter from Nadew Woreta to the EWCO, Debark, 7 December 1973 [ibid.].

75 Peter Hay, 'Monthly report Awash Park', Metehara, February 1967, n.p. [EWCA, JB 2].

76 Letter from Peter Hay to Gizaw Gedlegiorgis, Awash, 22 February 1967 [ibid.].

77 Peter Hay, 'Awash monthly report', Metehara, October 1966, n.p. [ibid.].

78 Peter Hay, 'Monthly report Awash Park', Metehara, April 1967, n.p. [ibid.].

79 Belete Ayele, 'Report by Belete Ayele', Metehara, April 1969, n.p. [ibid.].

80 Ali Ahmed, 'Report by temporary game guard Ali Ahmed', Metehara, April 1969 [ibid.].

81 Letter from John Blower to Mebratu Fisseha, Addis Ababa, 14 July 1969 [EWCA, JB 4].

82 Ibid.

83 Letter from George Brown to Gizaw Gedlegiorgis, Omo, u.d. [EWCA, JB 7].

84 Letter from George Brown to John Blower, Omo, 6 May 1969 [EWCA, JB 5].

85 Letter from George Brown to Mebratu Fisseha, Omo valley, 25 March 1970 [EWCA, 1.A.B.6 'Berhanu Bisetegn, 1960–1984 Et. c.'].

86 Letter from a storekeeper at the Omo Park to the Conservation department, Omo, December 1966 [EWCA, 2.B.5.3 '1962–1996 Et. c., Different issues'].

87 Letter from George Brown to John Blower, Omo valley, September 1966 [EWCA, JB 6].

88 Letter from George Brown to John Blower, Omo, 6 May 1969 [ibid.];

John Blower, 'Development of roads and tracks in national park: outline programme of work', Addis Ababa, 15 May 1968, n.p. [EWCA, JB 8].

89 Letter from Frederick Duckworth to Mebratu Fisseha, Addis Ababa, 1 March 1972 [EWCA, 2.B.5.1 '1959–1970 Et. c., Reports'].

90 EWCO, 'Symposium', Addis Ababa, 25 March 1968, n.p. [EWCA, 1.A.A.20 'Atekelet Ferede, 1958–1980 Et. c.'].

91 Letter from Clive Nicol to John Blower, Gondar, October 1966 [EWCA, JB 5].

92 Melvin Bolton, 'Simien mountains national park. Report on a ground survey of the park boundaries', Addis Ababa, 3 July 1970, n.p. [EWCA, 1.A.B.10 'Melvin Bolton, 1969–1972'].

93 Peter Hay, 'Monthly report – April, 1966', Awash camp, 4 May 1966, n.p. [EWCA, JB 2].

94 Peter Hay, 'Awash monthly report', Metehara, October 1966, n.p. [ibid.]; Peter Hay, 'November monthly report, 1966. Awash Falls Park', Metehara, December 1966, n.p. [ibid.].

95 Peter Hay, 'Awash monthly report – Sept. 1966', Metehara, October 1966, n.p. [ibid.].

96 Peter Hay, 'December monthly report, 1966. Awash Falls Park', Metehara, January 1967, n.p. [ibid.].

97 Peter Hay, 'Monthly report Awash Park. February 1967', Metehara, March 1967, n.p. [ibid.].

98 Peter Hay, 'Monthly report Awash Park', Metehara, April 1967, n.p. [ibid.].

99 Peter Hay, 'Awash monthly report. April – 1967', Metehara, May 1967, n.p. [ibid.].

100 Peter Hay, 'Monthly report Awash national park. February 1968', Metehara, March 1968, n.p. [ibid.].

101 John Bromley, 'People and domesticated stock in the national park', Awash, 6 June 1969, n.p. [ibid.].

102 Peter Hay, 'Annual report 1967. Awash Falls national park', Awash, 1968, n.p. [ibid.].

103 Letter from John Blower to Gizaw Gedlegiorgis, Addis Ababa, 4 January 1966 [ibid.].

104 Peter Hay, 'Awash monthly report. April – 1967', Metehara, May 1967, n.p. [ibid.].

105 Letter from Peter Hay to John Blower, Awash, 27 May 1967 [ibid.].

106 Letter from John Blower to Gizaw Gedlegiorgis, Addis Ababa, 21 July 1967 [EWCA, JB 6].

107 Peter Hay, 'Awash monthly report. July 1967', Awash, August 1967, n.p. [EWCA, JB 2].

108 Peter Hay, 'Monthly report Awash park. February 1968', Metehara, March 1968, n.p. [ibid.].

109 Letter from John Blower to Gizaw Gedlegiorgis, Addis Ababa, 24 June 1968 [EWCA, JB 3]; letter from Peter Hay to John Blower, Awash, 28 June 1968 [ibid.].

110 Peter Hay, 'Annual report 1968. Awash Falls national park', Awash, 1969, n.p. [EWCA, JB 6].

111 Tadesse Mikael, 'Monthly report March 1969. Awash national park', Awash, April 1969, n.p. [EWCA, JB 2].

112 John Blower, 'Notes for the wildlife conservation board', Addis Ababa, April 1966, n.p. [EWCA, JB 5].

113 Clive Nicol, *From the Roof of Africa*, op. cit., p. 71.

114 Letter from John Blower to Mebratu Fisseha, Addis Ababa, August 1969 [EWCA, JB 5].

115 For a definition of injustice in the context of human and social sciences, see in particular: Étienne Balibar, 'La justice ou l'égalité. Pascal, Hegel, Marx', *in* Julia Christ and Florian Nicodème (eds.), *L'Injustice sociale, quelles voies pour la citique?* Paris: Presses universitaires de France, 2013, pp. 17–38.

116 Ted Shatto, 'Report from Safaris International', Chicago, October 1965, n.p. [EWCA, JB 6].

117 James Mellon, 'The Abyssinian ibex, or walia: a shoot on the heights and abysses of Semien', *in African Hunter*, London: Cassell, 1975.

118 Melvin Bolton, 'Simien mountains national park. Report...', op. cit.

119 On the restrictions imposed on land use, see in particular: Imperial Ethiopian Government, 'Order no. 65. Wildlife conservation order', *Negarit Gazeta*, vol. 30, no. 4, 5 November 1970, pp. 30–3 [EWCA].

120 Imperial Ethiopian Government, 'Regulations issued pursuant to the game proclamation of 1944 and the wildlife conservation order of 1970', *Negarit Gazeta*, vol. 31, no. 7, 19 January 1972, p. 37 [ibid.].

121 Ethiopia Tikdem, 'A draft proclamation to provide for the conservation and management of wildlife', Addis Ababa, 1975, p. 18 [ibid.].

122 Lealem Berhanu, 'Development and utilization of wildlife in coordination with livestock and range management', Addis Ababa, 1976, p. 1 [ibid.].

123 Ermias Bekele, 'A description of the conservation status and future outlooks...', op. cit., p. 12.

124 Martin Heidegger, *The Fundamental Concepts of Metaphysics. World, Finitude, Solitude*, Bloomington and Indianapolis: Indiana University Press, 1995, p. 195.

125 Letter from Gizaw Gedlegiorgis to John Blower, Addis Ababa, 4 July 1967 [EWCA, JB 4].

126 Letter from George Brown to John Blower, Omo, 6 May 1969 [EWCA, JB 5].

127 David Turton, 'The Mursi and national park development in the Lower Omo valley', *in* David Anderson and Richard Grove (eds.), *Conservation in Africa. People, Policies and Practice*, Cambridge: Cambridge University Press, 1987, p. 177.

128 Letter from Frederick Duckworth to Mebratu Fisseha, Addis Ababa, 1 March 1972 [EWCA, 2.B.5.1 '1959–1970 Et. c., Reports'].

129 Letter from Mariam Demeke to the EWCO, Omo, 1 December 1973 [EWCA, 2.B.5.1 '1959–1970 Et. c., Reports'].

130 Letter from Teshome Demena to the EWCO, Omo, 2 February 1976 [ibid.].

131 EWCA, 1.A.A.15 'Amare Gebretsadik, 1957–1963 Et. c.'.

132 Jean-François Bayart, 'Africa in the world', op. cit., p. 112.

133 Letter from Teshome Ashine to Kassa Woldemariam, Addis Ababa, 23 October 1973 [EWCA, 10.A.6 '1967–1972 Et. c., Notes for ministers from general managers'].

134 Peter Hay, 'Monthly report March 1969. Awash national park', Metehara, April 1969, n.p. [EWCA, JB 2].

135 George Brown, 'Possible increase of game guards to deal with Surma', Omo, January 1969, n.p. [ibid.].

136 Letter from Tadele Kercha to Balcha Edesa, Kefa province, 6 June 1970 [EWCA, 1.A.A.7 'Abera Gebremariam, 1958–1971 Et. c.'].

137 Letter from Clive Nicol to Gizaw Gedlegiorgis, Addis Ababa, 25 June 1969 [EWCA, 2.B.8.1 '1961–1970 Et. c., Reports']; letter from Gizaw Gedlegiorgis to Clive Nicol, Addis Ababa, 30 June 1969 [ibid.].

138 Letter from Amare Gebru and Chane Tekele to the Department of Conservation of Wild Animals, Debark, 22 December 1969 [EWCA, 1.A.A.14 'Amare Gebru, 1959–1990 Et. c.'].

139 Letter from Peter Hay to John Blower, Awash, 27 May 1967 [EWCA, JB 2].

140 IUCN, 'Twelfth General Assembly', op. cit., p. 153.

141 UNESCO 'Intergovernmental Committee for the Protection of the World Cultural and Natural Heritage...', op. cit., p. 7.

142 Letter from Teshome Ashine to Teshome Mathias, Addis Ababa, 18 October 1977 [EWCA, 10.A.6 '1967–1972 Et. c., Notes for ministers from general managers'].

Epilogue

1 IUCN, 'Twelfth General Assembly', op. cit., p. 153.

2 Raymond Dasmann, 'Life-styles and nature conservation', *Oryx*, vol. 13, no. 3, 1976, p. 285.

3 IUCN, 'Categories, objectives and criteria for protected areas. A final report

prepared by Committee on Criteria and Nomenclature Commission on National Parks and Protected Areas', Morges, 1978, p. 20 [IUCN-1978-003].

4 Charles Pitman, 'The balance of nature', *Oryx*, vol. 2, no. 1, 1953, p. 9.

5 Raf de Bont, '"Primitives" and protected areas: international conservation and the "naturalization" of indigenous people, ca. 1910–1975', *Journal of the History of Ideas*, vol. 76, no. 2, 2015, pp. 215–36.

6 Mouloud Feraoun, *Journal. 1955–1962*, Paris: Seuil, 2011 [1962], p. 62.

7 IUCN, with the advice, cooperation and financial assistance of the UNEP and the WWF and in collaboration with the FAO and UNESCO, 'World Conservation Strategy. Living resource conservation for sustainable development', Gland, 1980 [UICN-WCS-004].

8 Jacques Verschuren, 'Burundi and wildlife: problems of an overcrowded country', *Oryx*, vol. 14, no. 3, 1978, pp. 237–40.

9 Eric Edroma, 'Road to extermination in Uganda', *Oryx*, vol. 15, no. 5, 1980, pp. 451–2.

10 Kes Hillman and Esmond Martin, 'Will poaching exterminate Kenya's rhinos?', *Oryx*, vol. 15, no. 2, 1979, pp. 131–2.

11 Eric Edroma, 'Road to extermination in Uganda', op. cit.; Kes Hillman and Esmond Martin, 'Will poaching exterminate Kenya's rhinos?', op. cit.

12 Maaza Bekele, 'The false prophets of doom', *UNESCO Courier*, 27th year, July–August 1974, pp. 42–5.

13 Malcom Largen and Derek Yalden, 'The decline of elephant and black rhinoceros in Ethiopia', *Oryx*, vol. 21, no. 2, 1987, pp. 103–6.

14 Awegeghew Teshome, 'Wild life quarterly report (3rd quarter)', Omo Valley, 9 April 1982, n.p. [EWCA, 2.B.5.5 '1971–1974 Et. c., Reports'].

15 Michael Ghiglieri, 'Wildlife log on the Omo River', *Oryx*, vol. 16, no. 2, 1981, pp. 142–3.

16 On the subject of tourism in the Omo see in particular: Tamás Régi, 'The art of the weak: tourist encounters in East Africa', *Tourist Studies*, vol. 13, no. 1, 2013, pp. 99–118.

17 Jesse Hillman, 'Simien mountains national park: visit report', Addis Ababa, 1991, p. 7 [Bureau du parc du Simien, Debark].

18 Letter from Tilahun Bezabeh to Kebele 4 Debre Febres Seber, 1985 [ibid.].

19 Chiara Bortolotto, 'L'Unesco comme arène de traduction. La fabrique globale du patrimoine immatériel', *Gradhiva*, no. 18, 2013, pp. 50–73. On the dualism of western nature-culture, Philippe Descola's book remains the classic text on the subject: *Par-delà nature et culture*, Paris: Gallimard, 2005.

20 UNESCO, 'Konso cultural landscape', 2011 (https://whc.unesco.org/fr/list /1333/, accessed 26 July 2023).

21 *Le Monde Afrique* with Agence France Presse, 'Au Botswana, ouverture de la saison de la chasse à l'éléphant', 7 April 2021 (www.lemonde.fr/afrique /article/2021/04/07/au-botswana-ouverture-de-la-saison-de-la-chasse-a-l-elephant_6075825_3212.html, accessed 26 July 2023).

22 Survival International, 'Tanzania: thousands of Masai flee into the bush after dozens shot and detained following eviction for trophy hunting and conservation', 13 June 2022 (https://survivalinternational.org/news/13051).

23 UNESCO, 'State of conservation of the properties inscribed on the List of World Heritage in Danger', Brasilia, 2010, pp. 16–21 [UNESCO, WHC-10/34. COM/7A.Add].

24 UNESCO, 'Decisions adopted during the 41st session of the World Heritage Committee', Krakow, 2017, p. 29 [UNESCO, WHC/17/41. COM/18].

25 Kalaeb Girma, 'Fire reignites and blazes in Simien mountains', *Addis Fortune*, 13 April 2019 (https://addisfortune.news/fire-reignites-and-blazes-in-simien -mountains/, accessed 27 July 2023).

26 Guillaume Blanc, *The Invention of Green Colonialism*, op. cit.

27 Ernesto Ottone Ramirez, 'En Afrique, "faire de la protection de la nature un grand dessein colonial n'est pas sérieux"', *Le Monde Afrique*, 1 November 2020 (www.lemonde.fr/afrique/article/2020/11/01/en-afrique-faire-de-la-protection -de-la-nature-un-grand-dessein-colonial-n-est-pas-serieux_6058115_3212.html, accessed 4 August 2023).

28 Oryx, 'African Special Project, stage I', op. cit., p. 143; Gerald Watterson, 'Conservation of Nature…', op. cit., p. 73.

29 Jaeger Tilman, 'Reactive monitoring mission to Simien National Park, Ethiopia', IUCN, 2017, p. 15 [UNESCO, WHC.17/41.COM/].

30 Leslie Brown, 'Wild animals, agriculture, and animal industry', *in* Gerald Watterson, 'Conservation of Nature…' op. cit., pp. 109–12.

31 Abdallah Said Fundikira et al., 'The Arusha Manifesto', op. cit., p. 12.

32 Gerald Watterson, 'Conservation of Nature…', op. cit., p. 25.

Bibliography

Abbink, Jon, 'Authority and leadership in Surma society (Ethiopia)', *Africa: Rivista trimestrale di studi e documentazione dell'Istituto italiano per l'Africa e l'Oriente*, vol. 52, no. 3, 1997, pp. 317–42.

Adams, William, *Against Extinction. The Story of Conservation*, London and New York: Earthscan, 2004.

Adams, William and Martin Mulligan (eds.), *Decolonizing Nature. Strategies for Conservation in a Post-Colonial Era*, London: Earthscan, 2003.

Addi, Lahouari, 'Sociologie du savoir sur autrui. Contributions au débat sur les études postcoloniales', *Mouvements*, vol. 72, no. 4, 2012, pp. 54–67.

Anderson, David and Richard Grove (eds.), *Conservation in Africa. People, Policies and Practice*, Cambridge: Cambridge University Press, 1987.

Anker, Peder, *Imperial Ecology. Environmental Order in British Empire, 1895–1945*, Cambridge, MA: Harvard University Press, 2001.

Arendt, Hannah, *The Human Condition*, Chicago and London: University of Chicago Press, 1998.

Bahru Zewde (ed.), *Proceedings of the Fifth Seminar of the Department of History*, Addis Ababa University, Addis Ababa, 1990.

Bahru Zewde, *A History of Modern Ethiopia 1855–1991*, Oxford: James Currey, 2002.

Baroin, Catherine and Jean Boutrais, 'Bétail et société en Afrique', *Journal des africanistes*, vol. 78, no. 1–2, 2008, pp. 9–52.

Bayart, Jean-François, 'Africa in the world', *African Affairs*, vol. 99, no. 395, April 2000, pp. 217–67.

Beinart, William and Lotte Hughes, 'Empire and the visual representation of nature, 1860–1960', *History Compass*, vol. 6, no. 5, 2008, pp. 1177–93.

Beinart, William and Katie McKeown, 'Wildlife media and representations of Africa, 1950s to the 1970s', *Environmental History*, vol. 14, no. 3, 2009, pp. 429–52.

Bennett, Brett and Joseph Hodge (eds.), *Science and Empire. Knowledge and*

Networks of Science across the British Empire, 1800–1970, Basingstoke and New York: Palgrave Macmillan, 2011.

Benson, Etienne, 'Territorial claims: experts, antelopes, and the biology of land use in Uganda, 1955–75', *Comparative Studies of South Asia, Africa and the Middle East*, vol. 35, no. 1, 2015, pp. 137–55.

Bertrand, Romain, *L'Histoire à parts égales*, Paris: Points Seuil, 2014 [2011].

Bhabha, Homi, 'Entretien avec Jonathan Rutherford. Le tiers-espace', *Multitudes*, vol. 26, no. 3, 2006, pp. 95–107.

BLACT (ed.), *Introduction à la coopération en Afrique noire*, Paris: Karthala, 1983.

Blais, Hélène, Florence Deprest and Pierre Singaravélou (eds.), *Territoires impériaux. Une histoire spatiale du fait colonial*, Paris: Publications de la Sorbonne, 2011.

Blanc, Guillaume, 'Violence et incohérence en milieu naturel: une histoire du parc éthiopien du Semēn', *Études rurales*, no. 197, 2016, pp. 147–70.

Blanc, Guillaume, 'Governing nature and Ethiopia: struggles around world heritage, nation-building and ecologies (1963–2012)', *Northeast African Studies*, vol. 18, no. 1–2, 2018, pp. 137–64.

Blanc, Guillaume, 'L'expert, le dirigeant et l'habitant. La fabrique globale de la nature éthiopienne (1965–1970)', *Genèses*, vol. 115, no. 2, 2019, pp. 53–74.

Blanc, Guillaume, *Décolonisations. Histoires situées d'Afrique et d'Asie (19ᵉ–21e siècle)*, Paris: Points Seuil, 2022.

Blanc, Guillaume, *The Invention of Green Colonialism*, Cambridge: Polity Press, 2022.

Blanc Guillaume, Mathieu Guérin and Grégory Quenet (eds.), *Protéger et détruire. Gouverner la nature sous les tropiques (20ᵉ–21e siècle)*, Paris: CNRS Éditions, 2022.

Bluwstein, Jevgeniy, 'From colonial fortress to neoliberal landscape in Northern Tanzania: a biopolitical ecology of wildlife conservation', *Journal of Political Ecology*, vol. 25, no. 1, 2018, pp. 144–68.

Booth, Martin, 'Cowie, Mervyn (1909–1996)', *Oxford Dictionary of National Biography*, 2004 (https://doi.org/10.1093/ref:odnb/39752).

Bortolotto, Chiara, 'L'Unesco comme arène de traduction. La fabrique globale du patrimoine immatériel', *Gradhiva*, no. 18, 2013, pp. 50–73.

Bourdier, Frédéric and Patrick Kulesza (eds.), *La Combustion du monde. Peuples autochtones, conservation et marchandisation de la nature en Asie du Sud et du Sud-Est*, Paris: L'Harmattan, 2024.

Brockington, Daniel and James Igoe, 'Eviction for conservation: a global overview', *Conservation and Society*, vol. 4, no. 3, 2006, pp. 424–70.

Chakrabarty, Dipesh, 'Subaltern studies and postcolonial historiography', *Nepantla. Views from South*, vol. 1, no. 1, 2000, pp. 9–32.

Chivallon, Christine, 'La quête pathétique des *postcolonial studies* ou la révolution manquée', *Mouvements*, no. 51, 2007, pp. 32–9.

Christ, Julia and Florian Nicodème (eds.), *L'Injustice sociale, quelles voies pour la critique?*, Paris: Presses universitaires de France, 2013.

Clarke, Sabine, 'A technocratic imperial state? The colonial office and scientific research, 1940–1960', *Twentieth Century British History*, vol. 18, no. 4, 2007, pp. 453–80.

Cooper, Frederick, 'Conflict and connection: rethinking colonial African history', *The American Historical Review*, vol. 99, no. 5, 1994, pp. 1516–45.

Cooper, Frederick, *Africa Since 1940. The Past of the Present*, Cambridge: Cambridge University Press, 2002.

Cooper, Frederick, *Africa in the World. Capitalism, Empire, Nation State*, Cambridge, MA: Harvard University Press, 2014.

Cooper, Frederick and Randall Packard (eds.), *International Development and the Social Sciences. Essays on the History and Politics of Knowledge*, Berkeley: University of California Press, 1997.

Cormier-Salem, Marie-Christine, Dominique Juhé-Beaulaton, Jean Boutrais and Bernard Roussel, *Patrimonialiser la nature tropicale. Dynamiques locales, enjeux internationaux*, Paris: IRD Éditions, 2002.

Cormier-Salem, Marie-Christine, Dominique Juhé-Beaulaton, Jean Boutrais and Bernard Roussel (eds.), *Patrimoines naturels au Sud. Territoires, identités et stratégies locales*, Paris: IRD Éditions, 2005.

Cormier-Salem, Marie-Christine, Dominique Juhé-Beaulaton, Yves Girault and Dominique Guillaud (eds.), *Ambivalences patrimoniales au Sud. Mises en scène et jeux d'acteurs*, Paris: IRD Éditions and Karthala, 2016.

Dalla, Bernardina Sergio (ed.), *De la bête au non-humain: perspectives et controverses autour de la condition animale*, Paris: Éditions du CTHS, 2020.

Davis, Diana, *The Arid Lands. History, Power, Knowledge*, Cambridge, MA: The MIT Press, 2016.

Davis Diana and Edmund Burke (eds.), *Environmental Imaginaries of the Middle East and North Africa*, Athens: Ohio University Press, 2011.

De Bont, Raf, ' "Primitives" and protected areas: international conservation and the "naturalization" of indigenous people, ca. 1910–1975', *Journal of the History of Ideas*, vol. 76, no. 2, 2015, pp. 215–36.

De Bont, Raf, *Nature's Diplomats. Science, Internationalism, and Preservation, 1920–1960*, Pittsburgh: University of Pittsburgh Press, 2021.

De Bont, Raf, Simone Schleper and Hans Schouwenburg, 'Conservation conferences and expert networks in the short twentieth century', *Environment and History*, vol. 23, no. 4, 2017, pp. 569–99.

Descola, Philippe, *Par-delà nature et culture*, Paris: Gallimard, 2005.

Dlamini, Jacob, *Safari Nation. A Social History of the Kruger National Park*, Athens: Ohio University Press, 2020.

Donham, Donald, *Marxist Modern. An Ethnographic History of the Ethiopian Revolution*, Berkeley and Oxford: University of California Press and James Currey, 1999.

Dovers, Stephen, Ruth Edgecombe and Bill Guest (eds.), *South Africa's Environmental History. Cases and Comparisons*, Athens: Ohio University Press, 2003.

Du Bois, W.E.B., *The Souls of Black Folk*, New York: First Vintage Books, 1990.

Dülffer, Jost and Marc Frey (eds.), *Elites and Decolonization in the Twentieth Century*, London: Palgrave Macmillan, 2011.

Eczet, Jean-Baptiste, 'Des hommes et des vaches: l'attachement entre les personnes et leurs bovins en pays Mursi (Éthiopie)', *Anthropologie et Sociétés*, vol. 39, no. 1–2, 2015, pp. 121–44.

Eczet, Jean-Baptiste, *Amour vache. Esthétique sociale en pays mursi (Éthiopie)*, Milan: Mimésis, 2019.

Eczet, Jean-Baptiste, *Cattle Poetics. How Aesthetics Shapes Politics in Mursiland*, New York and Oxford: Berghahn Books, 2021.

Feuerhahn, Wolf and Pascale Rabault-Feuerhahn, 'La science à l'échelle internationale', *Revue germanique internationale*, no. 12, 2010, pp. 5–15.

Garland, Elizabeth, 'The elephant in the room: confronting the colonial character of wildlife conservation in Africa', *African Studies Review*, vol. 51, no. 3, 2008, pp. 51–74.

Geisler, Charles and Ragendra de Sousa, 'From refuge to refugee: the African case', *Public Administration and Development*, vol. 21, no. 2, 2001, pp. 159–70.

Gibson, Clark, *Politicians and Poachers. The Political Economy of Wildlife Policy in Africa*, Cambridge: Cambridge University Press, 1999.

Gilmartin, David, 'Scientific empire and imperial science: colonialism and irrigation technology in the Indus basin', *The Journal of Asian Studies*, vol. 53, no. 4, 1994, pp. 1127–49.

Girma Tayachew, 'The Simen wild fauna under the protection of the government of Haile Selassie: from endangered prey to national symbol (1941–1969)', *Annales d'Éthiopie*, no. 31, 2018, pp. 65–80.

Girum Getachew, Degefa Tolossa and Getachew Gebru, 'Risk perception and coping strategies among the Karrayu pastoralists of upper Awash valley, central Ethiopia', *Nomadic Peoples*, vol. 12, no. 1, 2008, pp. 93–107.

Gissibl, Bernhard, *The Nature of German Imperialism. Conservation and the Politics of Wildlife in Colonial East Africa*, New York and Oxford: Berghahn Books, 2019 [2016].

Gissibl, Bernhard, Sabine Höller and Patrick Kupper (eds.), *Civilizing Nature. National Parks in Global Historical Perspective*, New York and Oxford: Berghahn Books, 2012.

Grevsmühl, Sebastian Vincent, *La Terre vue d'en haut. L'Invention de l'environnement global*, Paris: Seuil, 2014.

Grundmann, Reiner, 'The problem of expertise in knowledge societies', *Minerva*, vol. 55, no. 1, 2017, pp. 25–48.

Guha, Ranajit, Shahid Amin, David Arnold, Veena Das and Asok Sen, *Subaltern Studies. Une anthologie*, translated from the English by Frédéric Cotton, Toulouse: Éditions de l'Asymétrie, 2017 [1983]. [This book contains extracts from the review 'Subaltern Studies', Delhi: OUP, vols II, (1983) V (1987), VI (1989) and VII (1994).]

Guidi, Pierre and Ophélie Rillon, 'Penser les violences politiques au prisme de l'intime', *20 & 21. Revue d'histoire*, no. 151, 2021, pp. 3–19.

Hedinger, Daniel and Nadin Heé, 'Transimperial history – connectivity, cooperation and competition', *Journal of Modern European History*, vol. 16, no. 4, 2018, pp. 429–52.

Heidegger, Martin, *The Fundamental Concepts of Metaphysics. World, Finitude, Solitude*, Bloomington and Indianapolis: Indiana University Press, 1995.

hooks, bell, *Feminist Theory. From Margin to Centre*, New York and Abingdon: Routledge, 2015.

Hulme, David and Murphree Marshall, 'Communities, wildlife and the "new conservation" in Africa', *Journal of International Development*, no. 11, 1999, pp. 277–85.

Igoe, Jim, *The Nature of the Spectacle. On Images, Money, and Conserving Capitalism*, Tucson: The University of Arizona Press, 2017.

Jacoby, Karl, *Shadows at Dawn. An Apache Massacre and the Violence of History*, London: Penguin, 2008.

Jundt, Thomas, 'Dueling visions for the postwar world: the UN and UNESCO 1949 conferences on resources and the origins of environmentalism', *Journal of American History*, vol. 101, no. 1, 2014, pp. 44–70.

Kirk-Green, Anthony, 'Decolonization: the ultimate diaspora', *Journal of Contemporary History*, vol. 36, no. 1, 2001, pp. 133–51.

Kloos, Helmut, 'Development, drought, and famine in the Awash valley of Ethiopia', *African Studies Review*, vol. 25, no. 4, 1982, pp. 21–48.

Kott, Sandrine, 'Les organisations internationales, terrains d'étude de la globalisation. Jalons pour une approche socio-historique', *Critique internationale*, vol. 52, no. 3, 2011, pp. 9–16.

Leach, Melissa and Robin Mearns, *The Lie of the Land. Challenging Received Wisdom on the African Environment*, Oxford and Portsmouth: James Currey and Heinemann, 1996.

Le Goff, Jean, 'Des effets des discours positifs sur les angoisses liées au changement climatique', *Nouvelle revue de psychosociologie*, vol. 24, no. 2, 2017, pp. 145–56.

Lekan, Thomas, '*Serengeti Shall Not Die*: Bernhard Grzimek, wildlife film, and the making of a tourist landscape in Africa', *German History*, vol. 20, no. 2, 2011, pp. 224–64.

Lekan, Thomas, *Our Gigantic Zoo. A German Quest to Save the Serengeti*, Oxford: Oxford University Press, 2020.

Lévi-Strauss, Claude, *Structural Anthropology*, London: Hachette UK, 2008.

Locher, Fabien, 'Cold war pastures: Garrett Hardin and the tragedy of the commons', *Revue d'histoire moderne et contemporaine*, vol. 60, no. 1, 2013, pp. 7–36.

Longo, Fiore, *Décolonisons la protection de la nature! Plaidoyer pour les peuples autochtones et l'environnement*, Paris: Double ponctuation, 2023.

Macekura, Stephen, *Of Limits and Growth. The Rise of Global Sustainable Development in the Twentieth Century*, Cambridge: Cambridge University Press, 2015.

MacLeod, Roy, 'Nature and empire. Science and the colonial enterprise: Introduction', *Osiris*, no. 15, 2000, pp. 1–13.

Mann, Gregory, *From Empires to NGOs in the West African Sahel. The Road to Non-governmentality*, Cambridge: Cambridge University Press, 2015.

Matasci, Damiano, 'Internationalising colonial knowledge: Edgar Barton Worthington and the Scientific Council for Africa, 1949–1956', *The Journal of Imperial and Commonwealth History*, vol. 48, no. 5, 2020, pp. 892–913.

Matasci, Damiano and Miguel Bandeira Jerónimo, 'Une histoire transimpériale de l'Afrique: concepts, approches et perspectives', *Revue d'histoire contemporaine de l'Afrique*, no. 3, 2022, pp. 1–17.

Matheka, Reuben, 'The international dimension of the politics of wildlife conservation in Kenya, 1958–1968', *Journal of Eastern African Studies*, vol. 2, no. 1, 2008, pp. 112–33.

Mathis, Charles-François and Jean-François Mouhot (eds.), *Une protection de l'environnement à la française? (xixe–xxe siècles)*, Seyssel: Champ Vallon, 2013.

Mbembe, Achille, *De la postcolonie. Essai sur l'imagination politique dans l'Afrique contemporaine*, Paris: Karthala, 2000.

McCann, James, 'The plow and the forest: narratives of deforestation in Ethiopia, 1840–1992', *Environmental History*, vol. 2, no. 2, 1997, pp. 138–59.

Médard, Jean-François (ed.), *États d'Afrique noire. Formations, mécanismes et crise*, Paris: Karthala, 1991.

Neumann, Roderick, *Imposing Wilderness. Struggles over Livelihood and Nature Preservation in Africa*, Berkeley and Los Angeles: University of California Press, 1998.

Neumann, Roderick, 'The postwar conservation boom in British colonial Africa', *Environmental History*, vol. 7, no. 1, 2002, pp. 22–47.

Neumann, Roderick, 'Moral and discursive geographies in the war for biodiversity in Africa', *Political Geography*, vol. 23, no. 7, 2004, pp. 813–37.

Olivier de Sardan, Jean-Pierre, *La Revanche des contextes. Des mésaventures de l'ingénierie sociale en Afrique et au-delà*, Paris: Karthala, 2021.

Oslund, Karen, Neil Brimnes, Niklas Thode Jenson and Christina Folke Ax (eds.), *Cultivating the Colony. Colonial States and their Environmental Legacies*, Athens: Ohio University Press, 2011.

Pressac, Laure (ed.), *Sur les murs. Histoire(s) de graffitis*, Paris: Éditions du patrimoine et Centre des monuments nationaux, 2018.

Régi, Tamás, 'The art of the weak: tourist encounters in East Africa', *Tourist Studies*, vol. 13, no. 1, 2013, pp. 99–118.

Rist, Gilbert (ed.), *Les Mots du pouvoir. Sens et non-sens de la rhétorique internationale*, Paris and Geneva: Presses universitaires de France and Institut universitaire d'études du développement, 2002.

Robertson, Thomas, *The Malthusian Moment. Global Population Growth and the Birth of American Environmentalism*, New Brunswick, NJ: Rutgers University Press, 2012.

Ross, Corey, 'Tropical nature as global *patrimoine*: Imperialism and international nature protection in the early twentieth century', *Past and Present*, vol. 226, no. 10, 2015, pp. 214–39.

Ross, Corey, *Ecology and Power in the Age of Empire. Europe and the Transformation of the Tropical World*, Oxford: Oxford University Press, 2017.

Said, Edward, *Orientalism. Western Conceptions of the Orient*, London and New York: Vintage Books, 1979.

Saunier, Pierre-Yves, 'Les régimes circulatoires du domaine social 1800–1940: projets et ingénierie de la convergence et de la différence', *Genèses*, vol. 71, no. 2, 2008, pp. 4–25.

Schauer, Jeff, '"We hold it in trust": global wildlife conservation, Africanization, and the end of empire', *Journal of British Studies*, vol. 57, no. 3, 2018, pp. 516–42.

Schauer, Jeff, *Wildlife between Empire and Nation in Twentieth-Century Africa*, Cham: Macmillan, 2019.

Schleper, Simone, 'Conservation compromises: the MAB and the legacy of the International Biological Program, 1964–1974', *Journal of the History of Biology*, vol. 50, no. 1, 2017, pp. 133–67.

Schleper, Simone, *Planning for the Planet. Environmental Expertise and the International Union for Conservation of Nature and Natural Resources, 1960–1980*, New York and Oxford: Berghahn Books, 2019.

Scott, James, 'Infra-politique des groupes subalternes', *Vacarme*, vol. 36, no. 3, 2006, pp. 25–9.

Smouts, Marie Claude, *Forêts tropicales, jungle internationale. Les Revers d'une écopolitique mondiale*, Paris: Presses de Sciences Po, 2001.

Solomon Belay, Aklilu Amsalu and Eyualem Abebe, 'Awash National Park, Ethiopia: use policy, ethnic conflict and sustainable resources conservation in the context of decentralization', *African Journal of Ecology*, vol. 51, no. 1, 2012, pp. 122–9.

Sow, Alfâ Ibrâhîm (ed.), *La Femme. La Vache. La Foi. Écrivains et Poètes du Fuuta-Jallon*, Paris: Julliard, 1966.

Spivak, Gayatri Chakravorty, *Can the Subaltern Speak?* New York: Columbia University Press, 2010.

Stapleton, Tim, 'Gamekeepers and counter-insurgency in Kenya and Rhodesia (Zimbabwe), 1952–1980', *International Journal of African Historical Studies*, vol. 49, no. 2, 2016, pp. 213–34.

Steinhart, Edward, 'National parks and anti-poaching in Kenya, 1947–1957', *The International Journal of African Historical Studies*, vol. 27, no. 1, 1994, pp. 59–76.

Stoler, Ann Laura, *Along the Archival Grain. Epistemic Anxieties and Colonial Common Sense*, Princeton, NJ: Princeton University Press, 2009.

Surun, Isabelle, 'L'exploration de l'Afrique au xixe siècle: une histoire pré-coloniale au regard des *postcolonial studies*', *Revue d'histoire du XIXe siècle*, no. 32, 2006, pp. 21–39.

Tilley, Helen, *Africa as Living Laboratory. Empire, Development and the Problem of Scientific Knowledge, 1870–1950*, Chicago: University of Chicago Press, 2011.

Tilley, Helen and Robert Gordon (eds.), *Ordering Africa. Anthropology, European Imperialism, and the Politics of Knowledge*, Manchester and New York: Manchester University Press, 2007.

Turton, David, 'Wilderness, wasteland or home? Three ways of imagining the Lower Omo valley', *Journal of Eastern African Studies*, vol. 5, no. 1, 2011, pp. 158–76.

Unger, Corinna, *International Development. A Postwar History*, London: Bloomsbury Academic, 2022 [2018].

Van Schuylenbergh, Patricia, 'De l'appropriation à la conservation de la faune sauvage. Pratiques d'une colonisation: le cas du Congo belge (1885–1960)', doctoral thesis, Université catholique de Louvain, 2006.

Van Schuylenbergh, Patricia, 'Virunga, star des médias. Les tribulations du plus ancien parc naturel d'Afrique', *Le Temps des médias*, vol. 25, no. 2, 2015, pp. 85–103.

Vigier, Daniel, 'La Commission de coopération technique en Afrique au sud du Sahara', *Politique étrangère*, vol. 19, no. 3, 1954, pp. 335–49.

Weiskopf, Julie, 'Socialism on safari: wildlife and nation-building in postcolonial Tanzania, 1961–77', *Journal of African History*, vol. 56, no. 3, 2015, pp. 429–47.

Wöbse, Anna-Katharina, '"The world after all was one": the international environmental network of UNESCO and IUPN, 1945–1959', *Contemporary European History*, vol. 20, no. 3, 2011, pp. 331–48.

Wöbse, Anna-Katharina, 'L'Unesco et l'Union internationale pour la protection de la nature: une impossible transmission de valeurs?', *Relations internationales*, vol. 152, no. 4, 2012, pp. 29–38.

Wöbse, Anna-Katharina and Patrick Kupper (eds.), *Greening Europe. Environmental Protection in the Long Twentieth Century. A Handbook*, Berlin and Boston: De Gruyter Oldenbourg, 2022.

Yihew Biru, Zewdu Tessema and Mengistu Urge, 'Perception and attitude of pastoralists on livestock–wildlife interactions around Awash National Park, Ethiopia. Implication for biodiversity conservation', *Ecological Processes*, no. 6, 2017.

Ethiopian Wildlife Conservation Authority (EWCA), Addis Ababa

• EWCA library

Ermias Bekele, 'A description of the conservation status and future outlooks of Ethiopia's Semien mountains, Bale mountains, and Abijata-Shall lakes national parks. Unesco's world heritage mission to Ethiopia. April 24, 1982', Addis Ababa, 1982.

Ethiopian Tourist Commission, 'National Park information sheet', Addis Ababa, 1976.

Ethiopia Tikdem, 'A draft proclamation to provide for the conservation and management of wildlife', Addis Ababa, 1975.

Ethiopia Tikdem, 'Endangered species of wildlife conservation commemorative coins regulations', *Negarit Gazeta*, vol. 37, no. 13, 21 June 1978, pp. 76–9.

EWCO, 'Annual report', Addis Ababa, 1978.

EWCO, 'Fourth five year plan', Addis Ababa, 1973.

Imperial Ethiopian Government, 'Order no. 65. Wildlife conservation order', *Negarit Gazeta*, vol. 30, no. 4, 5 November 1970, pp. 30–3.

Imperial Ethiopian Government, 'Regulations issued pursuant to the game proclamation of 1944 and the wildlife conservation order of 1970', *Negarit Gazeta*, vol. 31, no. 7, 19 January 1972, pp. 35–52.

Lealem Berhanu, 'Development and utilisation of wildlife in coordination with livestock and range management', Addis Ababa, 1976.

• John Blower files (JB)

JB 1, 2, 3, 4, 5, 6, 7, 8, 9, 10 and 11, 1965–1972

• EWCA's Records [Et. c. = Ethiopian calendar]

1.A.A.7 'Abera Gebremariam, 1958–1971 Et. c.'
1.A.A.14 'Amare Gebru, 1959–1990 Et. c.'
1.A.A.15 'Amare Gebretsadik, 1957–1963 Et. c.'
1.A.A.20 'Atekelet Ferede, 1958–1980 Et. c.'
1.A.B.6 'Berhanu Bisetegn, 1960–1984 Et. c.'
1.A.B.7 'Berihun Asfaw, 1963–1984 Et. c.'
1.A.B.10 'John Blower, 1965–1970'
1.A.B.10 'Melvin Bolton, 1969–1972'
1.A.B.11 'George Brown, 1966–1970'
1.A.K.9 & 1.A.L.1 'Lealem Berhanu, 1958–1970 Et. c.'
1.A.M.12 & 1.A.N.1 'Nadew Woreta, 1959–1989 Et. c.'
1.A.S.9 & 1.A.T.1 'John G. Stephenson, 1967–1970 Et. c.'
1.A.S.9 & 1.A.T.1 'P.D. Stracey, 1963–1966 Et. c.'
1.A.T.11 'Teshome Ashine, 1964–1983 Et. c.'
2.A.6.1 '1960–1973 Et. c., Field visits'
2.B.5.1 '1970 Et. c., Reports'
2.B.5.3 '1962 Et. c., Omo. Different issues'
2.B.5.3 '1962–1996 Et. c., Different issues'
2.B.5.5 '1971–1974 Et. c., Reports'
2.B.8.1 '1961–1970 Et. c., Reports'
6.A.2 '1962–1973 Et. c., EWCO general reports'
9.B.10 '1969–2004, Frankfurt Zoological Society aids'
9.B.11 '1968–1975, UNESCO'
9.B.14 '1971–1974, IUCN meeting reports'
9.B.15 '1972–1974, Building conservation coins'
9.B.2 '1957–1961 Et. c., The World Wildlife Fund different aids'
9.B.3 '1961–1964 Et. c., College of African Wildlife Management'
9.B.3 '1962–1964 Et. c., Prince Bernhard of Netherlands visit'
9.B.4 '1962–1978, American different aids'
10.A.4 '1964 Et. c., Correspondence'
10.A.5 '1964 Et. c., Correspondence'
10.A.6 '1967–1972 Et. c., Notes for ministers from general managers'

British archives

• Cambridge University Library (CUL), Cambridge

GBR/0012/MS Scott, C. 400-403 'The Council for Nature, 1962'
GBR/0012/MS Scott, C. 434-438 'The Fauna Preservation Society'
GBR/0012/MS Scott, C. 853-859 'Correspondence etc., 1960–1961'
GBR/0012/MS Scott, D. 231-242 'East Africa, August–September 1969'
GBR/0012/MS Scott, M. 1040-1046 'General correspondence'
GBR/0012/MS Scott, M. 1278-1284 'General correspondence'
GBR/0012/MS Scott, M. 1785-1789 'General correspondence, B, 1973'

• National Archives (NA), Kew

CO 822/266 'Kenya Game Department. Annual reports 1961–1962'
CO 847/53/1 'International Union for the Protection of Nature 1950'
CO 847/58 'Resolution by UN Economic and Social Council on listing of national parks and reserves in Africa 1958–1959'
CO 847/61 'Conservation of game and natural resources in colonies in Africa 1959–1960'
CO 847/62, 'Preservation of wild life in colonies in Africa 1959–1960'
CO 847/63 'Preservation of national parks and game reserves in colonies 1957–1959'
CO 847/66 'Report for 1956 by Game Policy Committee of Kenya 1957–1959'
CO 847/75 'Colonial game policy in Africa 1960–1961'
CO 847/78 'Report on the wild resources of East and Central Africa, by Dr E. B. Worthington 1960–1962'
CO 847/79 'Royal national parks and game reserves in Kenya 1960–1961'
CO 936/62/2 'International Union for the Protection of Nature'
FT 3 'Overseas conservation organizations'

• Natural History Museum (NHM), London

MSS Fisher coll. G16 'Fauna Preservation Society. Printed papers'
MSS Fisher coll. G77 'World Wildlife Fund. Printed papers with some correspondence'
Z. MSS PIT-C27 'Correspondence and offprints on ornithology. Grimwood'

• Zoological Society of London (ZSL), London

7AP 'Travels in the Middle East and East Africa – by John Morton Boyd'
G66 'Report – Kenya National Parks'

Food and Agriculture Organization (FAO), Rome

Brown, Leslie with J. Cocheme, 'Technical report on a study of the agrocli-matology of the highlands of eastern Africa', UNESCO and WMO, Paris and Genève, 1969 [FAO, LIB, M, 551.5 F732].

Child G.S., 'Report on follow-up of graduates of the College of African Wildlife Management, Mweka, Tanzania, 1965–1972', FAO, 1976 [FAO-FO-AFC/WL-76/4.2].

FAO, 'African Forestry and Wildlife Commission. First session (Ibadan, Nigeria, 31 October–7 November 1960). Final report', 1960 [FAO-AFC-60/9 Rev. 1].

FAO, 'Papers presented at the third session of the working party on wildlife management of the African Forestry Commission (Lome, Togo, 15–18 Jan 1969)', 1969 [FAO-FO-AFC/WL/69].

FAO, 'Papers presented at the third session of the working party on wildlife management of the African Forestry Commission (Lome, Togo, 15–18 January 1969)', 1969 [FAO-AFC/WL-69/1].

FAO, 'Papers presented at the fourth session of the Ad hoc working party on wildlife management of the African Forestry Commission (Nairobi, Kenya, 1–3 February 1972)', 1972 [FAO-AFC/WL-72].

FAO, 'Report of the African Forestry Commission Ad hoc working party on wildlife management (Kampala, Uganda, 21–25 September 1965)', 1965 [FAO-AFC/WPWM-65/8].

FAO, 'Report of the fifth session of the working party on wildlife management and national parks of the African Forestry Commission (Bangui, Central African Republic, 17–19 March 1976)', 1976 [FAO-AFC/WL-76/Rep].

FAO, 'The economic value of wildlife in certain African countries', 1978 [FAO-AFC/WL-78/4.1].

Francis, G.R. and G.S. Child, 'College of African Wildlife Management, Mweka, United Republic of Tanzania. Report of the UNDP/FAO review and programming mission', FAO, 1975 [FAO-FO-DP/URT/70/530].

Hemingway, Patrick, 'Tourist hunting in Kenya', FAO, 1968 [FAO-FO-AFC/WL-69/7].

Huffnagel, H.P., 'Agriculture in Ethiopia', FAO, 1961 [FAO, 065241].

Mence, Anthony, 'College of African Wildlife Management, Mweka, Tanzania', FAO, 1971 [FAO-FO-WCFET/71/21].

Mence, Anthony, 'Training in control of dangerous animals by use of a high-powered rifle', FAO, 1968 [FAO-FO-AFC/WL-69/2].

Riney, Thane, 'Conservation and management of African wildlife', FAO, 1967 [FAO, 456443/719 R47 (E)].

Robinette, Leslie, 'Game animal survey', FAO, 1968 [FAO-FO-AFC/WL-69/15].

Watterson, Gerald, 'Can the harmful effects of shifting cultivation be restricted by cooperative movements?', FAO, 1955 [FAO, 062072].

Oryx. The International Journal of Conservation

Blower, John, 'New look in Indonesia', Oryx, vol. 15, no. 1, 1979, pp. 50–4.

Blower, John, 'Rhinos – and other problems – in Nepal', Oryx, vol. 12, no. 2, 1973, pp. 270–80.

Blower, John, 'The wildlife of Ethiopia', Oryx, vol. 9, no. 4, 1968, pp. 276–83.

Boyle, Charles, 'What of the Serengeti?', Oryx, vol. 3, no. 6, 1956, pp. 303–18.

Brown, Leslie, 'Wildlife v sheep and cattle in Africa', Oryx, vol. 10, no. 2, 1969, pp. 92–101.

Caldwell, Keith, 'Report on a visit to East Africa', Oryx, vol. 1, no. 4, 1951, p. 173–86.

Caldwell, Keith, 'The Bukavu Conference', Oryx, vol. 2, no. 4, 1954, pp. 234–7.

Cowie, Mervyn, 'Preserve or destroy?', Oryx, vol. 3, no. 1, 1955, pp. 9–11.

Curry-Lindahl, Kai, 'The New African Conservation Convention', Oryx, vol. 10, no. 2, 1969, pp. 116–26.

Dasmann, Raymond, 'Life-styles and nature conservation', Oryx, vol. 13, no. 3, 1976, pp. 281–6.

Edroma, Eric, 'Road to extermination in Uganda', Oryx, vol. 15, no. 5, 1980, pp. 451–2.

Elliott, Hugh, 'Ethiopian Episode, by Leslie Brown. Country life, 42s.', Oryx, vol. 8, no. 3, 1965, p. 202.

Elliott, Hugh, 'The 1966 East African tour', Oryx, vol. 9, no. 1, 1967, p. 16.

Fauna Preservation Society, 'The Serengeti', *Oryx*, vol. 4, no. 6, 1958, pp. 351–2.

Fitter, Richard, 'IUCN Nairobi, 1963', *Oryx*, vol. 7, no. 4, 1964, pp. 154–5.

Ghiglieri, Michael, 'Wildlife log on the Omo river', *Oryx*, vol. 16, no. 2, 1981, pp. 142–3.

Grimwood, Ian, 'Airlift for hunter's antelope: rescue operation in Kenya', *Oryx*, vol. 7, no. 4, 1964, pp. 164–7.

Grimwood, Ian, 'Operation Oryx', *Oryx*, vol. 6, no. 6, 1962, pp. 308–34.

Grimwood, Ian, ' "Operation Oryx". The second stage', *Oryx*, vol. 7, no. 5, 1964, pp. 223–5.

Harthoorn, Antonie, 'Translocation as a means of preserving wild animals', *Oryx*, vol. 6, no. 4, 1962, pp. 215–27.

Hayes, George Dudley, 'Conservation in Malawi – old and new', *Oryx*, vol. 12, no. 3, 1974, pp. 334–40.

Hayes, George Dudley, 'How independence saved an African reserve', *Oryx*, vol. 9, no. 1, 1967, pp. 25–7.

Hillaby, John, 'African Special Project. Stage two – The Arusha Conference', *Oryx*, vol. 6, no. 4, 1962, pp. 211–14.

Hillman, Jesse, 'Conservation in Bale Mountains National Park, Ethiopia', *Oryx*, vol. 20, no. 2, 1986, pp. 89–94.

Hillman, Kes and Esmond Martin, 'Will poaching exterminate Kenya's rhinos?', *Oryx*, vol. 15, no. 2, 1979, pp. 131–2.

IUCN, 'African Special Project, stage I', *Oryx*, vol. 6, no. 3, 1961, pp. 143–70.

IUCN, 'Warsaw and Cracow meeting', *Oryx*, vol. 5, no. 6, 1960, pp. 373–80.

Jewell, Peter, 'Wild life research in East and Central Africa', *Oryx*, vol. 7, no. 2–3, 1963, pp. 77–87.

Largen, Malcom and Derek Yalden, 'The decline of elephant and black rhinoceros in Ethiopia', *Oryx*, vol. 21, no. 2, 1987, pp. 103–6.

Nicholson, Max, 'The new outlook in ecology', *Oryx*, vol. 4, no. 3, 1957, pp. 196–8.

Oryx, 'African president looks at nature conservation', 1976, *Oryx*, vol. 13, no. 3, pp. 255–6.

Oryx, 'Should the elephants be killed?', *Oryx*, vol. 10, no. 2, 1969, pp. 101–2.

Oryx, 'The FPS East African tour', *Oryx*, vol. 8, no. 4, 1966, pp. 219–20.

Oryx, 'The FPS/WWF Revolving Fund', *Oryx*, vol. 10, no. 5, 1970, pp. 291–2.

Oryx, 'The International Union for Conservation of Nature and Natural

Resources. African Special Project, stage I', *Oryx*, vol. 6, no. 3, 1961, pp. 143–70.

Petrides, George and Wendell Swank, 'The status of wildlife and wilderness areas in East Africa', *Oryx*, vol. 5, no. 4–5, 1960, pp. 295–306.

Pitman, Charles, 'The balance of nature', *Oryx*, vol. 2, no. 1, 1953, pp. 9–15.

Russell, Walter, 'The elephant problem in the Serengeti', *Oryx*, vol. 9, no. 6, 1968, pp. 404–6.

Savidge, John, 'The introduction of white rhinoceros into the Murchison Falls National Park, Uganda', *Oryx*, vol. 6, no. 3, 1961, pp. 184–9.

Uganda National Parks, 'Notes from Uganda', *Oryx*, vol. 4, no. 3, 1957, pp. 177–9.

Urban, Emil and Leslie Brown, 'Wildlife in an Ethiopian valley', *Oryx*, vol. 9, no. 5, 1968, pp. 342–53.

Verschuren, Jacques, 'Burundi and wildlife: problems of an overcrowded country', *Oryx*, vol. 14, no. 3, 1978, pp. 237–40.

Worthington, Edgar, 'Dynamic conservation in Africa', *Oryx*, vol. 5, no. 6, 1960, pp. 341–5.

Worthington, Edgar, 'The future of the African fauna', *Oryx*, vol. 1, no. 1, 1950, pp. 44–50.

Accounts, reports, personal observations

Blower, John, *Banagi Hill. A Game Warden's Africa*, Moray: Librario, 2004.

Blower, John, *In Ethiopia. A Game Warden's Adventures in Haile Selassie's Medieval Empire*, Moray: Librario, 2005.

Blower, John, *The Plundered Forests*, Moray: Librario, 2007.

Brown, Leslie, *Conservation for Survival. Ethiopia's Choice*, Addis Ababa: Haile Sellassie I University Press, 1973.

Everett, Mike, 'Obituary. Leslie Hilton Brown, OBE, BSc, PhD (1917–1980)', *British Birds*, vol. 74, no. 5, 1981, pp. 223–6.

Feraoun, Mouloud, *Journal. 1955–1962*, Paris: Seuil, 2011 [1962].

Fitter, Richard and Sir Peter Scott, *The Penitent Butchers. The Fauna Preservation Society 1903–1978*, London: Collins, 1978.

Gary, Romain, *The Roots of Heaven*, London: Penguin, 1960.

Greene, Wade, 'Keeping "the African experience" African', *The New York Times*, 15 August 1971 (https://legendsandlegaciesof-africa.org/johnowen.php).

Gruhn, Isebill V., 'The Commission for Technical Co-operation in Africa, 1950–65', *The Journal of Modern African Studies*, vol. 9, no. 3, 1971, pp. 459–69.

Haile Selassie I, 'Address to the United Nations. Haile Selassie, an historical speech delivered to the United Nations General Assembly on October 4, 1963', *The Proud Reader*, 2022.

Harroy, Jean-Paul, *Afrique. Terre qui meurt. La Dégradation des sols africains sous l'influence de la colonisation*, Brussels: Marcel Ayez, 1949 [1944].

Hay, Peter, *One Long Safari*, Agoura: Trophy Room Books, 1998.

Hayes, George Dudley, 'Wildlife conservation in Malawi', *Society Malawi Journal*, vol. 25, no. 2, 1972, pp. 22–31.

Huxley, Julian, 'The treasure house of wildlife', *The Observer*, 13 November 1960, pp. 23–4 (www.theguardian.com/environment/2010/nov/07/wwf -world-wildlife-fund-huxley).

Kalaeb, Girma, 'Fire reignites and blazes in Simien mountains', *Addis Fortune*, 13 April 2019 (https://addisfortune.news/fire-reignites-and-blazes -in-simien-mountains/).

Le Monde avec Agence France Presse, 'Au Botswana, ouverture de la saison de la chasse à l'éléphant', *Le Monde Afrique*, 7 April 2021 (www.lemonde .fr/afrique/article/2021/04/07/au-botswana-ouverture-de-la-saison-de-la -chasse-a-l-elephant_6075825_3212.html).

McCormick, John, *The Global Environmental Movement*, Hoboken, NJ: John Wiley, 1995 [1991].

Mellon, James (ed.), *The African Hunter*, Huntington Beach: Safari Press, 1975.

Messerli, Bruno and Klaus Aerni (eds.), *Geographica Bernensia Simen Mountains – Ethiopia*, Berne: Geographische Institut der Universitat Bern, 1978.

Mok, Michael, 'The losing fight for game parks', *Life*, vol. 69, no. 22, 27 November 1970, pp. 56–9.

Morris, Brian, 'G.D. Hayes and the Nyasaland Fauna Preservation Society', *The Society of Malawi Journal*, vol. 50, no. 1, 1997, pp. 1–12.

Nicholson, Max, *The Environmental Revolution. A Guide for the New Masters of the World*, London: Hodder and Stoughton, 1970.

Nicol, Clive, *From the Roof of Africa*, London: Hodder and Stoughton, 1972.

Parker, Ian and Stan Bleazard (eds.), *An Impossible Dream. Some of Kenya's Last Colonial Wardens Recall the Game Department in the British Empire's Closing Years*, Moray: Librario, 2001.

Ramirez, Ernesto Ottone, 'En Afrique, "faire de la protection de la nature un grand dessein colonial n'est pas sérieux"', *Le Monde Afrique*, 1 November 2020 (www.lemonde.fr/afrique/article/2020/11/01/en-afrique -faire-de-la-protection-de-la-nature-un-grand-dessein-colonial-n-est-pas -serieux_6058115_3212).

Shepherd, Anthony, *Flight of the Unicorns*, London: Elek Books, 1965.

Survival International, 'Tanzanie: des milliers de Massaï ont fui – des dizaines de blessés et d'arrestations lors d'expulsions au nom de la chasse aux trophées et de la "conservation" de la nature', 13 June 2022 (www .survivalinternational.fr/actu/13101).

Worthington, Edgar, *Science in the Development of Africa. A Review of the Contribution of Physical and Biological Knowledge South of the Sahara*, London: CCTA-CSA, 1958.

Worthington, Edgar, *The Ecological Century. A Personal Appraisal*, Oxford: Oxford University Press, 1983.

Wright, Ian Michael, Letter to Richard H. Nolte (Institute of Current World Affairs), 'Arusha Wildlife Conference', Nairobi, 22 September 1961 (www.icwa.org/wp-content/uploads/2015/10/IMW-6.pdf).

WWF, 'We must save the world's wildlife. An international declaration', Morges, 1961 (https://wwfeu.awsassets.panda.org/downloads /morgesmanifesto.pdf).

UNESCO, Paris

Adams, Alexander B. (ed.), 'First World Conference on National Parks. Proceedings. Seattle, June 30–July 7, 1962', National Parks Service, Washington, 1964 [UNESCO, UIC/16].

Blower, John, 'Ethiopia. Wildlife conservation and national parks. September 1965–September 1969', UNESCO, 1971 [UNESCO, 2351/RMS.RS/SCE, FR/TA/ETHIOPES 5].

Brown, Leslie, 'Ethiopia: conservation of nature and natural resources (30 December 1964 to 1 April 1965)', UNESCO, 1965, pp. 8–12 [UNESCO, WS/0865.192-AVS].

Grimwood, Ian, 'Ethiopia: conservation of natural resources (November 1964–February 1965', UNESCO, 1965 [UNESCO, WS/0865.66 Rev.-AVS].

Huxley, Julian, 'The conservation of wild life and natural habitats in Central and East Africa: report on a mission accomplished for UNESCO, July–September 1960', UNESCO, 1961 [UNESCO, NS.61/D.31/F].

Huxley, Julian, Alain Gille, Théodore Monod, Lloyd Swift and Edgar Worthington, 'The conservation of nature and natural resources in Ethiopia', UNESCO, 1964 [UNESCO, NS/NR/47].

IUPN, 'Unesco. International Technical Conference on the Protection of Nature. Lake Success, 22–29 – VIII – 1949. Proceedings and papers', UNESCO, Paris and Brussels, 1950 [UNESCO, IUPN/ CONF.2].

Tilman, Jaeger, 'IUCN. Reactive monitoring mission to Simien National Park, Ethiopia', IUCN, 2017 [UNESCO, WHC.17/41. COM/].

UNESCO Courier [Unesdoc online].

UNESCO, 'Decisions adopted during the 41st session of the World Heritage Committee', Krakow, 2017 [UNESCO, WHC/17/41. COM/18].

UNESCO, 'Intergovernmental Committee for the Protection of the World Cultural and Natural Heritage. Second Session. Final report', Washington, 1978 [UNESCO, CC-78/CONF.010/10 Rev].

UNESCO, 'Konso cultural landscape', 2011 (https://whc.unesco.org/fr/list /1333/).

UNESCO, 'Records of the General Conference, 17th session, Paris, 17 October to 21 November 1972, v. 1, Resolutions, recommendations', Paris, 1973 [UNESCO, 17/C Resolutions].

UNESCO, 'Regional seminar on ecological methodology and the conservation of natural resources in tropical Africa', *Nature and Resources*, vol. 8, no. 2, 1972 [UNESCO, 339.5].

UNESCO, 'Report of the director-general on the activities of the organization in 1971, communicated to member states and the executive board in accordance with article VI.3.b of the Constitution', Paris, 1972 [UNESCO, 17 C/3].

UNESCO, 'Resolution adopted by the General Conference of Unesco at its 12th Session', Paris, 12 December 1963 [UNESCO, 12 C/DR/64].

UNESCO, 'State of conservation of the properties inscribed on the List of World Heritage in Danger', Brasilia, 2010 [UNESCO, WHC-10/34. COM/7A.Add].

UNESCO, 'Use and conservation of the biosphere. Proceedings of the intergovernmental conference of experts on the scientific basis for rational use and conservation of the resources of the biosphere. Paris, 4–13 September 1968', Paris, 1970 [UNESCO, SC.69/XII.16/A].

UNESCO and United Nations Economic Commission for Africa, 'Final report of the Lagos Conference', Paris, 1965 [UNESCO, NS.64/D.36/A].

UNESCO and United Nations Economic Commission for Africa, 'Lagos Conference. Selected documents. International Conference on the organization of research and training in Africa in relation to the study, conservation and utilization of natural resources, Lagos, 1964', Paris, 1965 [UNESCO, NS.64/ D.38/A/F].

International Union for the Conservation of Nature (IUCN), Gland

Elliott, Hugh (ed.), 'Second World Conference on National Parks, Yellowstone and Grand Teton National Parks, USA, September 18–27, 1972. Proceedings', IUCN, Morges, 1974 [IUCN-1974-002].

Harroy, Jean-Paul, 'Proceedings of the Third International Conference for the Protection of the Fauna and Flora of Africa, Bukavu, 26–31 October 1953, Belgian Congo', IUCN, 1953 [IUCN-1953-002].

IUCN, *IUCN Bulletin*, 1961–1978 [UNESCO, UIC/8].

IUCN, 'Categories, objectives and criteria for protected areas. A final report prepared by Committee on criteria and nomenclature commission on national parks and protected areas', Morges, 1978 [IUCN-1978-003].

IUCN, 'Cinquième Assemblée générale. Fifth General Assembly. Edinburgh, 20-28.6.1956. Procès-verbaux. Proceedings', Brussels, 1957 [IUCN-GA-5th-004].

IUCN, 'Eighth General Assembly. Nairobi, Kenya, September 1963. Proceedings', Morges, 1964 [IUCN-NS-SP-no.001].

IUCN, 'Eleventh General Assembly, Banff, Alberta, Canada, 11–16 September 1972: proceedings', Morges, 1973 [IUCN-NS-SP-no.040, Fr].

IUCN, 'International Conference for the Protection of Nature, Brunnen, 28 June–3 July 1947. Proceedings, resolutions and reports', Basel, 1947 [IUCN, Bios-Cons-Nat-040].

IUCN, *IUCN 1970 Yearbook. Annual Report of the International Union for Conservation of Nature and Natural Resources for 1970*, Morges: IUCN, 1971 [IUCN-1971-003].

IUCN, *IUCN 1971 Yearbook. Annual Report of the International Union for Conservation of Nature and Natural Resources for 1971*, Morges: IUCN, 1972 [IUCN-1972-001].

IUCN, 'Ninth General Assembly, Lucerne, Switzerland, 25 June–2 July 1966: proceedings', Morges, 1969 [IUCN-NS-SP-no.008, Fr].

IUCN, 'Ninth technical meeting. Nairobi, September 1963. Proceedings and papers. The ecology of man in the tropical environment', Morges, 1964 [IUCN-NS-no.004].

IUCN, 'Proceedings and papers of the Fourth General Assembly held at Copenhagen (Denmark), 25 August to 3 September 1954', Brussels, 1955 [IUCN-GA-4th-003].

IUCN, 'Seventh General Assembly, Warsaw, June. 1960. Proceedings', Brussels, 1960 [UICN-GA-7th-006].

IUCN, 'Sixième Assemblée générale. Sixth General Assembly. Athens, Sept. 1958. Procès-verbaux. Proceedings', Brussels, 1960 [IUCN-GA-6th-005].

IUCN, 'Tenth General Assembly, Vigyan Bhavan, New Delhi, 24 November–1 December 1969. Volume II. Proceedings and summary of business', Morges, 1970 [IUCN-NS-SP-no.027].

IUCN, 'The position of nature protection throughout the world in 1950', Brussels 1951 [UNESCO, UIC/10].

IUCN, 'Twelfth General Assembly, Kinshasa, Zaire, 8–18 September 1975: Proceedings', Morges, 1976 [IUCN-NS-SP-no.044, Fr].

IUCN, 'Conference for the establishment of the International Union for the Protection of Nature. Fontainebleau, France. 30 September–7 October 1948', Paris, 1948 [IUCN, NS/ UIPN/5 and UICN, NS/UIPN/8].

IUCN, with the advice, cooperation and financial assistance of the UNEP and the WWF and in collaboration with the FAO and UNESCO, 'World Conservation Strategy. Living resource conservation for sustainable development', Gland, 1980 [UICN-WCS-004].

IUCN, FAO, UNEP and WWF, 'Proceedings of a regional meeting on the creation of a coordinated system of national parks and reserves in Eastern Africa, Seronera Lodge, Serengeti National Park, Tanzania, 14–19 October 1974', Morges, 1976 [IUCN-NS-SP-no.045].

Scott, Peter (ed.), *The Launching of a New Ark. First Report of the World Wildlife Fund*, London: WWF and Collins, 1965 [IUCN, SPE-Inst-002].

Villiers, André, 'Our mother nature: the conservation of nature and natural resources in the Sudan-Sahel Zone of Africa', IUCN, Morges, 1963 [IUCN-NS-SP-no.002].

Watterson, Gerald (compiled by), with the help of other members of the

IUCN Secretariat, 'Conservation of Nature and Natural Resources in Modern African States. Report of symposium organized by CCTA and IUCN and held under the auspices of FAO and UNESCO at Arusha, Tanganyika, September 1961', Morges, 1963 [IUCN-NS-no.001].

Index